Assessment of Cognitive Processes

RELATED TITLES OF INTEREST

The Psychoeducational Assessment of Preschool Children, Second Edition
Bruce A. Bracken
ISBN: 0–205–12520–4

The Psychology of Human Cognition: Mainstream and Genevan Traditions
Mary Howes
ISBN: 0–205–14373–3 Paper 0–205–14374–1 Cloth

Clinical Assessment of Children's Intelligence: A Handbook for Professional Practice
Randy W. Kamphaus
ISBN: 0–205–14694–5

Assessing Adolescent and Adult Intelligence
Alan S. Kaufman
ISBN: 0–205–12390–2

Clinical Interpretation of the Woodcock-Johnson
Kevin McGrew
ISBN: 0–205–14801–8

Assessing and Screening Preschoolers: Psychological and Educational Dimensions
Ena Vazquez Nuttall, Ivonne Romero, and Joanne Kalesnik
ISBN: 0–205–13280–4

Handbook of Child and Adolescent Assessment
Thomas H. Ollendick and Michel Hersen
ISBN: 0–205–14592–2

ASSESSMENT OF COGNITIVE PROCESSES

The PASS Theory of Intelligence

J. P. Das
University of Alberta

Jack A. Naglieri
The Ohio State University

John R. Kirby
Queen's University

Allyn and Bacon
Boston • London • Toronto • Sydney • Tokyo • Singapore

A Division of Simon & Schuster, Inc.
160 Gould Street
Needham Heights, Massachusetts 02194

Library of Congress Cataloging-in-Publication Data

Das, J. P. (Jagannath Prasad)
Assessment of cognitive processes / J. P. Das, Jack A. Naglieri, John R. Kirby.
p. cm.
Includes bibliographical references and index.
ISBN 0-205-14164-1
1. Intelligence tests. 2. Cognition—testing. 3. Cognition in children—Testing. 4. Children—Intelligence testing. 5. Exceptional children—Intelligence testing. 6. Special education. I. Naglieri, Jack A. II. Kirby, John R. III. Title.
BF431.D284 1993
153.9'3—dc20 03-13843
CIP

Printed in the United States of America

10 9 8 7 6 5 4 3 2 97 96 95 94

To
A. R. Luria
whose work inspired us to build
a model of cognitive processes
and to
Gita, Diane, and Marlo

CONTENTS

ABOUT THE AUTHORS

J. P. Das is Professor of Educational Psychology and Director of the Developmental Disabilities Centre at the University of Alberta, where he has taught since 1968. He obtained an honours degree in Philosophy, a Master of Arts in Experimental Psychology in India, and a Ph.D. in Psychology from the University of London Institute of Psychiatry working with Hans Eysenck. His research on understanding cognitive processes has resulted in several scholarly books including *Verbal Conditioning and Behavior* (Oxford: Pergamon, 1969) and *Simultaneous and Successive Cognitive Processes* (New York: Academic Press, 1979). He has published some 200 research papers and book chapters. The model of cognitive processes that is the central point of the book has evolved over 20 years in collaboration with many colleagues. Some of them, like the two co-authors of the book, have made significant contributions to the fields of psychology and education. He has held visiting appointments at Peabody College-Vanderbilt University (as a Kennedy Foundation Professor), UCLA, Monach University in Melbourne, and Moscow State University.

Jack A. Naglieri is Professor of School Psychology and Coordinator of the School Psychology Training Program at The Ohio State University, where he has taught since 1982 and is a Senior Research Associate at the Devereux Foundation's Institute of Clinical Training and Research. Prior to 1982 he was on the faculty at Northern Arizona University (1979 to 1982) and he worked as a school psychologist in Bethpage, New York from 1974 to 1977. Since earning his Ph.D. from the University of Georgia in 1979, Dr. Naglieri has published over 100 scholarly papers in psychological and educational journals and has given over 100 presentations at national and international conferences. He has also conducted many training workshops on his tests, the Matrix Analogies Test Short and Expanded Forms and the Draw A Person: A Quantitative Scoring System and Draw A Person: Screening Procedure for Emotional Disturbance as well as the Kaufman Assessment Battery for Children. Dr. Naglieri published the Matrix Analogies Tests in 1985, the Draw A Person: Quantitative Scoring System in 1988, and the Draw A Person: Screening Procedure for Emotional Disturbance in 1991. He is also an author of the Devereux Behavior Rating Scale—School Form and Devereux Scales of Psychopathology (1993). Dr. Naglieri and his co-author, Dr. J. P. Das of the University of Alberta in Edmonton, Canada, have produced the Das-Naglieri: Cognitive Assessment System, which will be published by The Riverside Publishing Company in 1995.

John R. Kirby is an educational psychologist specializing in the study of intelligence and cognitive processes. Following his studies at McGill

University and the University of Alberta, he taught at the University of Newcastle (Australia) for 11 years. He is currently Professor of Education and Coordinator of Graduate Studies and Research in Education at Queen's University in Kingston, Ontario, Canada. He is the author of numerous research articles and has published the following books: *Simultaneous and Succsssive Cognitive Processes* (Academic Press, 1979, with Das and Jarman), *Cognition, Development, and Instruction* (Academic Press, 1980, with Biggs), *Cognitive Strategies and Educational Performance* (Academic Press, 1984), and *Learning Problems: A Cognitive Approach* (Kagan and Woo, 1991, with Williams). He is currently president-elect of the Canadian Association for Educational Psychology.

PROF. A. R. LURIA
UNIVERSITY OF MOSCOW
13 FRUNZE STR., MOSCOW G. 19.

Feb. 20. 1975

Dr J. P. Das
Director
Centre for the Study of Mental Retardation
Alberta.

Dear Dr Das,

I received your letter together with the paper on Simultaneous and Successive Synthesis, and red this paper at once.

It was really a delight to learn the further advance of the studies in this direction, and I highly appreciate the efforts you have made. Up to now the approach from this point of view showed it's reliability and validity in the studies of Neuropsychological syndromes; now it was shown that in a direct approach with factor analysis these ideas are of a certain value. Thank you so much.

I hope that in the beginning of June I shall be in Moscow and should be glad to see you. Please call the Department of Neuropsychology, Psychology Faculty, Moscow University by the telephone 203.29.47, and you will be connected with me.

Sincerely

Al Luria

PREFACE

Intelligence testing has long been recognized as an industry. Yet the concept of intelligence that makes testing possible is firmly rooted in academic psychology. That concept is undergoing drastic changes and reconceptualization. This book is an attempt to clarify the concept of intelligence and to restructure the approach towards its assessment.

Cognitive functions or processes rather than "intelligence" are the focus of discussion in this book. We have relied on research on cognitive psychology and neuropsychology. Both have endless supplies of information, and both are actively evolving fields that study how the mind works. We cannot, of course, claim to have used all existing knowledge in those fields. Even if anyone could, the accumulated information would require sorting and synthesizing; a workable framework is needed. We have created and used such a framework, admitting our debts to researchers and clinicians who have investigated the workings of the mind.

Assessment of cognitive processes is the tip of the pyramid of knowledge we have used. At the base of the pyramid is a theoretical framework, which we believe is a necessity for good practice. We think that a practitioner such as a school psychologist cannot *label* a child's behavior (e.g., hyperactivity, reading disability) without first establishing a *taxonomy,* and taxonomies can be recognized and be useful only when they are backed by a *theory*. Therefore, we discuss assessment within a theoretical context.

Assessments can be justified by themselves, but they become more useful when they lead to remediation of the cognitive deficit revealed in testing an individual. This book discusses remediation and presents a method that has been tried successfully.

The theory that forms the basis of the book is PASS, which stands for Planning, Attention, Simultaneous, and Successive processes. These processes form a complex and interdependent system, which (1) helps us understand the nature of individual differences, (2) provides a framework within which to conceptualize assessment, and (3) leads directly to theory-based remediation.

OUTLINE OF THE BOOK

This book is divided into four parts, each consisting of several chapters. In Part I (this chapter and the next), we present an overview of our theoretical approach-*PASS,* for planning, attention, simultaneous, successive. In Part II, we deal with each of the major components of the theory in separate chapters. Chapter 3 summarizes the extensive research literature on attention and arousal and shows how individual differences in attention processes affect performance. Chapter 4 describes the two major types of processing or coding, simultaneous and successive processing. (These types of processing were the primary focus of our earlier work [Das, Kirby, & Jarman, 1979]; in this book we emphasize as well the importance of the attentional and planning processes that control simultaneous and successive processing.) Chapter 5 deals with the complex planning system.

Part III describes the development of assessment procedures, including the DN:CAS battery (Chapter 6). The relations between these measures and others (primarily of the WISC-R and the K-ABC) are considered in Chapter 7.

Part IV is more oriented toward detection of deficits and remediation. Chapter 8 presents a theoretical analysis of various disabilities and data concerning the DN:CAS profiles of children with such disabilities. In Chapter 9 we outline how cognitive assessment should lead to remediation; it is essential that remediation be considered in conjunction with assessment, yet much research and development remain to be done. In Chapter 10 we present our view of the future; our goal here is not to predict, but rather to stimulate research and development work.

This book is intended both as a guide to new thinking on intellectual assessment and as a graduate-level textbook. It will be of interest to academic and practicing psychologists and educators in the fields of cognition, individual differences, applied psychology, school psychology, and special education.

Scholarship does not thrive without patronage. Support for this scholarly work has been given by our respective universities and by granting agencies in Canada and the United States. Our students too have contributed to the various studies included in this book; they have been acknowledged by citing their publications and unpublished dissertations. The manuscript and disks for this book were prepared in several stages by efficient secretaries of the Developmental Disabilities Centre. We wish to especially recognize Fran Russell and Henny de Groot. Thank you, Henny, for keeping us on track as well!

J.P.D.
J.A.N.
J.R.K.

PART I

RESTRUCTURING INTELLIGENCE

1

THE COGNITIVE APPROACH TO INTELLECTUAL ASSESSMENT

Psychology has undergone a remarkable revolution since 1960. Over the span of three decades the fundamental framework within which the discipline is conceived has changed; this change mandated new topics for psychology to address, and changed the way old subjects are handled (e.g., Hebb, 1960; Miller, Galanter, & Pribram, 1960). Though successful in the realm of theory and research, this revolution has yet to have much impact upon the *practice* of psychology (Kirby & Das, 1990; Naglieri, 1989). This book is intended to extend that revolution into the area of intellectual assessment, one of the most significant fields of applied psychology (Anastasi, 1988).

The revolution changed many psychologists' framework from behaviorist to cognitive. Whereas in the past, mental processes were considered to be unexaminable because they cannot be observed directly, psychologists are now more willing to make inferences about those hidden processes. Furthermore, they realize that they need to consider those hidden processes if behavior is to be understood. Observable behavior had been seen by the behaviorists as the only legitimate object of study; in contrast, cognitivists see behavior as an indication of mental processes, those processes being the proper object of psychological study. The cognitive revolution has been described extensively elsewhere (e.g., Gardner, 1985).

The study of intelligence in psychology, dates back at least to Galton (1883). Early attempts to define intelligence theoretically failed to attain a consensus or to provide a definition that could be used in applied work (e.g., *Journal of Educational Psychology*, 1921). Two influences guided the study of intelligence from the 1920s to the 1960s: the behaviorist approach, which emphasized behavioral products at the expense of mental processes; and the great need of applied psychology for measures of intellect that could be used for selection purposes. These influences encouraged an approach to intelligence that was atheoretical and emphasized the technology of measurement to the exclusion of psychology. The most telling comment on the approach of this period was Boring's 1923 definition of intelligence as "the capacity to do well in an intelligence test" (as cited by Guilford, 1973).

By definition the study of intelligence must consider higher mental processes, but psychology prior to the 1960s did not have comprehensive theories of those processes to offer. It is not surprising that the field of intelligence went off on its own, to became a distinct discipline of scientific psychology (Cronbach, 1957). This further insulated the study of intelligence from theoretical developments that were beginning to take place in mainstream psychology.

The cognitive revolution had its roots in the 1950s (e.g., Miller, 1956) and was in full bloom by the mid-1960s (e.g., Neisser, 1967). By the mid-1970s many writers were calling for an extension of the cognitive revolution into the field of intelligence (Carroll, 1976; Das, Kirby, & Jarman, 1975, 1979; Hunt, Frost, & Lunneborg, 1973; Sternberg, 1977). Considerable amounts of research and theorizing resulted, but the practice of psychology has hardly changed at all. Psychologists being trained today may learn a great deal about cognitive theory but are then taught to administer intelligence tests that were developed in the 1920s and have not changed substantially since. Psychologists who missed the cognitive revolution entirely may not even suspect the great chasm between their testing methods and current theory.

Why has applied psychology been so slow to respond to the cognitive revolution? Both testing psychologists and cognitive psychologists must share the responsibility. On the testing psychology side, the development and validation of testing instruments is expensive and slow, and there is much vested interest in the existing measures. The psychology of intelligence testing has developed separately from the areas in which cognitive theories have grown, and so testing psychologists may not have been exposed to the new cognitive theories. On the cognitive psychology side, a more subtle reason is that many cognitive psychologists would question the fundamental assumptions behind traditional intellectual assessment; these questions, combined with doubts about the fairness and social value of intellectual assessment, have deterred their interest in test development. The result has not been the decrease in intellectual assessment that some may have desired, but rather the continuation of dated testing practices that have no basis in current theory. We feel the time has come for a comprehensive approach to intellectual assessment, one that is well grounded in cognitive theory and provides practitioners with the tools they need.

Our purposes in this book are to (1) present a coherent theory of cognitive processes, (2) demonstrate how this theory provides a comprehensive basis for understanding individual differences and for identifying the needs of the children we assess, (3) demonstrate how this theory has been applied in the development of testing procedures, and (4) discuss the implications of a cognitive process approach to intellectual assessment. More specifically, we hope to extend the horizons of the psychology of assessment, beyond the narrow and traditional constraints implicit in tests such as the Stanford-Binet and the Wechsler. In order to achieve these goals, we will need to review many research studies, but our aim is not to present these studies in complete detail.

The test development work that will be described here has produced a complete individualized assessment battery, termed the *Das-Naglieri: Cognitive Assessment System,* which we will abbreviate as *DN:CAS* (Das & Naglieri, 1993). While the DN:CAS plays a fundamental role in this book, our prime focus is the theory that is the foundation upon which the battery rests. We see the DN:CAS as the best available implementation of our theoretical approach. A complete presentation of information regarding it can be found in the DN:CAS manual. Our goal in this book is to adopt a broader perspective: to discuss other approaches to assessment, special purposes of assessment, future directions for assessment, and the implications of the application of a cognitive approach.

No approach to intellectual assessment can avoid fundamental issues concerning (1) the purposes of assessment, and (2) the nature of what is being measured. In the remainder of this chapter we consider these issues and outline the effects our approach may have on the field of intellectual assessment. The chapter concludes with an overview of the chapters that follow.

THE PURPOSES OF INTELLECTUAL ASSESSMENT

Assessment is a normal component of everyday life. The essence of assessment is observation, the noticing of some characteristic. We assess when we observe a person's height, appearance, address, language, happiness, cleverness, age, ability to drive an automobile, or interest in rock music. There is nothing unusual about assessment, nor is there anything inherently wrong in assessing others. If we were unable to observe each other and to remember each others' characteristics, meaningful human interaction would be impossible. That does not mean that assessment is always accurate (reliable and valid), nor does it mean that we are correct in the inferences we draw from the observations we make. Furthermore, incorrect inferences may be based upon accurate assessment.

Assessment is not contentious when the characteristic being assessed has an agreed-upon definition. We all know what height is, so if a new "measure" of height gives us a different reading than the one we expect, we conclude that the new measure is invalid. Similarly, inferences based on assessment are not contentious when the inferences made have unambiguous tests; for instance, a prediction that the stock market will rise on days when the temperature is cool can be quickly evaluated (and discarded).

The task of assessment becomes much more difficult when the characteristic being assessed does not have an agreed-upon definition and when the inferences we want to make do not have any clear tests. The assessment of psychological characteristics illustrates this difficulty, but uncertain measurement and inferences of dubious validity are by no means confined to psychology; examples can be seen in any attempt to assess very complex phenomena, such as subatomic physics or meteorology.

In intellectual assessment the constructs we try to assess are intelligence and its components. While there may be general agreement on the broad nature of these constructs, there is little theoretical consensus about their exact nature and how they should be assessed. The history of intellectual assessment has seen a continual debate about how many "intelligences" there are to be measured (Gardner, 1983). The inferences made on the basis of intellectual assessment are usually predictions about future performance, whether it be in school achievement or in job performance.

Two broad purposes can be identified for intellectual assessment. The first and more easily justifiable purpose is scientific curiosity; intellectual assessment is the method for determining and mapping the diversity of human mental competencies. This purpose is driven by theory and research and does not necessarily have any impact upon psychological practice. The second and more controversial purpose is prediction: We measure a set of intellectual characteristics at a point in time in order to predict how individuals will perform on other measures or at other points in time or to predict the environmental conditions under which they will perform best. The second purpose is clearly oriented toward application; this second purpose may lead to danger if it is divorced from the first—that is, if application loses its theoretical basis. It is important to distinguish among several issues relevant to the second purpose.

Selection versus Diagnosis

One of the guiding influences upon the field of intelligence has been the need to select a small number of individuals among many applicants for some sort of position; examples of this are the selection of children for regular schooling or the selection of military conscripts for officer training (see Vernon, 1979, pp. 3–7). If tests of intelligence can reduce the number of "inappropriate" persons selected, they can be used to make the process more efficient; presumably the inappropriate individuals either drop out of the position, or fail to become adequate in the position, or at least fail to be as good in the position as someone else who was not chosen.

However, it is important to realize that it is not always necessary to select individuals for a limited number of positions. For example, in the western world today there are enough school positions for every child. In many areas of education we want to ensure that the maximum education is offered to every applicant. In such cases the role of assessment should be to guide how education takes place for different individuals, rather than who should receive it. In this way, assessment takes on a diagnostic role rather than a selection role.

Fixed or Changeable Abilities

Prediction raises the question of how predictable are mental characteristics. It has often been assumed that assessment and prediction require fixed mental abilities. Although some degree of stability is required for meaningful measurement, and it is certainly true that fixed abilities have featured prominently in many approaches, assessment need not assume absolutely fixed abilities. Normal cognitive development is a process of change, but that does not mean that the process is chaotic. It is possible that traditional mental measurement has concentrated too much on the more stable aspects of cognition, ignoring aspects that may have more relevance to the cognitive changes we wish to promote. At the worst, measurement for the simple purpose of prediction describes what is likely to happen if we do not intervene. Traditional mental measurement may deserve the label "the dismal science" more than economics does!

Contextual Limits to Prediction

Prediction also has its limits. Any prediction has its boundary conditions, beyond which it is no longer valid. This is important in psychological assessment because each person being assessed has developed within a context, and predictions are made with reference to performance within some context. The research basis of any prediction is developed within contextual limits (e.g., the cultural background of the test subjects) and may not be appropriate for other contexts.

Consider a situation common in education, in which the relationship between a predictor and an outcome changes as a result of training. Prior to training, subjects employ a certain process in performing a task, a process that is helpful but not optimal. Before training, a measure of that process should be predictive of success in the task. If subjects are trained to employ a more optimal second process, then after training the measure of the first process should not be predictive of success. The validity of prediction may disappear with a change in process, due to a change in context, knowledge, or experience.

Prediction versus Explanation

Prediction is not the same as explanation or understanding. When measurement is not theory based, it is impossible to know why prediction has been successful. Traditional tests of intelligence are made up of items and subtests that have been selected because they correlate with other measures, not because they are derived from theoretical notions of what is being measured. Thus, it is difficult to be sure that the process is not circular. Explanation and understanding, rather than blind prediction, are the proper goals of science; they should contribute toward making selection or diagnosis more efficient as well.

WHAT IS MEASURED: ABILITIES OR PROCESSES?

The cornerstone of the traditional approach to mental measurement has been the concept of abilities. An ability is a trait or characteristic of a person, with respect to some mental task, that has attained a stable level of performance. Abilities are normally thought of as capacities, which can be measured in a "how much" sense; a person is said to have so much "ability" in the same way that a container is said to be able to hold so much water.

Abilities are thought to be organized hierarchically. General abilities, involved in many performances, are high in the hierarchy, and more task-specific abilities are at the lower levels. When a familiar task is encountered, the task-specific ability or abilities that have developed to perform it are activated; the individual's success in the task is determined by "how much" of the relevant abilities he or she has. When an unfamiliar task is encountered, higher or more general or more "fluid" abilities are brought to bear. The most general of abilities has been termed "g" or general intelligence (Spearman 1927). Each lower-level ability represents a more specific or narrow form of intelligence.

Many mental abilities have been identified, at various hierarchical levels. A typical hierarchy is presented in Figure 1-1. In most cases these abilities have not been derived from theory, but rather have been justified by the observed correlations among test performances (tasks). When a group of tasks clusters together empirically, the tests are inspected for some common element, and that element is the defining characteristic of the ability represented by that cluster of tests. In some cases particular abilities were hypothesized to exist (perhaps because they had been found

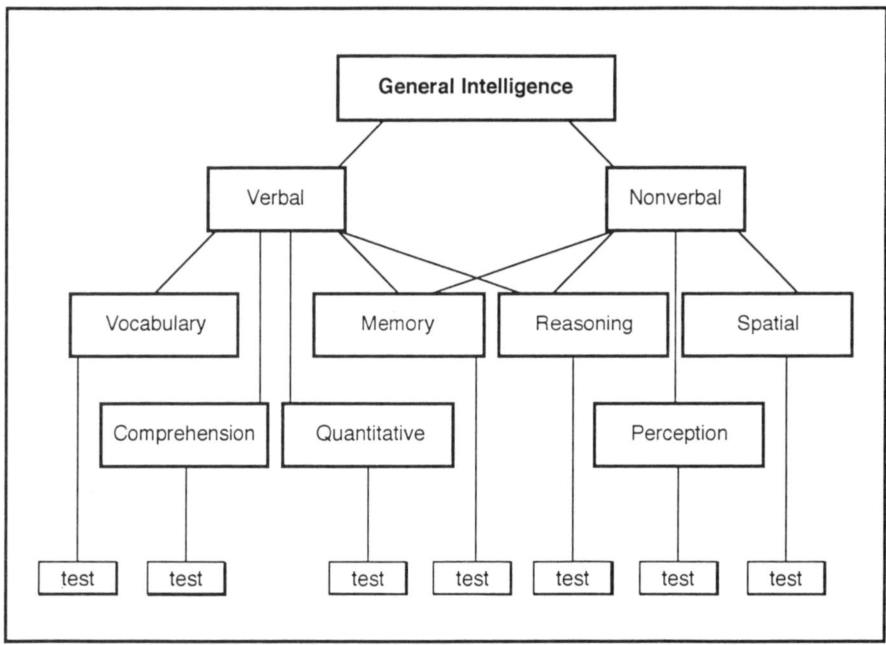

FIGURE 1-1 Hierarchy of General Intelligence

in a previous study), and tests were designed to tap them. In general, there has been no theoretical justification for which abilities exist, though theoretical interpretations of abilities have been made after the fact. This is shown by the nature of the abilities that have been found; as illustrated in Figure 1-1, some abilities refer to task content (verbal, spatial, quantitative) and others to the underlying mental process (reasoning, memory, perception). Traditional approaches to intelligence testing are dealt with further in Chapter 7.

The cognitive approach to intelligence emphasizes that capacities interact with processes that are dynamic and controllable, and that the processes themselves may be subject to capacity limitations. The existence of a capacity limit may be less important than the way in which that capacity is employed. Take for example the case of short-term memory. It is well known that short-term memory is limited, perhaps to seven items (Miller, 1956). Thus, one is limited to remembering seven sounds or words; however, with further or deeper processing, sounds or words can be formed into larger units ("chunked"), and remembering seven of those units results in memory for many more of the lower-level units. The capacity or ability stays the same, but the nature of the processing dramatically alters the performance (or functional level). Furthermore, new factors become relevant—e.g., one's capacity to carry out the process of chunking information.

Cognition emphasizes the mental operations that subjects execute, and clearly some of these are under conscious control. Individuals may have capacities that they do not know how to use, and they may not realize which they should be using. *Strategies,* conscious plans for performing tasks, are responsible for deploying abilities, yet traditional assessment avoided strategies and their assessment. Because strategies may be more relevant to changing performance, it seems crucial that they be the subject of assessment. Traditional approaches emphasized the stability of abilities and thus saw no need to investigate the more changeable components.

The notion of hierarchy illustrated above for abilities is also useful when considering processes (see Figure 1-2). Like abilities, processes may exist at various levels of generality; thus, we may have a specific strategy for dealing with a particular type of task, or a much more general strategy for dealing with a broader class of tasks (Kirby, 1989). The processes we deal with in this book are general processes, in that we are interested in generalizing to broad domains of behavior; however, each of these processes has its more domain-specific counterparts or aspects, and each of those may have task-specific equivalents. In order to fully understand a subject's behavior, we need to consider the general processes and also the extent to which that subject can apply those processes in a given task context (e.g., reading) and the task-specific knowledge regarding that context that the subject has attained (e.g., in reading, knowledge of phonics and of word meanings).

The adoption of a cognitive approach would seem to be beneficial for both clients and practitioners. The clients who are assessed benefit by having their competencies seen within a more valid and dynamic perspective. The other clients, those who asked that the assessment be done (e.g.,

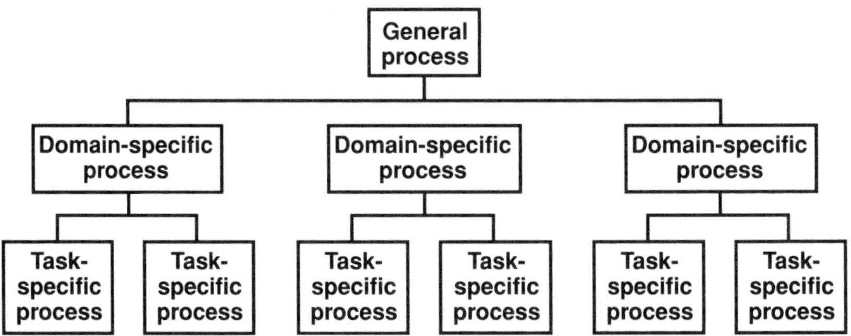

FIGURE 1-2 Hierarchy of Cognitive Processes

teachers and parents), benefit from receiving advice that is both more valid and more intrinsically related to cognitive improvement. Psychologists can drop their role as predictors of failure, become more in tune with theoretical developments in their profession, and serve their clients more productively. Furthermore, as the process of assessment becomes more valid, it should become easier for psychologists and clients to communicate about it, because it exists within a coherent theoretical framework. The result is not magic, however. Limits upon individuals' capacities or abilities continue to exist; the cognitive approach offers a new view of these limits, suggests some new factors that need to be addressed, and may help psychologists and clients alike in attaining those limits.

2

CONCEPTUALIZATION AND MEASUREMENT OF INTELLIGENCE: A COGNITIVE PROCESSING MODEL

Progress in the field of human intellectual assessment cannot be achieved if "improvements" consist mainly of revisions of old tests or reconceptualizations of the tasks included in old measures. We must be willing to expand the very concept of intelligence and, consequently, the scope of intelligence tests in order to effect a paradigm shift in this field. Das, Kirby, and Jarman (1975) and, more recently, Naglieri and Das (1990) have suggested that this reconceptualization should begin with the idea that intelligence is better viewed as *cognitive processes*. This conception should be followed by the construction of tests based on a theory that has been proposed, tested, modified, and deemed worthy of operationalization.

This chapter presents an overview of the model of cognitive functioning called *Planning, Attention, Simultaneous, and Successive (PASS) processing*. The model has been proposed as a new view of intelligence and evolved through many years of theoretical and empirical work. Initially described as an information processing model derived from Luria (Das, 1973b; Das, Kirby, & Jarman, 1975) and then as the Information-Integration model (Das, Kirby, & Jarman, 1979), recently the theory has been called the PASS model (Naglieri & Das, 1988, 1990). This view of intelligence is based on the neuropsychological work of A. R. Luria (1966, 1973, 1980) as well as cognitive psychological findings (Broadbent, 1958; Hunt & Lansman, 1986; Simon, 1981). We believe that it has a strong theoretical foundation, has been sufficiently operationalized, and is making significant contributions to understanding exceptionality, predicting academic and job performance, and intervention design.

THE PLANNING-ATTENTION-SIMULTANEOUS-SUCCESSIVE MODEL

A. Roots of the Model—Functional Units

According to Luria (1966, 1973, 1980), human cognitive processing involves three functional systems or units that work in concert and whose participation is "necessary for any type of mental activity" (1973, p. 43). The first functional unit is responsible for regulating cortical tone and maintenance of attention; the second unit receives, processes, and stores information using simultaneous and successive information coding; and the third unit programs, regulates, and directs mental activity. Luria states that the first functional unit is associated with the brain stem, diencephalon, and medial regions of the hemispheres. The second unit's functions are regulated by the occipital, parietal, and temporal lobes posterior to the central sulcus, and the third unit's functions are regulated by the frontal lobes, especially the prefrontal region. Although this model has a strong neurological foundation, our focus is on the cognitive processing components rather than their specific neurological locations. Each of these cognitive functions will be discussed in separate chapters.

The first functional unit is at the base of human mental processes because it maintains a proper state of arousal or cortical tone that allows for the focus of attention. Only when a proper waking condition is achieved can an individual receive and process information. Maintaining an appropriate level of arousal is especially important for effective activity since too much or too little interferes with proper information coding and planning. Appropriate levels of arousal also provide the opportunity for the specific direction of attention. Insufficient performance of this first functional unit, therefore, leads to difficulty with information coding (simultaneous and successive processes) and planning due to an underarousal or overarousal of the second and third functional units as well as difficulty in selective and organized responding (Luria, 1973).

The arousal aspect of the first functional unit is important because it provides the opportunity for the voluntary action of attention. Arousal and attention are closely related but at the same time distinct processes. Arousal is responsible for cortical tone and wakefulness, and attention is a more complex cognitive activity. While attention (selective and sustained, for example) is mainly under voluntary control, it is influenced by cortical arousal. Given an appropriate state of arousal, the two broad classes of selective and divided attention (Kahneman & Treisman, 1984) may occur. *Selective attention* tasks require the subject to focus or act on relevant stimuli and ignore irrelevant stimuli, while *divided attention* tasks measure the extent to which different activities can be performed without a loss of efficiency (Kahneman & Treisman, 1984). Any task involving the intentional discrimination between stimuli (e.g., trying to read a book in a distracting setting) requires selective attention, which is an important activity of the first functional unit.

The processing flow chart of attention presented in Figure 2-1 illustrates the structure of an attention task. According to this diagram, attention tasks require the individual to direct his or her responses to a particular stimulus and suppress reacting to a competing stimulus or stimuli. In this paradigm a multiple stimulus array is presented and instructions to respond to one stimulus and ignore the other are given. The attention test used by Das and Naglieri (1989) following the work of Stroop (1935) is an example of this type of task (see Chapter 3). The Stroop test materials present two variables to the subject; one is a word (e.g., *red, green, blue*) and the other is the color of the ink used to print the word (e.g., blue, red, green). The task requires the child to say the color in which each word is printed and not read the actual printed word. For example, the child sees the word *red* printed in green ink and must say "green" not "red." This task is congruent with the attentional paradigm because it requires the subject to suppress a response with a shorter latency (reading the word) in favor of a response with a longer latency (naming the color).

The second functional unit is responsible for receiving, processing, and retaining information a person obtains from the external world. Luria

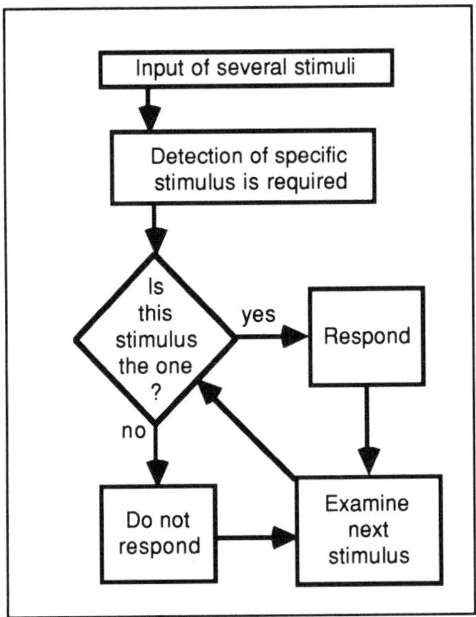

FIGURE 2-1 Attention Processes Path Diagram

(1966) states that "there is strong evidence for distinguishing two basic forms of integrative activity of the cerebral cortex, by which different aspects of the outside world may be reflected" (p. 74). These two types of processes are *simultaneous* (integration of stimuli into synchronous and primarily spatial groups) and *successive* (integration of stimuli into temporally organized serial order).

Simultaneous processing involves the integration of stimuli into groups, or the recognition that a number of stimuli share a common characteristic. Both of these aspects require that all the stimuli be related to one another. Simultaneous processing may take place with perceived stimuli (as when a child copies a design such as a cube), remembered stimuli (when the design is drawn from memory), or the conceptual aspects of stimuli (when the child reasons about a design as in Raven's (1956) or Naglieri's (1985a) figural matrices). These examples illustrate how the specific content of the task may vary considerably while the processing requirement remains the same.

The essence of simultaneous processing is that the elements of the stimuli are interrelated (i.e., surveyable). Simultaneously processed information is said to be *surveyable* because the elements are interrelated and accessible to inspection either through examination of the actual stimuli during the activity (as in the case of design copying) or through memory of the stimuli (as in the case of reproduction of a design from memory). Simultaneous processing is also involved when a person examines logical grammatical relations (for example, "the father's brother" and "the brother's father"). To further illustrate, a verbal simultaneous task may involve directions such as "draw a circle under a square to the right of a cross on top of a triangle." In this case the individual must examine the relationships and configuration among the circle, square, and cross based upon their spatial arrangement from the logical grammatical structure of the statement. The requirement is that the component parts of the task need to be interrelated. This critical aspect of surveyability (Das, Kirby, & Jarman, 1975) demands simultaneous processing (Naglieri & Das, 1990). The relationships among the components of a simultaneous task are illustrated in Figure 2-2.

Successive processing involves the integration of stimuli into a particular series where the elements form a chainlike progression. The critical aspect of successive processing is that elements must be ordered without surveyability. In contrast to simultaneous processing in which the elements are interrelated in various ways, in successive processing the elements are only linearly related. For example, successive coding is needed for skilled movements (e.g., writing) because this activity requires "a series of movements which follow each other in a strictly defined order . . . without surveyability" (Luria, 1966, p. 78). In the early stages of the formation of

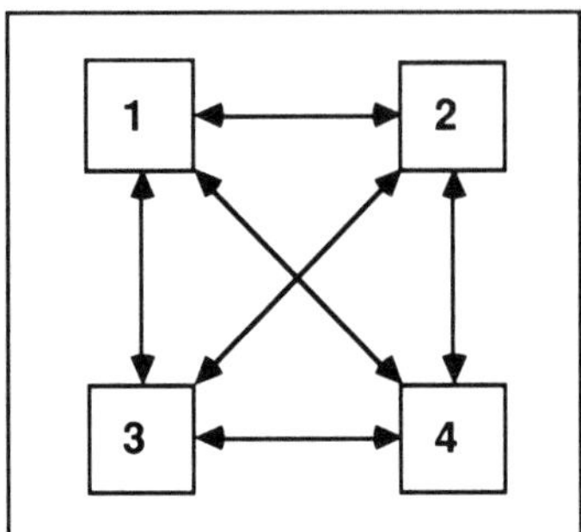

FIGURE 2-2 Simultaneous Processing Path Diagram

the skilled movement, each successive link exists as a separate unit and may be taught as a specific step in a larger behavior. Only when each aspect becomes automatic can the initial stimulus in the chain become the signal that leads to the automatic execution of the complete successive action. Linguistic tasks involving successive processing require the subject to appreciate the linearity of stimuli with no requirement for interrelating of the parts. For example, successive processes are involved to answer the question "The girl hit the boy—who got hurt?" because the ordering of the words within the sentence must be appreciated (Luria, 1984), as in repetition of words or numbers in proper order. The relationships among the components of a successive task are illustrated in Figure 2-3.

Evidence that simultaneous and successive processing are involved with the acquisition, storage, and retrieval of knowledge according to the demands of the task rather than its modality, method of presentation, or the task's content is available. Das, Cummins, et al. (1979) demonstrated that tasks of auditory (WISC-R Digit Span) and visual (Visual Short-Term Memory) modalities both involved successive processing. While the methods of presentation for tasks such as Figure Copying (drawing a design from an example) and Memory-For-Designs (drawing a design from memory) employed by Das, Cummins, et al. (1979) are very different, both have loaded on simultaneous factors. Research summarized by Jarman (1980) and Luria (1966) suggests that both forms of coding (simultaneous and successive processes) contribute a different component to language

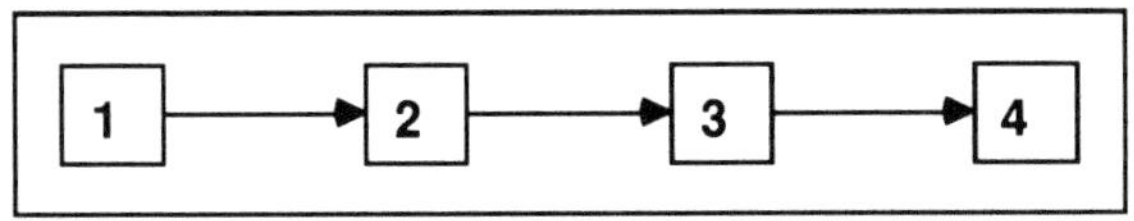

FIGURE 2-3 Successive Processing Path Diagram

usage. Understanding the syntax of a sentence involves the appreciation of the serial relation of one word to the next, which requires successive processing, and the comprehension of the meaning of a sentence involves simultaneous processing (Kirby & Gordon, 1988).

The third functional unit described by Luria (1973) allows the individual to form plans of action, carry them out, and verify the effectiveness of the plans. The third functional unit relies on the second functional unit for processing components and the first functional unit for proper attentional status. With the prerequisite functioning of these units, the individual can develop plans of action, inspect performance and regulate behavior so that it conforms to these plans, and then compare the effects of these actions with the original intention so that correction of mistakes is possible. The third functional unit is also responsible for activities such as impulse control, regulation of voluntary actions, and linguistic functions such as spontaneous speech (Luria, 1980). Das (1984a) and Arlin (1977) suggest that planning is the essence of human intelligence, as it involves the aptitude for asking new questions, solving problems, and self-monitoring as well as the application of information-coding processes.

Planning processes are distinct from simultaneous, successive, and attentional processes because they provide the individual the means to analyze cognitive activity, develop some method to solve a problem, evaluate the effectiveness of a solution, and modify the approach used as needed. These processes are necessary when an efficient and/or systematic approach to solving a problem is required. That is, planning processes provide the individual with the facility to determine and utilize an efficient way to solve a problem through the application of attention, simultaneous, and successive processes in conjunction with the base of knowledge.

The generation, selection, and execution of plans are the three main aspects of planning. As Figure 2-4 illustrates, the individual needs to become aware of the necessity of finding a plan before a method can be devised. Children and adults alike may not be aware that plans are necessary. If an appropriate plan is not within the individual's knowledge base, then one may not be used, or, alternatively, one may be sought and obtained, perhaps through instruction or by invention. If more than one is found, selecting the best one is important, and monitoring of the effectiveness of these solutions is always needed.

Good planning typically involves a series of executive actions that includes various components as shown in Figure 2-4. First, a task is presented to the individual and he or she must determine how it is to be solved. It may be a complex or simple task and may involve attentional, simultaneous, and successive processes, but the main requirement is to determine how to solve the problem. Next, the need for a plan is determined, and if a systematic approach to solving the problem is apparent,

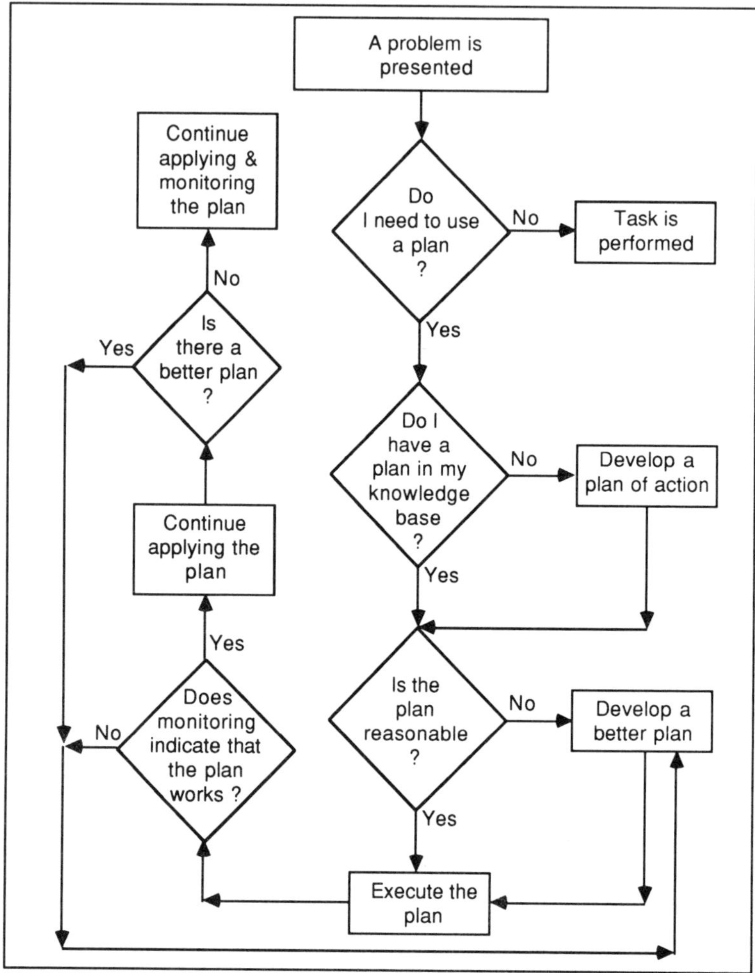

FIGURE 2-4 Planning Processes Path Diagram

then the individual searches his or her base of knowledge for an approach. If one is not within the knowledge base, an initial plan of action is developed and the plan is examined to determine if it is a reasonable one or not. If it is acceptable, the plan is implemented, but if not, a new plan is devised. If the plan is put into action, decisions are made to modify the effectiveness of the approach, continue applying the plan, modify it to achieve the most efficient approach to problem solving, or generate another one. This last step is iterated until the task is completed.

Knowledge base is the context within which all cognitive processes operate. Information is received and processed and the output is programmed depending on the knowledge base. This fund of accumulated knowledge can be thought of as the cumulative result of a person's experiences that have been stored in memory. Because all processes operate within the context of knowledge, this base of information influences all cognitive processes and motor programs.

Knowledge base includes information that has been accumulated through both formal and informal means. Formal knowledge is that acquired through instruction or reading; informal knowledge is that obtained by one's experiences. For example, in comprehending the meaning of a passage, the reader has to have acquired the knowledge of most of the words in order to understand each sentence and the necessary background knowledge related to the statements. The purpose of reading (e.g., to find out a particular fact or to follow the story) is also important because it allows the individual to transcend the letters and words to get at the meaning of the text. All of these activities use prior knowledge implicitly, without conscious effort.

Relationships among the PASS processes

The three functional units are dynamic in that they respond to the experiences of the individual, are subject to developmental changes, and form an interrelated system. The interactive and influential nature of attention, information coding, and planning is illustrated in Figure 2-5. As is evident from the figure, the functional units are all related while at the same time they maintain independence by having distinct functions. Additionally, the units rely on (and influence) one's base of knowledge. Coding and planning interact to perform various acts and facilitate acquisition of knowledge, but at the same time these higher functions depend on a proper state of arousal to provide the opportunity for learning. All the processes are influenced by the knowledge base, and, more exactly, knowledge acts as a moderator for processing. Therefore, effective processing is accomplished through the integration of knowledge with planning, attention, simultaneous, and successive processes as demanded by the particular task.

The information to be processed can arrive through any of the receptors (eyes, ears, skin, muscle movements, etc.) serially (ie., over time) or synchronously (i.e., concurrently). That is, several stimuli may be presented to the individual at one time or one at a time (e.g., hearing two different words at the same time or two words in a series). Auditory information is often presented serially, while visual information is frequently presented as a synchronous array. Despite the type of presentation, information processing is done according to the requirements of the task and is not dictated by the method (serial or concurrent) of presentation.

Because the PASS processes are viewed as interactive, they act in concert to provide specific functions to virtually all tasks performed in everyday life. This is not to say, however, that all the processes are equally involved in all tasks. In test development we attempt to identify tasks in which a particular process plays the dominant role, thus isolating that process to the extent possible. But in reality one process may be more related to some but not all other processes. This is illustrated by the close relationship between planning and attention described by Luria (1980) and Stuss and Benson (1986) resulting from the large number of neural connections between the first and third functional units in the brain. The reader should keep in mind, however, that all the PASS components are viewed as interactive; they act in concert to provide specific functions to virtually all tasks performed in everyday life, but not necessarily on an equal basis.

The relationship between the first and third functional units is a close one both theoretically and anatomically (Luria, 1980). Since planning requires an adequate state of arousal so that attention can be focused, an appropriate level of activation, attention, and arousal is needed so plans of action can be generated and utilized. Effective planning requires an appropriately aroused state as well as the inhibition of an inappropriate level of arousal. Selectively inhibiting or facilitating arousal is one of the important functions of the third functional unit associated with planning.

A similar strong relationship between coding and planning exists. Because real-life tasks can often be coded in different ways, how one manages the information is a planning function that influences the coding approach used. The application of simultaneous and/or successive processes will be influenced by the executive function of the third unit and, in addition, by the person's prior learning experiences. This has been illustrated by Hunt (1975), who described how Raven's Matrices could be solved using a gestalt or analytic approach, and by Lawson and Kirby (1981), Kirby and Das (1978b), and Kirby and Lawson (1983), who found that the application of these approaches and the effectiveness of solving the items can be influenced by training.

The output component of the PASS diagram is a complex function by itself. Following processing activities that are a result of the demands of the task, the output may require additional processes. For example, simultaneous processes may predominate in the solution of a task, but motor programming may be required if the response is a written one. An individual may have the competence in processing but fail to come up

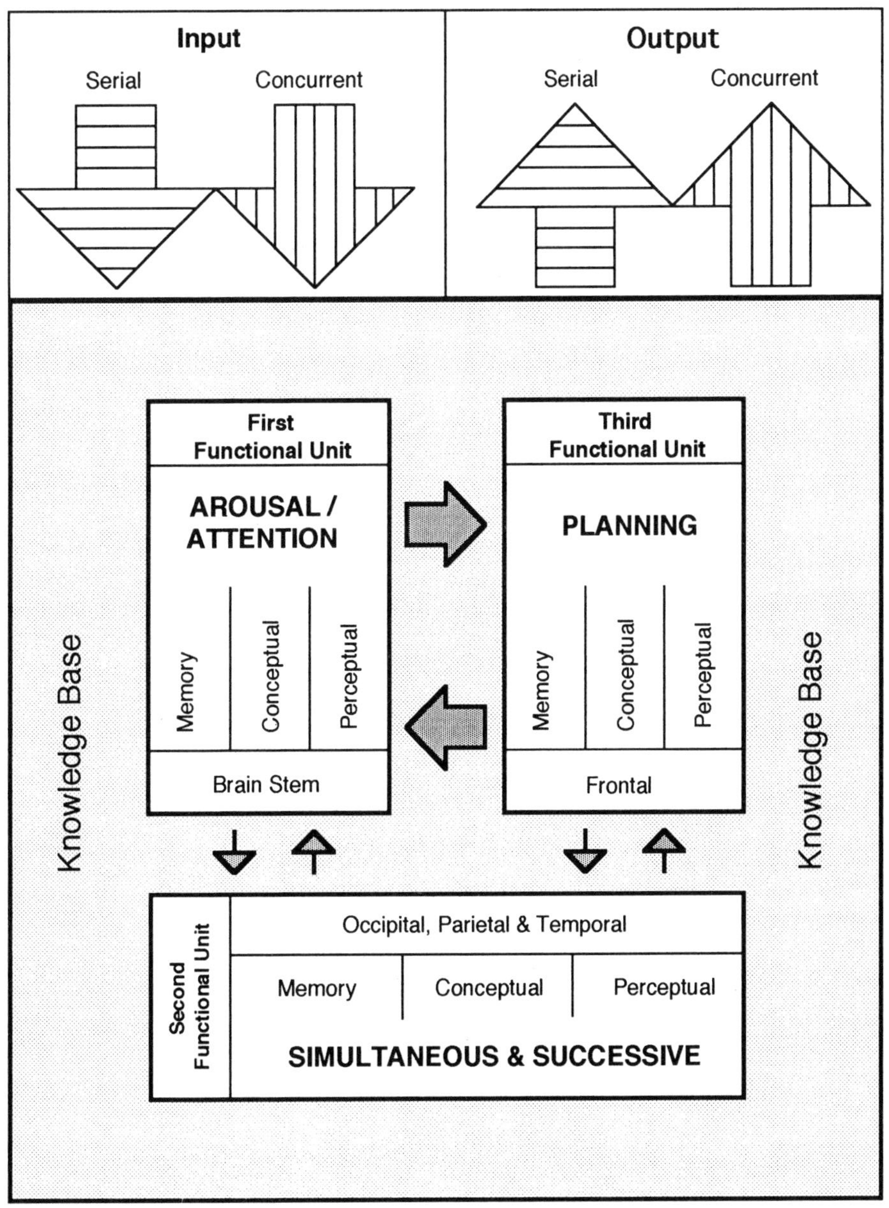

FIGURE 2-5 The PASS Model of Ability

with the motor program required to respond. This can be a problem in special groups such as brain-damaged and mentally handicapped individuals.

SUPPORT FOR THE PASS MODEL

Neuropsychological Base

At the base of the issue of the validity of the PASS model is the neuropsychological work of A. R. Luria (1966, 1973, 1980) and his identification of the cognitive processes. Luria's functional organization of the brain, as it relates to specific regions, is used as a way to conceptualize the important aspects of human ability. We have used the three functional unit model as a base for identifying the four important processes involved in human cognitive competence. The value of the PASS model rests on the extent to which it provides a thorough means to conceptualize and measure human cognitive competence. Luria's conceptualization of neuropsychological functioning is used, therefore, as a base upon which to build a model of the important cognitive processes related to successful human functioning (Das & Varnhagen, 1986). It is important to note, however, that at this time the PASS tasks are used to assess cognitive processes rather than as direct measures of neurological status. That is, the test battery has not been specifically developed for the purpose of neuropsychological assessment and, therefore, should be used to assess cognitive functioning rather than neurological stauts until the appropriate evidence for validity is provided.

Factorial Validity

Simultaneous and Successive Processing

Complementing Luria's work is the simultaneous and successive processing research initially reported by Das (1972) and Das, Kirby, and Jarman (1975, 1979), which has clearly shown that the simultaneous and successive information coding component of the model has construct validity. These researchers and others have found simultaneous and successive factors and evidence of developmental differences by chronological and mental age using tests such as Progressive Matrices, Memory for Designs, and Figure Copying (simultaneous) and Digit Span forward, sound blending, and Sentence Repetition (successive). The studies have involved samples of elementary and middle school age students (Das, 1972, 1973 a,b; Das & Molloy, 1975; Garofalo, 1986; Jarman & Das, 1977; Kirby & Das, 1978a; Kirby & Robinson, 1987; Naglieri & Das, 1988), high school age samples (Naglieri & Das, 1988; Biggs & Kirby, 1984), and adults (Das & Heemsbergen, 1983; McCallum & Merritt, 1983; Merritt & McCallum, 1983; Wachs & Harris, 1986; Ashman, 1982). We discuss these and other studies in Chapter 3.

Simultaneous and successive factors have been identified in a range of culturally distinct settings. Leong, Cheng, and Das, (1985) found evidence of simultaneous and successive processing (as well as planning) in a sample of normal Chinese students in Hong Kong, and a significant relationship between reading and each of these processes, as did Naglieri and Das (1988). In other cross-cultural investigations, Mwamwenda, Dash, and Das (1984) and Dash, Puhan, and Mahapatra (1985) found support for simultaneous and successive factors with samples of children in India. Additionally, several investigations have reported simultaneous and successive factors in samples of Canadian (e.g., Das, 1973; Das, Bisanz, & Mancini, 1984), Native Canadian (e.g., Krywaniuk & Das, 1976), American (e.g., Naglieri & Das, 1988; Wachs & Harris, 1986), Australian (e.g., Schofield & Ashman, 1986), and Australian Aboriginal (Klich & Davidson, 1984) children. These studies and others provide evidence that tasks used to operationalize simultaneous, successive, and planning processes have functioned similarly despite wide differences in culture, language, and socioeconomic status.

Validity for tasks used to measure the second functional unit has also been found with various types of exceptional children. Simultaneous and successive factors have been identified by several researchers for samples of normal (Das & Dash, 1983; Das, Kirby & Jarman, 1975; Naglieri & Das, 1988), mentally retarded (Ashman, 1982; Cummins & Das, 1980; Das, 1972; Das & Cummins, 1979; Das, Cummins, et al., 1979; Das & Molloy, 1975; Jarman, 1978; Leong, 1980), learning disabled (Das, Leong, & Williams, 1978), and gifted (Karnes & McCallum, 1983; Snart, O'Grady, & Das, 1982) children and adults. Detailed treatment of this topic will be provided in a subsequent chapter.

Planning

Tasks intended to measure the third functional unit of planning have been examined recently along with simultaneous and successive tasks. In this research, planning has emerged as a separate factor distinct from simultaneous and successive processing. Planning tasks ranged in complexity from the simple connection of numbers on a page (Trail Making) to more complex tasks such as writing a story and playing a strategic game (Das &

Heemsbergen, 1983). Results of factor analytic studies have found simple tasks such as Trail Making and Visual Search to load with complex ones such as those involving written composition of a story (Ashman & Das, 1980; Das & Heemsbergen, 1983), solving syllogistic reasoning items (Das & Heemsbergen, 1983), the Wisconsin Card Sorting task (Garofalo, 1982), and a pictorial category task (Schofield & Ashman, 1986). Two recently developed tasks involving identification of two out of six identical numbers on a row (called matching numbers) and completion of a page of symbol/letter pairs (called planned codes) have also loaded with visual search and/or trail making in studies by Naglieri and Das (1988) and Stutzman (1986).

The separation of planning processes from speed of processing has been an important issue because most planning tasks are timed. While timing a task does not mean that the score will reflect speed, since time may reflect efficiency as well as rate, analysis of these two components has shown that they are different. Das (1984), Das and Dash (1983), and Naglieri, Prewett, and Bardos (1989) showed how speed of reading words and speed of saying the color of an object did not load with planning factors identified using the timed tasks Visual Search and Trail Making. Additionally, Ashman and Das (1980) showed that simple reaction time (latency to press a switch following an auditory and visual stimulus) did not load on the same factor as planning defined by Visual Search and Trail Making. Thus, the interpretation of planning as speed has not been supported.

Attention

Finally, tasks to operationalize the first functional unit of attention have recently been included. Naglieri, Das, et al. (1991) and Naglieri, Prewett, and Bardos (1989) have found selective attention measures similar to those used by Posner and Boies (1971) and Stroop (1935) to be useful in assessment of attention. While researchers studying the PASS model have only recently begun to incorporate attentional tasks into the battery, the results of these initial investigations are encouraging. For example, Reardon and Naglieri (1991) found that these attentional tasks were effective in the assessment of individuals with attentional deficit disorder. (This will be discussed more in Chapter 3).

In considering the degree to which these factor analytic findings are supportive of the PASS model, the issue of the use of this particular statistical approach warrants discussion. Although factor analysis has been important in the development of the validity research on this model, the interpretation of the factors has been based on the theory articulated by Luria and is not a post hoc interpretation of patterns of tests from a factor analysis. The approach taken has been to first choose measures that fit the theory based on an analysis of their anticipated and suggested processing requirements and then to test the degree to which each task is an efficient measure of the process using correlational, as well as other (e.g., ANOVA), analyses.

The factorial investigations inform us about the efficiency of the tasks used to represent planning, attention, simultaneous, and successive processes and are not intended to be a definitive test of the theory. As such, the results provide an indication of the extent to which a group of variables used to operationalize the theory reflects some common influence (the specific process) as well as the extent to which variables can be organized into different dimensions (Carroll, 1983). This helps in the determination of a group of robust measures that may be useful in research and clinical settings. This information should then be used to examine validity issues that test the utility of the theoretical model of human cognitive functioning for differential diagnosis, sensitivity to neurological status, and so on. The value of these factorial analyses is, therefore, to illustrate that Luria's constructs can be operationalized and therefore may have potential for use in research and clinical settings.

Another factorial method currently available for estimating the degree to which the hypothesized PASS model can describe the interrelationships of the variables and the extent to which this corresponds to the observed pattern of covariances among the variables is the LISREL confirmatory approach. This approach provides an index of the goodness of fit of theoretical models and can also examine the relative fit of several theoretical models.

LISREL confirmatory factor analytic results reported by Naglieri, Das, et al. (1991) clearly demonstrated that the four-factor PASS model provided the best conceptualization of the underlying interrelationships among a set of tasks administered to a sample of 247 individuals ranging in age from 5 to 19 years. Using a number of criteria for evaluating model goodness of fit, the PASS model was found to provide a good fit. Relative comparisons of four models also indicated that the PASS model was a significant improvement over other models tested. In comparison to Verbal-Spatial-Speed, Verbal-Nonverbal, Memory-Reasoning, and "g" alternative models, the PASS model consistently provided a significantly better fit to the observed data. These results have since been replicated by Naglieri, Braden, and Gottling (1993) and Naglieri, Braden, and Warrick (1993).

PASS and Achievement

PASS is not just a theory of intelligence test performance, but of cognition in general. It is, therefore, quite unlike traditional approaches to intelligence, which not only lacked a theoretical basis, but also had no basis for a theoretical connection to school achievement. PASS provides a framework within which achievement skills may be understood and thus provides a firm basis for diagnosing and remediating children's learning problems.

The planning and attention components of PASS processes are particularly important for understanding achievement. While much research has implicated these areas in the poor achievement of many children, neither has featured prominently in theories of intelligence, and neither has been the focus of psychometric assessment. In fact, these processes may provide the key to understanding and predicting behavior that has eluded previous approaches. Take, for instance, the prediction of success in a profession. While traditional intelligence measures predict who will enter a particular profession, they seem unrelated to success in a particular field. It is very possible that achievement within a particular narrow domain is a function of the interaction of planning, attention, simultaneous, and successive processes with a particular knowledge base. For example, planning processes are most critical in activities requiring the use of unique or nonroutinized solutions to problems. In such cases the worker must evaluate the information provided and select relevant from irrelevant information (attention) to apply the appropriate process or processes (simultaneous and/or successive) and, most importantly, determine how these three processes will be applied and maintained (planning) to bring the task to a successful completion.

For the present purposes it is only necessary to demonstrate that PASS measures are empirically related to achievement measures. This has been done in numerous studies employing many different PASS and achievement measures in many different subject populations, as discussed in detail in subsequent chapters. For example, various aspects of reading achievement have been shown to be significantly related to simultaneous and successive processes (Cummins & Das, 1978; Kirby & Das, 1977; Naglieri & Das, 1987) and to planning (Das, 1984a; Naglieri & Das, 1987). Measures of mathematics achievement have been shown to be related to simultaneous and successive processing (Garofalo, 1986; Naglieri & Das, 1987), to planning (Ashman & Das, 1980; Das & Heemsbergen, 1983; Garofalo, 1982; Kirby & Ashman, 1984), and to attention (Warrick, 1989).

Diagnostic Utility

One aim of diagnosis is to determine if a congruence exists between an individual's cognitive processing competence and academic, or job, requirements. Due to the relatively greater complexity of the PASS model and the increased perspective with which it views cognitive processes, there is an increased potential for sensitivity to personal variations. Through the changed perspective from which intelligence is viewed, more efficient diagnostic power for exceptional children, such as the learning disabled, is possible. This has been supported by Bardos (1988), who found that through the addition of planning and attention measures, identification of individuals as learning disabled and mentally retarded was improved over the use of information coding (simultaneous and successive) measures alone. This finding is consistent with those by Naglieri (1985b) and Naglieri and Haddad (1984) in that measures of simultaneous and successive processing alone were not sufficient to diagnose a learning disability. The limited success of current intelligence tests, such as the WISC-R and K-ABC, to be sensitive to the deficiencies of many disabled children is well documented (Naglieri, Das, & Jarman, 1990) and, as suggested by Naglieri and Das (1990), may be the result of the limited perspective of intelligence these measures use. The sensitivity of the PASS model to the difficulties of reading disabled students has been examined and is summarized in Chapter 8.

SUMMARY

The Planning, Attention, Simultaneous, Successive cognitive processing model (PASS) provides a new approach to intelligence and its assessment of individual status that is based on the neuropsychological model of A. R. Luria. The conceptualization of PASS and their assessment has been based on contemporary research on cognitive psychology as well. Individual PASS processes are assessed by tasks that normally require the engagement of the specific cognitive process regardless of the test's content (e.g., verbal or nonverbal) or modality (e.g., visual or auditory). Simultaneous processing will be apparent when the child is required to interrelate the components of the task where each stimulus must be considered in relation to every other. Successive processing will be apparent when the child is required to appreciate the linearity of stimuli. Attentional processes require the direction of cognitive activity to a particular stimulus and inhibition to a competing stimulus. Planning processes will be involved when the individual is required to analyze a task, develop a means of solving the problem, evaluate the effectiveness of the solution, modify the plan as needed, and, finally, demonstrate some efficient and systematic approach to problem solving. Planning processes provide the individual with the means to utilize simultaneous and successive processes for tasks that are the focus of attention. The research conducted on the PASS model suggests that it is a viable alternative to the traditional psychometric view of intelligence because it (1) has been shown to have factorial validity, (2) can be effectively operationalized, (3) is related to achievement, and, (4) provides a theoretical perspective from which to understand and identify exceptional students.

PART II

PROCESSES OF COGNITION

3

ATTENTION

Before we can assess attention, we of course need to know what it is. The concept of attention is used widely by educators and psychologists. Teachers in elementary school demand attention from their young students. Psychologists and psychiatrists diagnose children as suffering from an attentional deficit disorder (ADD). Children of drug abusers may demonstrate deficits in cognitive functions including attention. Babies born to mothers who have frequently used alcohol during pregnancy may grow up to develop ADD with hyperactivity. Activity or arousal level and its relation to attention should be understood both in terms of physiological as well as behavioral changes. In this chapter we present the concepts of arousal and attention, discuss the theories, and describe the attention tests used in our research. This will include information that is neuropsychological in nature and details of cognitive functions whose application to assessment is not immediately apparent. We believe, however, that this information is necessary to appreciate the intricate nature of attention and provide a critical background for its assessment.

Attention and arousal are difficult to define, yet there is no reason to doubt that we experience both. Typically, attention has been observed to entail focus and selectivity. Things and ideas come in and out of focus; at one time we are clearly aware of certain objects or thoughts, and at other times they fade away. Fluctuations of attention or shifts in attention occur as long as we are awake. In the history of psychology, Titchener (1908), who was one of the proponents of structuralism, thought of attention in terms of "sensible clearness" or clarity of sensation. William James (1890), a contemporary of Titchener, thought of attention as a process of selection, simply because we need to select from the large number of stimuli that impinge on us during our waking moments.

There are several problems that make it difficult to arrive at one definition of attention. First of all is its relationship to consciousness. Is it always a conscious behavior? The second problem is its relationship with arousal and the localization of arousal and attention in the brain. It has been claimed for a long time (Wundt, 1904) that attention is probably linked with the functions of the frontal lobe. A third difficulty is philosophical, concerning the mobilization of attention, the very process of selecting what to attend to and what not to. The selection must be conducted by something or someone. Who makes the selection? This is the old problem of the little person, a homunculus, who resides in the brain, orchestrating the focusing of attention and selecting what is relevant and what is irrelevant. We shall address each of these issues in this chapter, following a survey of current perspectives on attention.

INFORMATION PROCESSING AND NEUROPSYCHOLOGICAL PERSPECTIVES

Arousal and attention can be examined from two broad but often interactive perspectives: physiology, including neuropsychology, and information processing. In Chapter 2, we have established a need to consider these two perspectives *together* for understanding all cognitive processes. We begin with the distinction between arousal and attention.

Arousal and Attention

According to Luria's conceptualization of arousal and attention, arousal is the function of the first block of the brain, a unit for regulating the level of activity of both body and mind. The unit includes subcortical structures such as the reticular formation and the thalamus and interacts with the frontal lobes more intensively than with the other areas of the brain. There are three sources of influence on arousal: (1) metabolic processes of the individual regulated by the hypothalamus (different people have different metabolic processes—some are mostly lazy and sleepy, whereas others are more energetic due to their higher levels of metabolism); (2) orienting response registering the arrival of a stimulus from outside (as described in detail later in this chapter), when the stimulus is novel, intense, or confusable; and (3) internal sources of stimuli from intentions, plans, and other thoughts arriving from the frontal lobes. Of these three sources, the second and third are most related to attention.

Arousal can be modulated by outside conditions such as heat, cold, and noise, as well as by internal affective or cognitive conditions such as anxiety, anger, and fear. Attention to the task at hand may increase under loud levels of noise or anxiety and decrease when the level is excessively high. A prolonged period of attention may reduce arousal, making the individual sleepy. Arousal is seen as a psychophysical change in decreased or increased heart rate, blood flow, and respiration, but the same changes can be used as measures of attention as well. We shall discuss this later in some detail. But for now, what can we conclude about the relation between attention and arousal? *Arousal* is the state of being active. Arousal, for example, is low when one is drowsy and high after drinking coffee. During mental activity we need more arousal while solving a difficult problem. It is a general rather than a specific state of alertness. *Attention*, on the other hand, is specific; we attend to something in particular, whereas we can be generally alert. Although it is not easy to separate arousal from attention, it is safe to say that arousal is subcortical whereas attention is also partly controlled by the cortex, especially by the frontal lobe. Arousal and attention are next discussed from the point of view of information processing.

Information Processing Approach

The information processing theories assume that what has happened before must determine the significance of any event that happens now. In other words, an event is significant only if it is novel or if it has been given special meaning or significance. There are many determinants of attention. Some signals become important because of *genetic predisposition*. Even very young children are predisposed to attend to language and to a human face. Animals, too, are predisposed to attend: the rabbit to the rustling sound of leaves, dogs to smell, and so forth. Another factor that influences us to attend to certain things and not to others is the *need state* of the individual, such as the physical need to satisfy hunger and thirst. Needs can be made salient through self-instruction as well. The child in a class creates the need or motivation to pay attention to the teacher. Needs are also produced through social interactions, and thus direct our attention.

Broadbent's Filter Theory

The most notable information processing theory in regard to attention was the filter theory proposed by Broadbent in his book *Perception and Communication* (1958). The theory assumes that the processing capacity of an individual is limited; in other words, he or she has only a limited amount of resources that can be allocated. Since our receptors, such as the eyes and the ears, have many parallel inputs, a bottleneck in the flow of information develops. To function efficiently and to prevent an overloading of the limited capacity that a person has, selection is necessary. Broadbent proposed a filter that screens the information and only allows information to pass that is more meaningful or is necessary for the individual at a certain moment, in preference to the competing information. What happens, then, if more than one message arrives at the same time? The unattended message is held in short-term store, whereas the attended one is transmitted instantly. The filter has built-in preferences. It allows new stimuli, or significant stimuli (such as your own name) to pass easily, even if they are contained in the unattended message.

The filter theory of Broadbent with its assumption of a limited capacity has had a great influence in the conceptualization of attention. It was also important for understanding the correlates of attention, perception and short-term or working memory (Baddeley and Hitch, 1974). More recent theories of working memory show the great extent to which Broadbent's conceptualization has been influenced information processing theory. These key concepts are discussed in the next section.

Filters, Limited Capacity, and Short-term Memory

Children have a limited capacity for processing information. Mentally retarded children are further limited in their capacity, which affects their attention and short-term memory. How can we understand children's attention in terms of information processing?

Recent developments in limited capacity and filtering notions following Broadbent (1958, 1977, 1984) can be useful in this regard. Beginning with *selection,* at least two stages of perceptual selection can be proposed. First there is a passive stage of perceptual selection; information from our sensory environment is packaged into different segments. These can be subsequently attended to or rejected. In the later stage, more detailed information is brought in for verification. If it is verbal information, then the individual's attention is perhaps more affected at this stage by its meaning, importance, or by the pleasantness of the word.

More recently Broadbent (1984) has placed attention, memory, and perception in one theoretical context. He proposes a "simplistic model," a cross with four arms. Each of the four arms of the cross represents a memory store; i.e., it holds representation for a short time. The four arms contain, respectively, a sensory store, a motor output store, an abstract working memory store, and a long term associative store.

The following points are made in the model and have direct relevance for our purposes in this book. (1) Processing does not proceed in a passive way from sensory to central processes. Instead, there is an interaction. In other words, information does *not only* flow from input toward output. (2) Processing is influenced by the context in which the information occurs, such as the emotional state, attitudes, and strategies for information processing of the individual. Each of these factors is extrinsic to the stimulus itself because the factors exist in the social and personal realm of the individual. For example, learning-disabled and hyperactive individuals may have limited capacities in some cognitive areas because of one or more of the three contexts—emotional, attitudinal, or strategic.

One philosophical criticism of Broadbent's model concerns the necessity of proposing an executive who has the four different kinds of desktops, each represented by one arm of the cross. Somehow this executive manages the flow of information. Attentional control or strategies guide the flow of information and thus are used for explaining variations of attention among individuals. Therefore, the question is: Who makes the selection and allocates the limited resources of the individual? This is not answered by empirical research. A homunculus does not do this, yet the model seems to require such an assumption. The structures of the brain do not provide any evidence of an executive at the desk or of a conductor in charge of the orchestra of the activities of the nervous system.

MAJOR FORMS OF ATTENTION

Attention is related to arousal both at the information processing and at the neurophysiological level. We discussed the close connection between arousal and the first functional unit of Luria's model in Chapter 2. Here we continue the discussion, showing that the two levels blend together, and explain the basis of individual differences in attention and arousal, which are reflected in the task performance of children and adults.

Arousal

The concept of arousal has often been linked to the orienting response, and both are interpreted more frequently from the perspective of neuropsychology rather than from an information processing perspective. However, let us look at the information processing perspective at this point and postpone the neuropsychological description of arousal and the orienting response to the next section.

There is no doubt that arousal interacts with attention and, in a more global sense, with cognition. A certain amount of arousal is recognized to be necessary for learning to occur. This was assumed in the drive theory of Hull and others (Hull, 1943; Hilgard, 1956). Hull thought of the *excitatory potential* as a multiplicative function of habit and drive. High arousal leads to a narrowing of attention (Easterbrook, 1959), so that individuals do not take advantage of alternatives of responding, nor do they utilize all the cues that might be presented before them. The state of high arousal may be created by drugs such as caffeine, or psychological states of anxiety and stress. High arousal can be experienced by mentally handicapped children or children with other cognitive handicaps, even in a relatively simple task, as it may create anxiety and fear. Therefore, it is important to understand not only the positive but also the negative role of arousal while assessing test performance.

Let us understand how the three concepts *attention, arousal,* and *effort* have been related (Kahneman, 1973). We agree that the levels of arousal and effort are high if the task is difficult, and when more effort is expended, arousal impedes rather than helps. However, people may be aroused either because of the effort given to their performance or because of internal conditions such as stress. Kahneman suggests that there is really no physiological correlate of effort. In other words, there is no unique physiological change that reflects effort; the changes in arousal level as shown by heart rate and pupillary dilation do accompany effort, but these can occur due to other conditions as well. Notwithstanding the lack of a unique physiological base of effort, we need to understand the effort variable for interpreting test performance. In assessing attention it is important to consider the factors that inherent in the task itself, which result in greater investment of effort. For instance, the cognitive load caused by the task may impede effort in intellectually handicapped individuals. Strategies such as rehearsal are necessary for them, but such strategies produce a greater effort and the concomitant physiological changes such as acceleration of heart rate. Thus, what appears to be an effortless task for a normal child may be extremely effortful for a mentally handicapped child of comparable age and therefore would produce a greater arousal. The greater the arousal during the performance of a difficult task, the worse is the performance. We shall come back to a discussion of effort and the physiological changes that indicate excessive use of energy when we consider the neuropsychological aspects of attention.

Sustained and Selective Attention: Definition and Assessment

Sustained Attention

According to Parasuraman (1984), *sustained attention* is defined as the maintaining of attention to a single source of information for an unbroken period of time. If the source of information is interesting and absorbing, then attention will be easily maintained over time. However, if it is monotonous and dull, attention cannot be sustained for a long time. The word *vigilance* means the same as sustained attention in recent writings. It is that form of attention that is most closely associated with alertness or arousal over time and indicates the state of the person's physiological efficiency. Vigilance or sustained attention decreases when it is maintained over a period of half an hour when targets that appear irregularly and infrequently need to be detected. Parasuraman cites Mackworth's definition of vigilance as "a state of readiness to detect and respond to certain small changes occurring at random time intervals in the environment" (Parasuraman, 1984, p. 244). Sustained attention or vigilance tasks are sometimes equated with *continuous performance tasks.* However, these tasks have a much faster rate and thus may not reflect a loss of alertness as slow vigilance tasks do.

Typically, in a vigilance task the individual may watch the face of a clock as a minute hand moves steadily and predictably over the clock face but infrequently jumps a mark, moving two places rather than one place. One of the auditory vigilance tasks that Das and his students (e.g., Das & Melnyk, 1989) have used asks children to listen to the names of four boys and four girls that occur randomly at a rate of one per second, the target being a specific combination of a boy's name (Pete) followed by a specific girl's name (Liz). The child is asked to signal when he or she hears "Pete" followed by "Liz."

The performance on a vigilance task is affected not only by how frequently the target or the signal occurs, but also by the length of the task. Decrement in vigilance performance is attributed to two causes: (1) a decrement in the individual's sensitivity, and (2) a shift in the individual's criterion for deciding what a target or signal is. It is argued that in prolonged vigilance, both sensitivity decrement and criterion shift jointly determine the worsening of performance.

There are many reasons for individual differences in the efficiency in maintaining vigilance. Some of these are the state of arousal and attitude to the test, whereas others are more stable personality traits. According to Eysenck (1957), introverts are better equipped for work on prolonged and monotonous tasks compared to extroverts, because introverts have a higher level of cortical arousal and the extroverts have the reverse, i.e., a higher level of cortical inhibition. Poor vigilance is also observed among some kinds of brain-damaged individuals (Davies & Parasuraman, 1982).

Selective attention is either focused or divided. In focused attention the individual is required to attend to one source or kind of information and exclude the others, whereas in divided attention the individual shares time between two or more sources or kinds of information or mental operations (Davies, Jones, & Taylor, 1984). Many different tasks have been used to measure selective attention. We describe some of them, such as the Stroop test and Number Finding, later in this chapter.

We divide selective attention tasks further into those in which the selection occurs at the time of receiving and encoding the stimuli, in contrast to tasks in which the selection occurs at the time of response or expression. The Stroop is an example of selection at the *expression stage.* This is the stage at which the individual inhibits the automatic response of reading the word and gives the response of naming the color. Selection at the encoding or *reception stage* is seen in dichotic listening, central and incidental learning, as well as in Picture and Letter Matching tasks, which we have devised after Posner; we will describe these tasks in some detail in a later section.

Although there are many kinds of selective attention tasks, all of them test three distinct components: selectivity, resistance to distraction, and shifting or switching strategies. Attentional selectivity can be further distinguished as data-driven or memory-driven. Data-driven attentional selectivity is instantiated in the Posner's task, which requires detecting physical identity (letter pair AA is identical, AB is not), whereas memory-driven selectivity is instantiated in detecting category or name identity (letter pair Aa is identical, Ab is not). Similarly, research on old age has shown that selective attention decreases in old people due to the failure of memory driven processes (Davies, Jones, & Taylor, 1984).

A Summary of Recent Reviews

Contemporary reviews of attention have brought together 30 years of research since Broadbent proposed his filter theory. This section offers a summary of our knowledge about this complex cognitive function which, in conjunction with some fundamentals of neuropsychology (discussed in the next section), should facilitate the ability to assess attention and critique tests.

Attention can be focused or divided between two or more things and ideas. Individuals control their attention by focusing or dividing. However, research suggests that there is no general ability to focus attention on one stimulus or to shift attention from one to another (Lansman, Poltrock, & Hunt, 1983). Assessment of attention, therefore, does not include the capacity for focusing and time sharing.

A recent review of selective attention identifies the two key concepts discussed in the previous section: (1) the process of selection and (2) the expenditure of varying degrees of mental effort (Johnston & Dark, 1986). Mental effort itself is based on the two attributes of attention that we have mentioned before. These are an individual's limited capacity and control of attention.

The process of selection is determined in two different ways: (1) by an internal top-down process comprising such *internal* sets as priming the individual's attitude towards the stimuli to be attended to and (2) and by bottom-up external processes such as stimulus properties of intensity and size. These are the main determinants of attention.

Controlled as opposed to automatic attention must be selective. It uses long-term memory as described by Cowan (1988):

> *[T]he parts of perception that proceed automatically are the coding processes that take place as the stimuli activate long-term memory. However, more complete perceptual interpretations occur when the stimulus information passes the filter. The central executive calls up additional relevant information and forms broader associations among the stimuli and between the stimuli and prior memory. (p. 177)*

The interdependence between perception, attention, and memory is emphasized. Is attention related to a higher cognitive function as well? The answer is yes, to planning (see Chapter 5) and problem solving. For its link to problem solving, there is a comprehensive theoretical review by Hunt and Lansman (1986). These links make attention an extremely complex form of information processing. The complexity is reflected and reinforced further by linking intelligence to attention.

NEUROPSYCHOLOGY OF ATTENTION

Attention and arousal are not only experienced subjectively, but also have their physiological correlates. The neuropsychological approach to attention typically considers the physiological correlates along with the subjective experience of attention and arousal.

Orienting Response—Pavlov and Sokolov

We start with the historical and history-making work of Pavlov, who observed attentional behavior in dogs. During his experiments on digestion and, later, on conditioning, he often observed that the dog attended to the signal that preceded food. In fact, the amount of salivation elicited by the signal, such as a metronome beat, was almost equal to the salivation elicited by the unconditioned stimulus, which was food.

Orienting Response (OR)

Attention must be elicited by a signal *before* it is associated with a response, such as food; otherwise, conditioning will not occur. In other words, in order for a neutral signal such as a metronome sound to become an instigator for salivation through its association with food, the signal itself must have attentional value. The dog perks up its ears and turns toward the metronome on hearing the sound, as though saying, "What is it?" Therefore, the *orienting response (OR)* is the building block of attention and learning. It is a basic unit of attention, and attention is a prerequisite for learning and for higher levels of cognitive functions. Therefore, OR is usually regarded as a basic aspect of intelligent behavior.

The OR has two characteristics. First, it is a general response initiated by a stimulus that is novel. The unspecific orienting response is an arousal response. The second characteristic of OR is that it habituates. That is, a repeated presentation of a stimulus wipes out the OR. We notice these two properties in our daily experience. A novel event attracts our attention because it evokes an orienting response. But when novelty dies away, we do not pay much attention to the same event.

The purpose of an orienting response is to increase the discrimination capacity of the receptors. Beyond receptors, in higher cognitive functions, OR may be analogous to what is described as a priming stimulus. This is clearly seen when we present the word *bread* before presenting the word *butter* and observe that the perception of the word *butter* is facilitated; i.e., it is faster than the condition in which *butter* is not preceded by the word *bread*. Habituation of OR is linked to novelty; they are like the two faces of a coin.

Evocation of the OR is itself a response to discrepancy or novelty, and its decay or fading away is a sign of selective inhibition. The implication of these aspects of OR for the classroom is that children respond to a novel event, but if the event does not acquire any significance, they habituate and stop attending to it. We can support this theoretically by considering Sokolov's (1960, 1963) model of OR.

Sokolov's Neuronal Model

In the basic model of OR the elementary component of attention has a filtering as well as an amplifying function. In Sokolov's (1960) words: "The nervous system apparently forms a certain program of stimulation. This program is compared with the real stimulation. If the stimuli do not coincide in all parameters, an orienting reflex is evoked at each point of disagreement" (p. 206). These basic ideas are still useful in understanding attention and are illustrated in Figure 3-1.

The neuronal model assumes two separate systems, a screening system and an amplifying system. The *screening system* preserves information about the stimulus, i.e., its intensity, duration, and, if the stimulus is verbal, its semantic properties. If a new stimulus does not match with the information stored in the screening system, OR is produced, facilitated by the amplifying system. The *amplifying system* amplifies or enhances the autonomic responsivity and the sensitivity of the receptors that will receive the mismatched stimulus. Consequently, the OR appears at the very moment when the stimulus does not coincide with the neuronal model. If

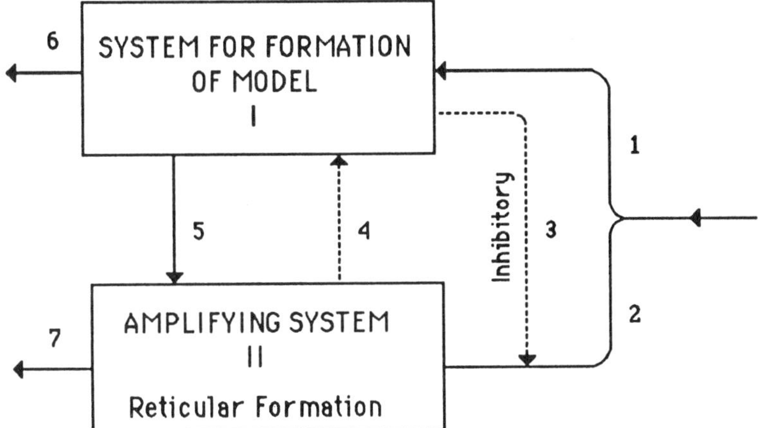

FIGURE 3-1 Sokolov's Model: How Does OR Work?

Adapted from Sokolov, 1960.

I. Modeling system. II. Amplifying system. 1 = specific pathway from sense organs to cortical level of modeling system; 2 = collateral to reticular formation (represented here as an amplifying device); 3 = negative feedback from modeling system to synaptic connection between collaterals from specific pathway and R.F.; 4 = ascending activating influences from the amplifier (R.F.) upon modeling system (cortex); 5 = pathway from modeling system to amplifying system (this is the pathway through which the impulses signifying concordance are transmitted from the modeling system to the amplifying system); 6 = to the specific responses caused by coincidence between the external stimulation and the neuronal model elaborated in the cortex; and 7 = to the vegetative and somatic components arising from the stimulation of the amplifying system (R.F.).

the new stimulus matches with an existing neuronal model, the cortex either inhibits it, or, if the stimulus is a previously conditioned one, then it produces a conditioned response. This describes the process by which meaningless and repetitive stimuli are not attended to, whereas meaningful stimuli, on repetition, produce the appropriate response that the individual has learned.

Orienting Response and Higher Cognitive Processes

The foregoing summary of orienting response as a neuronal model serves as an appropriate background for regarding even this basic element of attention as a cognitive process. There is no doubt that the OR is a reflection of higher cognitive functioning. This is the kind of attention that has been used for assessing intellectual function in babies. The experiments on OR presented years ago by Luria and Vinogradova (1959) are examples of studying higher cognitive processes, such as the semantic systems, through the OR.

Selective Attention—Its Correlates in Brain Activity

The OR is essentially an instance of selective attention. Selective attention can be measured physiologically as well as behaviorally. Physiological measures provide an objective index that is not affected by the necessity of pressing a key or making a verbal response. It is therefore good to understand what kinds of functions, subsumed in selective attention behavior, have correlates in brain activity.

A common objective correlate of selective attention is the evoked potential. *Evoked potentials* are small changes in the EEG (electroencephalogram) that arise shortly after a stimulus has been presented. A classical study (Spong, Haider, & Lindsley, 1965) demonstrated that even this elementary brain response accompanying attention is controlled by the individual's intention. The subjects in this study could attend to light flashes and ignore clicks to the ear, or do the opposite, when they were instructed to do so. The researchers found that the evoked potential to light flashes was greater when the individuals were asked to attend to flashes, and likewise it was greater to clicks than to flashes when they were asked to attend to the clicks. This study shows that selective attention is subject to verbal control; i.e., it can be regulated by the individual's internal "speech."

Luria used the evoked potential to study both attentional selectivity as well as the mobilization of active attention. The results are described in *The Working Brain* (Luria, 1973) and demonstrate precisely the cognitive control of arousal and attention. Does the evoked potential reflect active expectancy? It undoubtedly does, as evidenced in both experiments of Luria and new studies as reviewed by Naatanen (1982). Luria (1973) showed that evoked potential increased in amplitude when sensory stimuli were presented following an instruction to attend to them. This regulation by speech, however, is not apparent before the child reaches school age, but it becomes effective in later stages of development. "Physiological changes produced by a spoken instruction and lying at the basis of voluntary attention are formed only gradually and do not appear in a precise and stable form until the age of 12 to 15 years" (Luria, 1973, p. 270). How this influences planful behavior is discussed next.

Mobilization of attention in a situation that has many demands on attention must require planning, and hence the involvement of frontal lobe functions. Therefore, developmentally speaking, optimal capacity for mobilization of attentional resources seems to occur as children reach late childhood.

The other notable finding is in regard to the location of the evoked potential in the brain. As a child develops, the changes are found not only in the sensory areas, such as the occipital area for visual stimuli, but also they begin to appear in the frontal areas. Thus, regions in the frontal lobes become closely involved and play a more intimate part in complex and stable forms of voluntary attention.

Localization of Attention and Attentional Deficit

Besides evoked potentials there are other correlates of attention, such as slow potentials and contingent negative variations. These include the autonomic measures of heart rate, galvanic skin response, blood flow, and respiration. We refer to the brain and autonomic correlates simply to clarify the relation between the cognitive characteristics of attention and arousal on the one hand, and their neurophysiological bases on the other. Our examples from Luria's work are consistent with the overall model of information integration related to PASS processes. In spite of the apparently dated source, Luria's functional organization of the brain has been surprisingly insightful and valid in the background of contemporary research, as has been recently pointed out (De Sonneville & Njiokiktjien, 1988).

Is attention or its malfunctioning localized in the top or bottom part of the brain? Recent research on neuropsychology of attention implicates *both* the upper and the lower structures in the brain. As long as autonomic responses such as heart rate are attentional responses, the controlling centers must be in the subcortical region. However, not only involuntary but also voluntary attention is controlled subcortically through pathways that can modify synaptic transmission at a precortical level as far away as the retina. Posner and Petersen (1990) more recently studied the involvement of cortical regions, investigating selective attention and its relation to the brain. They support the involvement of two posterior brain systems in selective attention. This includes selection of spatial information and selection of semantic information. Higher levels of the system can act to prevent sensory events from inappropriate control of performance of many cognitive tasks. The hypothesis is that the dorsolateral prefrontal cortex plays an important part in this higher level of attention.

It is clear from the review of both central and autonomic changes that accompany attention that the frontal lobes and the limbic system play an equally important role. The frontal lobes play a more important role in the mobilization of attentional resources in voluntary attention. If the frontal lobes are intact but the hippocampus is damaged, it is possible to restore selectivity in attention through verbal instruction. The frontal lobes, as is well known, are concerned with goal-directed, planful behavior (see Chapters 2 and 5), and selective attention requires planning. The failure of selectivity is seen in impulsive behavior of hyperactive children. The role of the frontal lobes in controlling attention and in inhibiting impulsive responses therefore is quite important.

Along with the frontal lobes, the limbic system controls arousal and attention, as we have seen in the early models of attention. For instance, the brain stem reticular formation together with the limbic system regulates attention, motivation, and emotion. The hypothalamus plays a central role in all these processes, and we can understand attention-arousal as an interactional process involving cortical structures as well as subcortical ones. Nowhere is this interaction more clearly seen than in attention deficit.

In attention deficit all components of attention beginning with OR are adversely affected. For example, in regard to OR, when the frontal lobes do not control the direction of attention, then any stimulus may evoke the unspecific OR and thereby promote distractibility. We suggest that in attention deficit disorder the limbic system and the frontal region do not work in cooperation as they should. The failure of the frontal region leads to nonselectivity of attention. Then are we to assume that an executive fails to select?

Conclusions of Neuropsychological Studies

The overwhelming conclusion from OR and other attentional studies involving the brain is that the frontal lobes play an important part. Luria (1966) suggested this many years ago, and Naatanen (1982) has provided more recent evidence supporting both the neuronal model of Sokolov as well as the involvement of the frontal lobes. Pribram and McGuinness (1975) have suggested that there are specific control mechanisms; arousal is controlled in the amygdala circuits, activation in the basal ganglia, and the hippocampus circuit works to overcome the constraints that keep these two control systems from functioning. In short, attention and arousal go hand in hand, modulated by activities both in the top and bottom parts of the brain.

The Organization of Attention in the Brain

We have provided an answer to the question: How is attention organized in the brain? The upper part of the brain (neocortex), thalamus, and the brain stem are very closely involved in regulating attention, and the neocortex is predominately in control of guiding complex attentional behavior. In contrast, the reticular formation plays a major role in maintaining arousal or keeping the individual wakeful. Voluntary forms of attention that are relevant for solving a problem or listening to instructions during a learning situation are only possible when the upper parts of the brain, especially the frontal lobes, are engaged. The regulation of attention develops as the frontal lobes and limbic system work cooperatively. Children may be aroused by bodily needs or by situations that arouse emotions such as fear or pain. But as they grow, they become aroused by situations that have social-cultural significance (disapproval by peers and motivation for excellence are some examples). Then arousal is mediated by situations that are not physically stimulating but are cognitively interpreted. Sokolov's model showing the amplification or inhibition of arousal suggests that perhaps most of the messages for facilitation or inhibition originate in the frontal lobes.

ASSESSMENT OF ATTENTION AND INTELLIGENCE

A transition from neuropsychology to information processing has been made easy by prominent researchers in neuropsychology, the foremost among whom must be Geschwind (1982), who identified five major characteristics of the attentional systems. These characteristics place attention squarely among other complex cognitive systems.

Geschwind lists five characteristics of the attentional system:

1. Attention is selective.
2. Attention is coherent, as it is maintained for some time once the selection is made.
3. It is necessary to shift attention.
4. It is important to monitor a broad range of stimuli before focusing attention.
5. Individuals may have special sensitivity to certain kinds of stimuli.

These characteristics describe higher cognitive functions that manifest themselves in intelligent behavior. Thus, there is no doubt that at least in human beings we are dealing with intelligent activity when we consider attention.

Support for this view is also found in psychometric studies, as exemplified by Stankov (1983). In reviewing factor analytic evidence he comes to the conclusion that all phenomena considered to be attentional have a common link with intelligence.

Measures of Attention and Application to School Psychology

In this section we review some measures of attention that have been used in our research. First we describe these measures, and then we summarize the empirical studies on diverse populations such as mentally handicapped, learning-disabled, and hyperactive children. It will be evident from the various studies reported that an integration of the two different approaches, information processing and neuropsychology, has proved to be useful in understanding attentional processes and their use by the special groups of children.

Vigilance

A typical characteristic of vigilance is a decrement in efficiency over time. Levine, Romashko, and Fleishman (1973) analyzed 53 studies on vigilance and concluded that both perceptual and cognitive function are involved in vigilance. Within the perceptual category many of the tasks can be described as *perceptual speed.* This is the speed with which the subject may detect the similarity between patterns or configurations that are presented simultaneously, or one after another in succession. Another component of the perceptual domain is described as *flexibility of closure.* From the generic description given by the authors, it seems to be a facility to recognize the stimulus when it is embedded in a field of distractors.

The tasks in the cognitive domain fall into two categories. One, called *selective attention,* involves the ability to concentrate on the task and filter out the distracting stimuli. This is, of course, a general description of selective attention, but what makes the task more like a vigilance performance is when the signal is a simple one occurring in a background of monotonous distractors. The other category of cognitive tasks was *time sharing.* This is the ability to utilize information that can only be obtained by shifting between two or more sources of information.

It is important to note the difference between perceptual speed tasks and the other kinds. The typical example of perceptual speed is watching light flashes that occur at intervals of 3 seconds and to detect a flash that lasts for slightly longer than usual, 0.8 seconds rather than the usual 0.5 seconds duration. Flexibility of closure, in contrast, is a continuous performance task in which the subject watches a clock face for a minute hand that moves steadily except that it stops infrequently for 0.2 to 0.8 seconds. It seems to us that efficiency in the perceptual speed task may be deteriorating for two reasons, the stress on the sensory system itself and the interaction between the efficiency of the sensory system and the efficiency for judgment of small differences in duration. In any case, the tasks we have chosen in DN:CAS for measuring attention do not fall into the perceptual speed category, as will be evident from our discussion below.

In choosing a vigilance task that measures sustained attention, we should seek the following four characteristics (Warm & Birch, 1985):

1. The task is prolonged and continuous, often lasting for half an hour or more.

2. The signals to be detected are weak.
3. The signals occur randomly without warning.
4. The subject's response does not change the probability of the signal's occurrence.

Two kinds of scores are computed, which are the number of *signals omitted* and the number of *false detections*. From these basic scores, several derived scores may also be obtained following signal detection theory. Omissions and false detections can be calculated in 5-minute blocks of performance; therefore, it is possible to distinguish groups of individuals on the basis of these two error scores, as well as the decrement of efficiency in detection of signals by plotting the omission scores over contiguous blocks of 5 minutes. In other words, the groups may be contrasted both in terms of their omissions and false detections, even if the performance decrement is not observed. It is well known that consistent decrement cannot be seen unless the task lasts for half an hour or more. That is why it may be difficult to observe a consistent decrement function with special populations with whom it may not be possible to prolong the task beyond a few minutes. An example of a vigilance task used by Das follows.

Sustained Attention Test

This attention task requires that the child listen to a tape recording of a list of names. Four boys' names (Doug, Paul, Dave, and Pete) and four girls' names (Jane, Liz, Sue, and Ann) are presented using a tape recorder. The names are presented at the rate of one every second. The task can be as long as 30 minutes. Three signals occur each minute. The child is required to tell the examiner when the signal was presented (in this case the name Pete followed by the name Liz). The child is instructed to tell the examiner when the signals occurred by tapping his or her hand on the table. The examiner records every time a tap occurs after the word was spoken (see transcript used as a record sheet in Figure 3-2). Omissions and false errors are scored.

Measures of Selective Attention

Selective attention can be described as either focused or divided. In the first, attention is focused on one source of information disregarding other competing sources, whereas in divided attention it is shared between two or more sources. Several tasks have been used for measuring selective attention. These include dichotic listening, central-incidental learning, the Stroop test, and the physical versus name match task of Posner (Stroop, 1935; Posner & Boies, 1971; Proctor, 1981). For a general description of

Minute 1

Doug__Paul__Paul__Pete__Jane__Ann__Sue__Doug__
Pete__Liz__Ann__Jane__Jane__Doug__Jane__Paul__Doug__Jane__
Doug__Jane__Ann__Dave__Sue__Paul__Pete__Liz__Sue__Pete__
Jane__Jane__Liz__Ann__Paul__Doug__Ann__Jane__Liz__Paul__Ann__
Liz__Paul__Doug__Pete__Jane__Liz__Liz__Pete__Liz__Doug__
Doug__Liz__Sue__Sue__Pete__Jane__Sue__Jane__Liz__Pete__Doug__

FIGURE 3-2 Transcript of Name Response Tape

selective attention and the review of major research on it, we recommend the book by Parasuraman and Davies (1984).

We have used the Stroop test and the tasks such as those modified from Posner & Boies (1971) as measures of expressive and receptive aspects of selective attention, respectively. The notion that attention requires central processing capacity and that selective attention tasks may vary in terms of the amount of this capacity has been advanced for some time (Baddeley & Hitch, 1974; Posner, 1973). Both the Stroop and Posner tasks are appropriate measures of selective attention in that both are measures of discrimination, selectivity, and the ability to handle more than one task at the same time. Examples of these tasks are given in Chapter 6, which describes how PASS has been operationalized.

Selective Attention Receptive—Posner's Physical and Name Match Tasks

Posner's (1978) ideas for matching pairs of letters that are visually identical (AA, TT, etc.) and identical in name (Aa, Tt, etc.) have been used in constructing two sets of tasks, Picture Matching and Letter Matching (examples in Chapter 6). In both, the pairs are either physically same (same picture or letter presented in pairs) or name same (two different pictures of flowers, upper- and lowercase forms of same letter). Physical identity for simultaneously presented pictures or letter pairs is faster than name identity. But a comparison of Picture and Letter Matching will show that pictures take longer than letters to match. The reason is that each picture has to be given a meaning and a name has to be found for it. Scores in this test are omissions (or the reverse, number hits) and time taken to complete the task.

Selective Attention, Expressive: Stroop Test

The Stroop test comprises word reading, color naming, and naming the color of the ink with which the colors are written (Stroop, 1935). The parts critical for our experiments are color naming, which has a minimal cognitive processing requirement, and color-word naming, in which the subjects has to inhibit the reading of the word but instead say the color. The Stroop test has been used as a measure of selective attention for hyperactive and learning disabled children (Campbell, Douglas, & Morgenstern, 1971; Cohen, Weiss, & Minde, 1972; Santostefano, Rutledge, & Randall, 1964; Lazarus, Ludwig, & Aberson, 1984). Although the Stroop test has been modified in many studies, the general format consisting of word reading, color naming, and naming of colors from a conflict part has been maintained by most. However, when experimental psychologists have attempted to isolate the different cognitive processes that contribute to Stroop interference, the stimuli have been presented individually, rather than in a chart or card to be read line by line. Either way, there is a growing consensus in the literature in regard to the Stroop interference phenomenon that it relates to inhibitory processes, most probably at the time of response (expressive stage) rather than at the time of encoding (receptive).

Selective inhibitory processes in attention, as a neuropsychological construct, has been used by Sokolov as a major factor in explaining the nature of OR. However, in terms of information processing theory, selective inhibitory mechanisms have not been invoked, except by Neill and Westberry (1987). They explain Stroop interference as just one of the instances of selective inhibition, which according to them is a pervasive function in the control of cognitive processing.

In children beyond the first grade, and even in older students, the interference condition is a measure of selective attention. Usually three basic scores are obtained from the Stroop: the speed of reading words (first condition), which has sometimes been called *speed of personal tempo* (Das, 1969); color naming (second condition); and interference (third condition). The interference score has been variously estimated. One method is to subtract the color reading time from the color-word reading time and divide it by color naming time. A simpler one is to divide color naming time by the color-word reading time. The simplest, of course, is to treat all three scores separately and to show that even when color naming time remains the same across two groups or individuals, the interference time may vary.

Comments on Selective Attention Tasks

Selective attention has been linked to distractibility, and for this reason the concept is all the more muddled. Krupski (1986) objects to regarding distractibility as a general trait of the individual and criticizes studies that try to show that learning disabled children are distractible.

The notion that attention requires central processing capacity and that selective attention tasks vary in terms of the amount of the capacity they may use has been advanced for some time (Baddeley & Hitch, 1974; Posner, 1973), although neither of the key concepts, attention and central processing capacity, has a general acceptable definition. Nevertheless, it can be assumed that whenever attention tasks are used as measures of cognitive capacity comprising discrimination, selectivity, and the ability to handle more than one task at the same time, they have separated the learning disabled from nondisabled children (cf., Ford, Pelham, & Ross, 1984; Copeland & Reiner, 1984). On the other hand, if the load on central processing capacity is minimal, as in vigilance or other sustained attention tests excluding CPT (which has a fast presentation rate and degradation of the signal stimulus, which increase the difficulty of the task without increasing the load on higher cognitive processes), no reliable difference between learning-disabled and nondisabled children has been obtained.

Receptive and Expressive Selective Attention—Locus of Interference

In discussing selective attention performance of the learning disabled, both Posner and Stroop performance can be explained by a common model of stimulus matching (Posner & Snyder, 1975) that suggests two separate locations for selection. In the Posner task it is at the time of encoding the letter pairs, and in the Stroop color-word conflict card it is at the stage of response. The Posner physical matching requires a low-level perceptual encoding, whereas in name matching a relatively higher level of cognitive coding is required. The Stroop interference arises at the output stage; the information about the word is reached earlier than information about color. The first has to be suppressed. This theoretical explanation in terms of a relative speed difference between word and colors has been questioned (Dunbar & MacLeod, 1984). What is certain, however, is that the Stroop interference, even when correlated with the physiological measure of activation (event-related potential in the form of the duration of P300), occurs at the output stage (Duncan-Johnson & Kopell, 1981).

SUMMARY

To be attentive implies that the individual is alert. Alertness can be sustained for a period of time and is selective. From the information processing as well as from neuropsychological points of view, these three aspects of attention have spawned much research. These three aspects of attention are found in humans and animals. Arousal or alertness is a common prerequisite for learning and memory. Maintenance of the attentional set and selectivity are the basis of discrimination and generalization. Attention, through its relation to learning and problem solving, becomes an essential component of intelligent behavior. Attention cannot only be manipulated in learning and problem solving, but can be assessed by appropriate tasks. The assessment of selective attention more than that of sustained attention has been useful in distinguishing between groups of special children.

4

THE CODING OF INFORMATION

The role of the processing system is crucial to the PASS model of information processing. Whereas the attention-arousal and planning systems can facilitate (or interfere with) information processing, it is in the processing system that most of the actual "action" takes place. It is in this system that the incoming information is received, combined with prior knowledge in the knowledge base, transformed according to prior knowledge and to the operating plan, and stored for later usage. The stored knowledge adds to the individual's knowledge base.

The processing system has also been referred to as the "coding" system, because it is this system that "encodes" incoming information, "recodes" existing information according to the demands of the task, and stores information in coded form for later use. The term *coding* is more precise than *processing*, because *processing* can refer to the operation of any or all of the three systems. However, *coding* does not capture the broad scope of this system; for this reason, we will continue to use both terms, using the context to specify our meaning.

Coding is what happens when new or incoming information is interpreted in terms of what we already know. Meaning does not exist in the stimuli that occur in the world (such as sounds, sights, and smells); rather, we have to bring meaning to those stimuli. The stimuli have to be *coded* so that we can understand or react to them. The same stimulus can be coded in different ways; for instance, a mud puddle may be interpreted as a nuisance by a well-dressed person, as the location for an imaginary naval battle by a child, and as the source of a life-saving drink by a person dying of thirst. The mud puddle itself has no meaning; meaning is the result of what you do with it, how you code it. The coding that takes place is a function of the knowledge base that we possess and of what we are trying to do in the task at hand. Prior knowledge sets the limits on how incoming information can be coded. If you know nothing about the game of cricket, watching a cricket match will be very confusing, and you will try to interpret it in terms of games you do understand (perhaps baseball). If you are trying to remember some words in a language you do not know, you must either remember the individual sounds (a very difficult task, after a word or two) or search for English words that sound similar and remember those (this is also difficult and could lead to serious errors).

The meaning we attach to incoming information also depends on what we are trying to do at that moment, upon our current plan. The mud puddle example illustrates this. Our plan facilitates paying attention to stimuli that are currently relevant (for instance, food for a hungry person) and influences the way in which we code what we have attended to (for instance, a hammer may be seen as a way to hold a door open, as a weapon, or even as a way to insert nails into walls!). (The role of attention is discussed in chapter 3, and the role of planning in Chapter 5.)

In the following sections we discuss a number of aspects of coding. The coding of information is very much like operating upon it, and the result of coding is the formation of some sort of mental representation, which can later be recoded. Coding may take place automatically, or it may be the result of conscious effort. Codes can exist in long-term memory, or in working (or short-term) memory. Three critical aspects are: *how much coding* is involved in a task, *the content of the codes* formed, and *the types of coding* that can be involved. Two types of coding, simultaneous processing and successive processing, are the major focus of the chapter. We examine recent evidence regarding the nature of these these two types of processing, techniques for measuring them, and the consequences of individual differences in them for school learning.

REPRESENTATIONS AND OPERATIONS

Incoming information (e.g., a physical signal in the acoustic or optic nerves) needs to access some sort of internal representation or code and must be processed. The representations that input accesses, and the operations performed upon them, are a function of what the person knows (the prior knowledge base) and of what the person is trying to do (the current plan).

Let us consider representations first. If you were shown the numbers "2 4 6 8 2 4 6 8," you would probably recognize them as the first four even numbers, repeated once; so your representation of them, your code for them, would be something like "first four even numbers, twice." Young children, who just barely knew their numbers but who did not understand odd and even numbers and who did not notice that the first four were repeated, would have to represent the same input information in a more cumbersome way, probably as "two, four, six, eight, two, ..." Finally, someone who did not know our number system would have to represent the numbers as a very long list of curved and straight lines; i.e., each number would have to be broken down into two or more line features.

This variety of representations, from features (the line segments) to elements (the numbers) to patterns (taking account of odd and even, and repetition), provides a simple example of how coding can vary from simple to complex. More complex codes require more prior knowledge and perhaps more conscious effort to be used, but they result in more durable memories because there are fewer separate bits to remember.

Processing always takes place under the control of a plan, even if the plan is a simple or habitual one of which we are not conscious (see Chapter 5). Plans usually call for operations to be performed upon the newly represented input information; an operation is a form of coding. For example, if the information were a series of words "cat, sheep, goat, dog, goldfish, pig," you might decide to pronounce each one (a naming operation), to repeat the series several times, or to form the set into two groups (pets and farm animals) and rehearse within groups (a clustering and rehearsal operation). (In terms of the PASS theory, repeating the series is an operation that requires successive processing, while clustering requires simultaneous processing; naming may require a combination of simultaneous and successive processing, depending on the person's reading skills.) As tasks become more complex, the number of possible processing operations grows quickly. The result of carrying out these processes upon the input representation is a new representation (a new code), which may contain information not previously known (as when several numbers are added to give a new number) and which can then be entered into further stages of processing.

A key concept in understanding operations is that of *automaticity*. An automatic operation is one that takes place without any conscious effort or attention; if an operation is not automatic, then attention or effort must be devoted to it, and this will limit the attention or effort that can be given to other aspects of the task. Normally we want to have our lower level operations working automatically, so that we can use our mental resources on the higher levels of the task.

The processes of representation and operation have been described here separately for purposes of clarity. Keep in mind that they are very similar, always occur together, and depend heavily on each other. Operations usually depend upon the nature of the representations on which they operate, and operations usually produce new representations. *Operation* describes the act of coding, while *representation* describes the results of coding; one cannot have one without the other.

SHORT-TERM AND LONG-TERM MEMORY

The codes we produce and use can exist in several sorts of state or memory. The two familiar categories are short and long-term memory. *Short-term memory (STM)* has been seen as a relatively passive, temporary store of what we are currently thinking of or aware of; information in STM that is not further processed quickly fades away. STM is also limited in the number of codes it can hold at any one time, estimates varying from four to seven. Because of this limitation it is important for each code to contain as much information as possible. This is also the reason for the importance of automaticity; if we have to attend to the lower levels of a task's processing, we may have to fill our STM with line segments, rather than with words—seven line segments may only give us two or three letters, whereas seven words could contain considerable information.

Long-term memory (LTM), on the other hand, is a permanent store of all that we know. As far as we understand at the moment, much of what is stored there is in the form of *schemes,* high-level coded representations that are richly interconnected. Long-term memory comprises our knowledge base; incoming information is matched against long-term memory knowledge in the process of accessing its initial representation. It also comprises our knowledge of procedures or operations to apply to representations. As we learn new representations, or links between representations, or new operations, these are added to our long-term memory.

Recent research and theory have shown the short- and long-term memory distinction to be an oversimplification. What was previously termed STM is now thought to consist of primary and working memories, as well as an articulatory "loop" and a visual-spatial "scratch-pad." Estes (1982) proposed that STM be divided into *primary memory,* which is very short-term, and *working memory.* Information coded in primary memory is transient and fades away unless it is either worked on in working memory or sent to LTM. Consider the following example: We see for a very short time, a display in which the letter *E* is embedded among distracting lines. If we recognize the letter as *E*, then it is transferred from primary memory to LTM and we can remember having seen this letter even after several minutes. If we do not recognize the letter, then all we see is a haphazard set of lines, which must fade quickly (from primary memory) because it does not have a meaning for us. If we do not immediately recognize the letter but succeed in constructing it from the lines presented (perhaps because we are searching for a letter to complete a word), the letter exists in working memory and would also be transferred to LTM.

Working memory itself can be subdivided (Baddeley, 1986, 1990) into a central processing space, an articulatory loop, and a visual-spatial scratch-pad. The central processing space is where information is transformed, while the articulatory loop and visual-spatial scratch-pad are mechanisms for recirculating auditory and visual information. Working memory provides us with a temporary knowledge base, a set of currently active information.

The memories stored in both STM and LTM can also be divided into those that are episodic and those that are semantic (Tulving & Donaldson, 1972). *Episodic memory* is personal and historical; we remember what has happened to us, in what order, when it happened, and where. Episodic memory can be short-term (e.g., when we remember a list of numbers in a memory span test), or long-term (e.g., when we remember the events of a football game from 20 years ago). *Semantic memory* instead refers to our memories for the meanings of words or events, all richly interconnected and related. Short-term semantic memories would include recognizing the meanings of words as they are read; long-term semantic memories concern our knowledge of the world and language—e.g., that snow is cold and may require shoveling. Yet more divisions in memory have been proposed (Graf & Schacter, 1985; Tulving, 1985).

The complexity of this new view of STM and of the role of strategies in determining the path processing takes emphasizes that STM can no longer be seen as only a passive, short-term store. The new model is more complex but is essential for understanding the relationship between coding processes and memory.

LEVEL, CONTENT, AND TYPE OF CODING

There are many dimensions of coding that could be discussed. For example, we could think about the sensory modality of the original stimulus (visual, auditory, tactile, etc.) and about whether the codes were learned in school or not, and so on. In this section we describe three dimensions of coding that we think are important for understanding children's thinking and learning; these are the dimensions of *level of coding, code content,* and *type of coding*. The last of these is a central feature of the PASS theory.

Level of Coding

Level of coding concerns the amount of coding required for a given representation. In the example used in the previous section, a low level of coding for "2 4 6 8 2 4 6 8" would be a list of the individual numerals; a higher level would be the names of the numbers; and a higher one still would be the pattern, "the first four even numbers, twice." We can see the same type of hierarchy in other tasks. Consider reading: The lowest level of coding would be the letter features, the next higher letters, then letter groups (syllables), words, phrases, and so on (Kirby, 1988; Kirby & Williams, 1991).

What is involved in going to higher levels of coding? Each higher level is more complex than the preceding one, i.e., more dependent upon abstractions and inferences from the lower-level information. The higher levels also depend more upon information already in the knowledge base, and less upon the raw information coming in. As higher levels are attained, more and more raw information is represented in a single code; thus, less and less working memory space is required. In order to proceed to the next higher level of coding, the codes at the preceding level need to be organized or structured; this means that they need to be held in some sort of order while the higher-level analysis is performed to produce or recognize the pattern that is the basis of the higher level code. Finally, it is clear that lower levels of coding often occur automatically, without any conscious effort, while the higher ones occur much more effortfully.

Code Content

The second important dimension is *code content*. With respect to school learning, the two most important kinds of content are verbal and spatial. Much psychological research (e.g., Bryden, 1990; Corballis, 1989; Gazzaniga, 1970) has suggested that the left hemisphere of the brain is specialized for processing verbal codes, the right for spatial codes. The code content dimension is relevant when considering children's learning problems because problems may occur primarily in verbal (language, reading, spelling, writing) or spatial (mathematical) areas. However, this dimension has been overemphasized in recent years, particularly by educators insufficiently cautious in generalizing from experimental results (see Corballis's 1980 review of some of the myths that have risen around the hemispheric differences research). The code content dimension is clearly important; for instance, the verbal content domain is clearly the locus of many children's reading problems. It is still necessary, however, to probe further to discover exactly how those problems occur—i.e., to investigate the processes or types of coding involved.

It is important to recognize that code content is not the same as type of coding (see next section). Among the many confusions surrounding the brain laterality work is one that sees verbal coding as essentially linear or successive, while spatial coding as holistic or simultaneous. This confounds two dimensions that in our view should be kept distinct; verbal codes may be simultaneous (as in knowing the referent of a word or the relationship between two words), and spatial codes can be successive (as in recognizing a sequence of actions or remembering a series of pictures). Kaufman and Kaufman (1983) have fostered this confusion by suggesting that their K-ABC simultaneous and sequential tests may refer either to Luria's processes or to the left brain—right brain distinction (the K-ABC is discussed in Chapter 7).

Type of Coding: Simultaneous or Successive

The "how" of coding is dealt with more by the *type of coding* dimension. We have proposed that there are two major types of coding, either simultaneous coding or successive coding. In simultaneous coding or processing, relationships between pieces of input information are used to produce a single or integrated code (cf. Kirby & Das, 1990); for example, you do simultaneous coding when you realize that "cat, dog, and goldfish" are all pets, when you see the pattern underlying "2 4 6 8," or when you see that a set of lines in a drawing forms a square. There are several key features to simultaneous coding:

1. The pieces of information (words, numbers, or lines) have to possess some relationship with each other (group membership, numerical rule, geometric pattern.
2. That relationship, or the basis for discovering it, must exist in long-term memory.
3. The resulting code is a holistic unit, taking up only one space in working memory.
4. The parts of the code—i.e., the information that initially elicited the code—do not necessarily retain any intrinsic order after simultaneous coding (e.g., you don't have to remember that "cat" came first).
5. Some initially coded information may even be lost (e.g., you remember that several pets were listed, but not which ones, or that a square was drawn, but not the location or color of the lines).

Simultaneous processing is illustrated schematically in Figure 2-2.

While simultaneous coding involves the production of a single code from an ordered set of information, successive coding is required to produce and hold that ordered set. In successive coding, information is put in sequence; it may or may not have been presented sequentially. The only relationship seen to exist in the information is the sequential or temporal one (cf. Kirby & Das, 1990). For example, you use successive coding or processing when you remember the sequence of numbers that forms a telephone number or when you follow a set of sequential instructions ("go down to the first set of traffic lights, turn right, go as far as the first church, turn left, . . ."). The key features of successive coding are:

1. No relationship other than the sequential one is perceived (any other relationship would provide the basis for a simultaneous code;
2. The successive code originally takes up as much space in working memory as there are units within the code.
3. With practice or overlearning the sequential links within the code can be automated to a point at which the whole sequence can be produced smoothly and effortlessly, thus taking up less working memory space.
4. The order or sequence of the items is critical, as in learning a series of dance steps or numbers.

Successive processing is illustrated schematically in Figure 2-3.

How do simultaneous and successive processing relate to the features and divisions of memory referred to earlier? Both types of processing occur in working memory, and the results, simultaneous and successive codes, are stored in LTM. It is important to recognize that we are not identifying successive processing with STM, even though many of the tests that measure successive processing involve STM. Depending upon the nature of the material and the subject's knowledge base about it, simultaneous processing is just as likely to be involved in STM. The two holding mechanisms that serve working memory, the articulatory loop and the visual-spatial scratch-pad, are ideally suited for retaining, respectively, auditory-successive and visual-simultaneous information. Auditory information is by its very nature presented successively, while visual information is presented simultaneously; however, once the information enters working memory, mode of presentation becomes irrelevant, or at least less relevant than what is done to the information, that is, the type of processing applied to it. Both simultaneous and successive processing may be applied to information that is verbal or spatial, episodic or semantic.

From this description it should be clear that simultaneous and successive coding are complementary; the units that are part of a successive code are themselves simultaneous codes at a lower level, and the successively coded units are the basis for the next higher level of simultaneous coding. Neither type of coding is in this sense superior to the other, as both are required at various levels. In most tasks a *cyclical hierarchy* of simultaneous and successive coding can be seen, successive coding of simultaneous units at level 1 being the basis for simultaneous and then successive coding at level 2, and so on.

Consider the cyclical hierarchy in a simple memory task. The initial recognition of the individual numbers requires simultaneous processing, in the sense that the patterns of the individual stimuli must access representations in LTM. These representations are activated in STM, and successive links are formed between them. At this point, patterns among the items (such as 2-4-6) may be recognized, again requiring simultaneous processing.

The same cycle of processes can be seen in a more complex task such as reading. Kirby (1988) has argued that processing in reading may occur at eight distinct levels of increasing complexity and abstraction: features, letters, sound or syllable units, words, phrases, ideas, main ideas, and themes. At each level, items of information are recognized (simultaneous processing) and ordered (successive processing), so that higher-level units can be recognized (simultaneous processing). This is illustrated in Figure 4-1; both simultaneous and successive processing are required at each level of the hierarchy.

While both types of coding are involved in virtually all tasks, many tasks can be identified as depending primarily on one or the other type of coding; this happens because one of the types of coding in a particular task

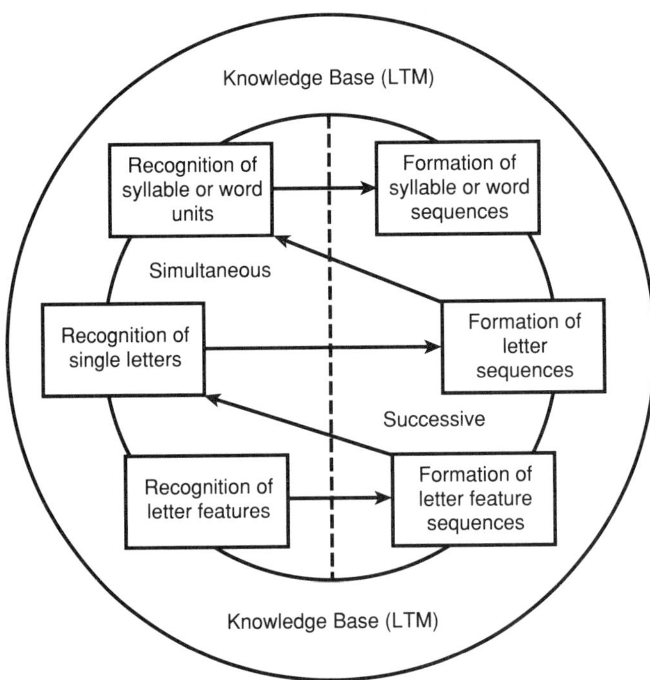

FIGURE 4-1 Cyclical Hierarchy in Reading

is more difficult than the other or because processing in a task does not go beyond a certain level, and thus either simultaneous or successive processing represents the highest level of processing. Consider the task of remembering a telephone number after hearing it once (see Figure 4-2). The highest level of simultaneous processing usually required is the recognition of the individual numbers. For normal, adult, English speakers (for English numbers), this is not a source of difficulty, so persons will not differ much in their ability to perform this part of the task. In other words, individuals' levels of simultaneous processing will not be related (correlated) with performance in the task. On the other hand, the highest level of successive processing normally involved, the retaining in order of the number units, is relatively difficult, and therefore individual differences in successive processing should be related to individual differences in memory for telephone numbers. However, if there were some pattern underlying the telephone number, as in "248-1632," then simultaneous processing may well be related to performance in the task, in which case the successive processing component would become less difficult and less related to success.

This demonstrates that the type of coding measured by a task depends

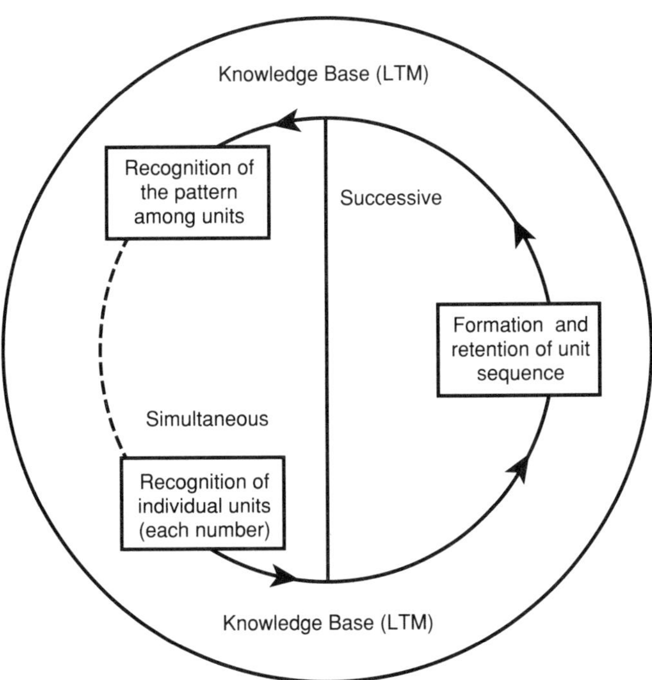

FIGURE 4-2 Processing in Remembering a Phone Number

on both the nature of the task and the knowledge and strategy employed by the person performing the task. Remembering telephone numbers with no underlying pattern calls at the highest level for successive processing; however, if one is unfamiliar with the basic units (the numbers), then simultaneous processing at a lower level will determine success. If there is an underlying pattern, and if the person decides to look for it (that is, uses such a strategy), then simultaneous processing at the next higher level will determine success; if the person doesn't decide to use that strategy, then successive processing will determine success. The decision to employ a pattern-based strategy is a function of planning.

It should be clear by now that our thinking about tests and what they measure becomes much more complex when we adopt an information processing approach. This complexity may make our task appear harder, but in reality that difficulty was always there; what has changed is our awareness of it. That awareness, however, should lead to improved diagnostic assessment and remedial instruction.

Types of Coding: Abilities, Strategies, or Styles?

A major difficulty in discussing coding is to determine what exactly are the "things" being discussed; this is most apparent with respect to types of coding. For example, is simultaneous processing an ability—that is, something some people are generally good at and others generally poor at? Or is it a strategy—that is, something you could decide to use or not, depending upon the situation and how you feel? Even further, perhaps it is a style, a relatively stable and characteristic method of approaching the world in general. We see coding as having all three of these aspects.

Take for example the simultaneous processing involved in recognizing patterns of numbers in order to remember them more successfully. Some sort of ability factor seems to be involved: individuals do differ in being able to recognize such patterns, some patterns are more difficult to detect than others, and training in mathematical patterns would probably increase your skill at detecting them. The ability factor appears to have two aspects, those of knowledge and skill. The knowledge aspect concerns whether you know (understand and remember) a particular pattern; for example, the pattern of raising to the third power could produce the following sequence: 1 (= 1 × 1 × 1), 8 (= 2 × 2 × 2), 27 (= 3 × 3 × 3), and so on. If you don't know about multiplication and powers, you cannot be expected to detect this pattern.

The skill aspect concerns how well you can detect the patterns you do know. If you were to practice pattern recognition, without learning any new patterns, you would probably get better at it; you would probably recognize patterns in more number sequences, and you would probably recognize them more quickly. It would appear in this case that your pattern recognition skills are improving, by becoming more automatic and less effortful. At the moment our point is only that abilities are involved in coding and that abilities have knowledge and skill aspects. These two aspects may be strongly related to each other, and both may be able to be increased (in spite of the common initial prejudice that abilities are fixed). We use the term *ability* here to refer to a competency in a task that has reached a relatively stable level; subsequent events (such as instruction, experience, or even mental development) may cause a change in this level.

Coding also clearly has a strategic component, in that particular *strategies* determine which type of coding is to be employed and for which aspects of the task and, therefore, which types of coding are likely to be related to success in the task. Strategies also have knowledge and skill aspects, in that you may or may not possess (know) a certain strategy, and you may or may not be efficient (skilled) in its use. Strategy use is also affected by the manner in which tasks are presented. For instance, in a task requiring recall of a set of words (e.g., animals and furniture), we can arrange the task in such a way that most individuals in a certain age-education-culture group will use successive processing (present the words in random order and require that they be recalled in order) or so that they will use simultaneous processing (ask them to recall in two categories). Unlike abilities, strategies may be able to be changed relatively quickly. Strategies will be dealt with more fully in Chapter 5, as they are most properly a function of planning, but they are very relevant to coding because they determine how coding will proceed.

Coding also has a stylistic component. A *style* is a habitual manner of approaching certain types of tasks or even the world in general. Styles can be characterized in many ways, including in terms of the types of coding that predominate in them. For example, a style of learning may be to relate new information to old, to produce a new integration (Biggs, 1987); this style clearly relies on simultaneous processing (Biggs & Kirby, 1984). The alternative style could be to maintain new information in its input form, comprehended but not integrated with old information (Biggs, 1987); this style would rely upon successive processing (Biggs & Kirby, 1984). Our point here is that many cognitive or learning styles can be characterized partly by the type of coding upon which they rely. To the extent that individuals vary in their facility in using the two types of processing, in required knowledge, and in willingness to employ certain strategies, it may be possible to characterize some students as preferring simultaneous processes and others as preferring successive processes, though the status of such a characterization is unclear (Das, 1988a). We are *not* suggesting that all individuals can be usefully assigned to one or the other group.

Abilities, strategies, and styles interact, in that individuals are more likely to adopt a given style if they know many of the strategies consistent with that style and if they have good levels of the required abilities. The interaction is complex, however, because some people may have the requisite abilities and strategies without adopting that style exclusively, and because others may prefer a given style even though they lack the appropriate abilities and strategies (cf. Kirby, Moore, & Schofield, 1988).

This point has profound implications for the measurement of cognitive processes: As we argued in Chapter 1, adoption of a *processing* approach (rather than one of fixed abilities) lessens one's certainty about what exactly is being measured by any given task at any given time but increases one's understanding of the variety of mental processes that may be involved. When we measure a single performance, we do not know to what extent that performance has been limited by ability or strategy or style factors; as a result, we do not know whether or not performance can be improved.

It is important to keep in mind that coding has the three aspects of abilities, strategies, and styles. All of these will have an effect on how persons approach tasks in general and how well they perform in a given task. To some extent, type of coding can be used to classify people according to their general preferences (styles), or according to their situation-specific choices (strategies), or according to their information processing abilities. While abilities and styles will tend to produce stable classifications, strategies are likely to be more variable and thus subject to instruction. We will see in Chapter 9 that an important question in remediation is whether the child's poor performance is due to low coding ability in a certain area or to the lack of use or knowledge of the related strategy.

Categories of Processing

A common misunderstanding of simultaneous and successive processing is to consider them only as two abilities and as the only two important abilities. As we have indicated in the previous section, abilities are certainly relevant to the two types of coding. However, we believe it is wrong to identify simultaneous and successive processing as only abilities. Rather, we see them as *categories* of abilities, i.e., as groups of more basic or narrow abilities that share the common type of coding characteristic; we also emphasize that they are fundamentally processes, determined both by abilities and strategies.

At the broadest level, simultaneous and successive processing can be seen as types of coding underlying all forms of behavior. Within each type of coding, tasks from similar areas (e.g., reading or spatial tasks) would be expected to be more related to each other than to other manifestations of the same type of coding from a different area. For this reason, for instance, we would expect measures of simultaneous coding using spatial content to be more highly correlated with each other than with a simultaneous coding test that used verbal content. In fact, because of the possible importance of verbal content, that verbal test may even be highly correlated with a verbal test of successive processing. Thus, our theory does not lead us to predict uniformly high correlations among tests tapping the same type of coding, nor uniformly low correlations between tests tapping different types of coding; as we have emphasized throughout this chapter, there are more factors determining test scores than just type of coding. Simultaneous and successive processing are theoretically defined constructs, whose construct validity relies on more than the correlations among tests. Of course, if two tests of a type of coding are not correlated at all, then individual differences in at least one of them are not being affected by that type of coding; in this case the particular test would not be a very effective indicator of that type of coding.

If each type of coding is conceived as a *hierarchy* of abilities and strategies, then a person with a coding difficulty could have that problem high in the hierarchy, which implies that it would be apparent in many forms of that type of processing, or low in the hierarchy, implying that it would only be seen within a narrow range of tasks. Thus, for example, a child could have a general simultaneous coding problem, which would be seen in reading, language, mathematics, and spatial tasks. Another child could have a more narrow problem, only showing up in tests measuring simultaneous coding in reading.

Research to date has supported the existence of general coding problems (e.g., Das, Kirby, & Jarman, 1979). In fact, if it were not for belief in, and evidence for, consistency between general and specific levels of processing, then most existing psychometric assessment would be obsolete: Why assess general intelligence, or any other general skill, if it is not related to specific (e.g., school-related) tasks (Kirby, 1989)? Further, how could any general process be assessed, if there were no consistency among different tasks? The fact that consistency has been observed, however, does not mean that it should always be expected, or that the consistency is by any means perfect. The most likely result is that test scores will be most correlated when the tests share the maximum number of characteristics (e.g., type of coding, content, etc.) and that consistency should drop as tests (and the processes they evoke) become more dissimilar. This is by no means a new proposal, nor counterintuitive, but it is often overlooked when theories attempt to explain the correlations among tests.

MEASURING PROCESSING

In this section we describe a general approach to measuring coding processes, as well as several of the actual tests that have been used in previous studies. We describe general coding process tests, which could be used in a standardized battery of processing measures, and a number of tests that would assess the coding processes within specific achievement areas. The tests that form the DN:CAS battery (Das & Naglieri, 1993) will be completely described in Chapter 6.

General Concerns

Several of the cautions that have been made in the preceding section merit emphasis here. Most important of these is that there is no such thing as a pure measure of either simultaneous or successive coding. All tests involve various levels of both types of coding. When we describe a test as measuring either type of processing, we are saying that the highest level of processing normally involved in that task is primarily dependent on that type of processing. (*Normally* here refers to the way in which average, English-speaking persons of Western culture and education would approach the task; persons from different cultural and educational backgrounds may well approach these tasks differently. This is an empirical issue, which does not challenge the theory but might alter the classification of the tests or invalidate particular measures in other contexts.)

While all the measures described are ability tests, in the sense that they measure how well people are able to do them, it should not be forgotten that (1) strategy or style factors could be involved (i.e., the person could be bringing the wrong abilities to bear upon the task) and (2) the "abilities" in question may be able to be improved. Accordingly, no subject's score should be regarded as carved in stone. This raises the related point of dynamic assessment. Most previous and current psychometric assessment is essentially static; the person's current ability to perform the task is measured, with minimal guidance from the tester about how to approach the task. Based largely upon the work of Vygotsky (1962), several current researchers (e.g., Feuerstein, 1980; Palincsar & Brown, 1984) are suggesting that potential should be assessed more dynamically—that is, in the context of instruction. In this case, assessment seeks not to find out what the person can do without instruction, but rather how much better the person can do with instruction. Although there is little research evidence to go on, we will indicate where possible how a dynamic approach could employ these tests. (Dynamic assessment is also relevant to strategy assessment and teaching; see Chapter 5.)

Tests of Successive Coding

The goal of measuring successive coding is to tap the person's skill at keeping things in a particular order. Usually this means that we have to increase the number of items to be kept in order until we reach a level at which the person fails. Another way to make tasks more difficult is to increase the amount of work (coding) the person must do before doing the successive coding. This latter technique relies on either forcing the person to discover the ordering by him- or herself, or requiring processing to proceed to higher levels (through several cycles of simultaneous and successive coding) before reaching the level at which the successive coding of interest takes place.

In assessing successive coding it is crucial to ensure that the only links between items that should be apparent to the subject are temporal or ordinal. If the subject can find an underlying pattern or rule, or if the items can be combined to form a new integration, then simultaneous processing may take place and thus be assessed by that test instead.

Memory Span

The most straightforward of successive coding tests is called Digit Span. The tester reads a series of one-digit numbers and the subject tries to repeat all of them in exactly the same order. Digit Span subtests are used in many test batteries, including the WISC-R (Wechsler, 1974). Instead of using digits as items, other stimuli such as words, sounds, pictures, or even hand movements can be used. Stimuli can be presented via the visual, auditory, or tactile modes, and responses can be made verbally, in writing, by rearranging stimulus objects (e.g., pictures or words on cards), or by recognizing (selecting) the correct copy. Verbal memory tests as well as gestural hand movements tests have been used as successive tasks (Das, Kirby, & Jarman, 1979; Naglieri & Das, 1988).

A different type of successive processing measure is Naming Time (Das & Siu, 1989). In this test, children are asked to read 30 unrelated familiar words as quickly as possible, and their time is recorded. This is a measure of successive processing because it is necessary to maintain a fast rhythm while naming the words and because the words must be decoded sequentially (there are no context cues to word identity). Children with fast naming times have longer memory spans and are more able to recall narratives; learning-disabled children have slower naming times and recall fewer details in stories (Das & Siu, 1989).

Higher-level Successive Coding

Memory span tests typically require little coding prior to the successive coding in which we are interested; for instance, there is usually little difficulty in recognizing the stimulus items (numbers, words, etc.). However, it is possible to devise tests in which considerable processing is required to produce the units that are then successively coded, such as in the recall of narrative texts. The type of test used most frequently has been one in which sentences are to be repeated. Because sentences usually contain more words than can be held in working memory (as separate, unintegrated words), it is necessary to recode them, through simultaneous processing, into a smaller number of units (essentially phrases). This smaller number of units can then be held as a successive code in working memory.

Kirby and Gordon (1988) used a set of sentences which increased in number of phrases from two to seven and found that this correlated with Digit Span to define a successive processing factor. Das and Naglieri (1989; Naglieri, Das, et al., 1989; Naglieri, Prewett, & Bardos, 1989) have used a similar test, Sentence Repetition, in which the sentences have a coherent syntax (so phrases can be formed) but no real meaning (preventing simultaneous coding between phrases). In the latter test, subjects are asked to repeat sentences such as "Red blues to pink the green purple but not the brown purple" and then, to check that they have understood the syntax, are asked a question such as "Which purple does the red blue?"

It is important that the units to be held in order cannot be easily integrated. An example of the failure to do so is provided by Kaufman and Kaufman (1983). They developed a test called "Photo Series" to measure successive (in their terms, sequential) processing; the subject's task is to arrange a number of photographs so that they tell a story. While the story does involve a successive coding of events, the events depicted by the photos are clearly related, and therefore simultaneous coding of them into a unitary plot scheme takes place. Given this analysis, it is not surprising that Kaufman and Kaufman found Photo Series to measure simultaneous processing. Story element sequencing could be a good measure of higher-level successive coding, but the test designer would have to ensure that those elements could not be easily integrated.

Discovering Order

In the tests mentioned so far, the order of items is essentially supplied to the subjects, the order being basically the input temporal order. To some extent this is an oversimplification, because in visual presentations there is no necessary or inherent order. Our writing system leads us to scan (read) visual displays from left to right, so that direction becomes the "natural" order. Of course, other cultures read in other directions, and people who haven't learned to read may not have developed a standard order of visual scanning at all. With that qualification, however, it is fair to say that the preceding tests do not require the subjects to discover the underlying order.

A test that does require discovering of order is Visual Short-Term Memory (see Das, Cummins, et al., 1979; Kirby & Biggs, 1981). A set of numbers is presented on a grid (such as those shown in Figure 4-3), and

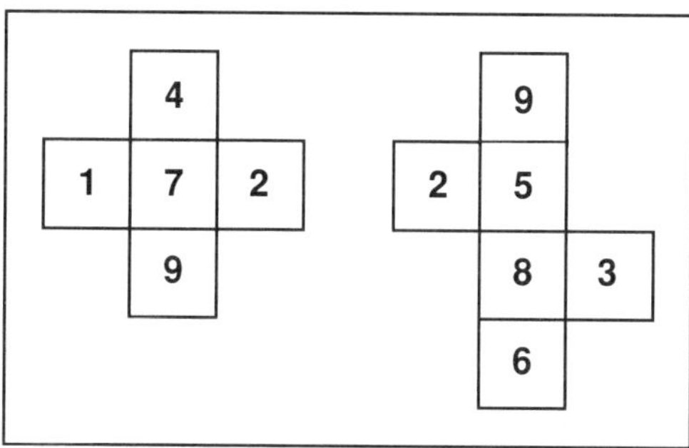

FIGURE 4-3 Samples of Visual Short-term Memory Items. Source: Das, Cummins, et al., 1979; Kirby & Biggs, 1981

then, after the display is removed, the subject has to reproduce the numbers on a blank grid of the same shape. To do so, particularly for larger grids, requires scanning the original display in a systematic order, rehearsing the numbers in that order, and then reproducing them in the same order. If grid shape stays the same, then a single scanning pattern could be learned and the "discovery of order" factor minimized (this is the way the test was administered in the studies described by Das, Cummins et al., 1979). If grid shapes change unpredictably, however, effort must be expended on each trial to create an order and use it (Kirby and Biggs [1981] presented it this way).

Successive Coding in Reading

The easiest tasks to develop in reading that measure successive coding are essentially memory span ones using written letters and words. It could be useful to compare spans with and without reading, for instance, with reading-disabled children who would be expected to show higher spans when reading was not involved. It may also be worthwhile to test for successive coding of auditorially presented sounds, as some authors have suggested that reading-disabled children have difficulty in phonologically coding and retaining sound sequences (e.g., Shankweiler et al., 1979; Stanovich, 1982a; however, see Das, Bisanz, & Mancini, 1984).

A reading span technique has been developed by several authors (e.g., Daneman & Carpenter, 1980; Masson & Miller, 1983) that uses the same principle underlying the sentence repetition tests described earlier. Typically, they give subjects several sentences to read and then ask them to recall the last word of each of the sentences. Other questions about the sentences are then asked, to ensure that all of the sentences were being attended to and were comprehended. While the units recalled are still only words, considerable higher-level processing of meaning must already have happened. (For more on such "working span" measures, in which considerable coding occurs along with the span task, see Kirby and Williams [1991], chapter 12.)

More sophisticated examples of successive coding in reading could be developed, but they await experimental verification. For example, a reader could be asked to recreate the sequence of events that took place in a text. In such a case it would be important to make the events unrelated, so that no unitary plot scheme could be produced by simultaneous processing. While this is seldom typical of texts, it is not uncommon for information or an event to be presented in the beginning or middle of a text, without its relevance or relatedness being made clear until much later. The reader with better successive coding can retain this information in the correct ordinal place, waiting for the later information that indicates how to integrate it. The reader with less effective successive coding forgets this information, so that there is nothing left to integrate when the later information is supplied.

It is also important to demonstrate that the general measures of successive processing (those without any specific achievement area content) are predictive of achievement skills. Numerous studies have shown successive processing to be correlated with reading skills (e.g., Cummins & Das, 1977; Kirby & Das, 1977; Krywaniuk & Das, 1976; Leong, 1980; Naglieri & Das, 1987); the relationship is particularly strong for decoding skills (i.e., the recognition of words out of context using phonological and visual cues). Kirby and Robinson (1987) found that a successive processing factor was difficult to identify in a sample of reading-disabled children; they suggested that these children were poor at successive processing and tended to employ simultaneous processing (inappropriately) in its place. Kirby and Das (1990) have described the way in which successive processing is involved in the naming or articulation of words (see also Das and Siu [1989], whose study was discussed earlier in this chapter).

Successive Coding in Mathematics

Simple equivalents of the memory span tests could be devised in mathematics by using numbers or mathematical symbols as items. Similarly, most of the reading measures described are also relevant, as they are involved in the reading and comprehending mathematical word problems.

Successive coding measures that are specific to mathematics are more difficult to devise, perhaps due to that domain's predominant reliance on the relating and integrating operations of simultaneous processing, and also due to the planning component involved in step-by-step computation and in problem solving. While experimental work has yet to be done, some measures could be constructed that require the execution of a series of steps that are not obviously related to each other and which require only minimal planning. Retention of this sequence of steps would be an example of successive coding, and this could be much more difficult for a child with a learning problem in mathematics.

Some children may use successive processing in the early stages of learning arithmetic tables—for instance, if they learn the number fact "3 plus 6 is 9" in a rote fashion, without much comprehension. However, it seems more common for children to begin by carrying out the actual computations by counting and then to shift to direct retrieval of the answer from the stimulus, which is recognized as a single pattern (Ashcraft, 1982; Kirby & Becker, 1988).

Successive processing has been found to be correlated with mathematics achievement, but generally at a lower level than simultaneous processing (Das, 1988b; Garofalo, 1982; Kaufman & Kaufman, 1983; Leong, Cheng & Das, 1985). These studies are described, in the following section on simultaneous processing.

Tests of Simultaneous Coding

The goal in assessing simultaneous coding is to measure the person's facility in relating and integrating discrete pieces of information—i.e., in processing two or more pieces of information to produce one piece. In order for two pieces of information to be so combined, some sort of relationship must exist (or be constructed) between them. Such relationships can be at relatively low levels of coding, for instance two lines forming a right angle, or at very high levels of coding, for instance when two paragraphs reflect exactly opposite views of democracy without saying so explicitly. Tests of simultaneous coding can be made more difficult by increasing the amount of coding that precedes the simultaneous coding, by increasing the amount of information that must be included in the new simultaneous code, or by decreasing the familiarity of the relationship that must be recognized. We describe examples of general tests from the areas of spatial relations, verbal relations, and analogical reasoning, and then achievement area measures in reading and mathematics.

Spatial Relations

If tests of memory span are the most obvious examples of successive coding, tests of spatial relations are the most obvious examples of simultaneous coding. Because of this, it is necessary to emphasize that these are *not* the only measures of simultaneous coding. Many different spatial relations tests exist, most sharing the characteristic that discrete stimulus lines must be related to each other so that the unitary figure they form can be recognized. The tests differ in what is done next and in what sort of response is made.

One group of tests is exemplified by the Figure Copying test (see Das, Cummins, et al., 1979), in which the subject's task is to copy a visible geometric figure (another familiar figure copying test is the Bender Gestalt test [Koppitz, 1964]). Because copying is presumed to be easier if the overall figural relations are used to guide drawing, this test relies on simultaneous coding. Simultaneous coding is also emphasized by the scoring criteria, which stress maintenance of geometric relations and proportions. Memory-for-Designs (Graham & Kendall, 1960) is a similar measure, in which the figures are reproduced from memory. Both Figure Copying and Memory-for-Designs have been used extensively as measures of simultaneous coding (Das, Cummins, et al., 1979). The two tests have recently been combined in Figure Memory, in which the figure has to be remembered but traced when embedded in a background of lines and other figures (Naglieri & Das, 1988; Naglieri, Prewett, & Bardos, 1989).

A more easily scored test would be any of the various spatial ability tests: Typically subjects are asked to perform some sort of mental operation (such as a rotation) upon a figure and answer a simple yes/no question (e.g., would it form a square when combined with a second figure?). Kirby and Das (1978b) showed that such tests were strongly related to measures of simultaneous coding.

Somewhat more complicated is the Embedded Figures test, in which a simple figure is concealed within a complex figure and the subject's 's task is to locate or identify it. While the Embedded Figures test has been used to assess the cognitive style of field independence (Witkin et al., 1977), Heemsbergen (1980) has shown it to be related to other measures of simultaneous processing.

Verbal Relations

Relationships also exist between verbal concepts. For example, if you were asked how a dog and a horse were alike, you would have to produce a feature list for each word and compare the lists. Relating verbal concepts requires simultaneous processing (Cummins & Das, 1978).

A more elaborate example is provided by Das and Naglieri's (1989) Tokens Test. Subjects are shown a set of colored plastic shapes of different sizes and asked to select, for example, "all the large blue ones" or "all the large blue ones that aren't triangles." Simultaneous processing is required to construct (integrate) the appropriate verbal concepts ("big and blue" or "big and blue, but not triangle") that guide selection.

Further verbal relations tests could rely upon imagery, whereby verbal concepts are translated into pictures. For example, when faced with a problem such as "Bill is taller than Sue, but Mary is taller than Bill; who is the tallest?" many subjects mentally represent the three persons as figures of different sizes and make their judgment from the resulting mental image (e.g., Huttenlocher, 1968).

Analogical Reasoning

In analogical reasoning problems (such as cat is to pet as table is to ?) subjects need to discover a relationship (between cat and pet), and then apply this relationship to a third item (table) to produce the missing item (?). Both of these acts rely heavily on simultaneous processing. Overall performance on such items may also depend on other factors (such as familiarity of the items, familiarity of the relationships, how similar the first pair of items is to the second pair, and so on), but at least simultaneous processing is being employed.

The analogical reasoning test that has most often been used to measure simultaneous processing is Raven's Progressive Matrices (Das, Cummins, et al., 1979). (While some of this test's items are clearly spatial relations items (see Kirby & Das, 1978; Kirby & Lawson, 1983; Lawson & Kirby, 1981), the majority of the items, and all of the more difficult ones, are nonverbal analogies.) Das and Naglieri (1989) use the Matrix Analogies test developed by Naglieri (1985a). Other examples, particularly from the verbal area, could be produced (See figures in chapter 6).

Simultaneous Coding in Reading

In reading, as in any other activity, simultaneous coding is used to integrate a set of items to produce a new single item. Examples would include integrating letter parts into letters, letters into words, words into phrases or ideas, and ideas into main ideas (see Kirby [1988] and Kirby & Williams [1991] for further examples).

Reading is usually divided into decoding and comprehension; in our early research we found that decoding at the early elementary grades required successive processing, while comprehension at any age required simultaneous processing (Das, Cummins, et al., 1979); some studies indicated that both simultaneous and successive processing were required for comprehension (Kirby & Das, 1977). Recent research has confirmed the importance of both simultaneous and successive processing, as well as planning, in comprehension (Das, Mensink & Janzen 1990; Das, Snart, & Mulcahy, 1982; Kirby & Gordon, 1988; Naglieri & Das, 1988). These studies demonstrate that simultaneous processing measures with no reading component are good predictors of reading comprehension achievement.

Simultaneous Coding in Mathematics

Just as reading can be divided into decoding and comprehension, mathematics can be divided into computational and problem-solving components. Simultaneous processing should be related to the immediate recognition of individual numerals and of number patterns (such as "2 + 3 = ?"), which are essential skills underlying computation. If the problems to be solved are word problems, then successive processing becomes important through decoding; whereas simultaneous processing becomes involved for comprehension of the sentence, deciding what parts of the word problem are important. Computation, however, because of its step-by-step nature and its requirement of a plan, should also be dependent upon planning.

Many skills in the mathematics problem-solving area can be seen to rely heavily upon simultaneous processing. Examples include the understanding of geometric relations, the formation of mental representations of problems, and the recognition that a particular problem fits a general pattern (e.g., "This seems to be a distance-rate-time problem").

A number of studies have confirmed the importance of simultaneous processing in mathematics. For example, Leong, Cheng, and Das (1985) found that simultaneous processing was the strongest predictor of standardized mathematics achievement for Hong Kong Chinese students. Simultaneous processing accounted for 16.7% of the variance for fourth-grade children (compared to 5.7% and 2.5% respectively for successive and planning); in sixth-grade simultaneous processing accounted for 18.6%, the other two factors making negligible contributions.

Garofalo (1982) related simultaneous and successive processing and planning to the Problem Solving and Computation subtests of the Iowa Test of Basic Skills in fifth-grade students. He found that Problem Solving was more strongly related to simultaneous than to the other two factors, while Computation was more strongly related to planning than to simultaneous or successive processing.

Garofalo's results as well as those of Warrick (1989) demonstrated that simultaneous processing is predictive of mathematics achievement. It is important to realize, however, that the actual pattern of results is dependent upon the mathematics measures used and the skill levels of the subjects. The critical point here is that simultaneous processing is involved whenever the task requires the relating or integrating of information. Further examples of simultaneous processing are discussed by Kirby and Williams (1991).

SUMMARY

In this chapter we have reviewed the two types of coding in which the processing system engages, simultaneous and successive. These processes have been defined theoretically. Those conceptual definitions were employed to derive measures and to predict relationships with achievement skills. Evidence has been presented concerning how these processes have been observed and the impact they have upon achievement skills. We emphasize that simultaneous and successive processing need to be considered in the context of the complete information processing model (PASS), that is, in conjunction with the attention and planning systems.

5

PLANNING

The processes underlying planful behavior relate to all the other processes and components of the PASS model. Attention and simultaneous and successive processing interact with planning. They are also dependent on knowledge base, as is planning; otherwise, plans will be uninformed and useless. Output programs, by definition, involve planning. We may ask, then, if planning processes can be separated from the other processes and components in our model; if the answer is negative, planning cannot be assessed separately.

At least two points can be immediately made in favor of treating planning processes as separate and distinguishable, if not independent. First is the critical role of planning in higher levels of cognitive activities such as problem solving: Strategies, plans, and executive functions are commonly used in describing problem solving behavior. Second, the disturbance of planning functions is uniquely associated with damage to the frontal lobes, specifically, to the prefrontal region. We shall discuss each of these points and, further, present empirical evidence from our own research in support of planning as a distinct process. But let us start with a definition of planning.

DEFINITION OF PLANNING

Planning consists of programming, regulation, and verification of behavior (Luria, 1966). Planning is a set of decisions or strategies an individual adopts and modifies to solve a problem and to reach a goal (Das, 1980). *Planning* refers to a process involved in nonroutine selection of programs for action, labeled as a supervisory attentional system (Shallice, 1982).

These definitions are drawn from both cognitive psychology and neuropsychology and share one element, the directive and evaluative role of planning. Planful behavior is not routine or entrenched behavior. But to say that it is concerned with merely novel behavior would be to ignore the regulatory function of planning. It directs behaviors, resisting distractions and overcoming discontinuities. Regulation also requires responding to feedback. Planning is characterized by purpose. It is self-generated and occurs in advance of action. It regulates behavior, probably by using inner speech. Yet planning may not be always accessible to introspection, as in the case of perceptual tasks that involve planning. Even in tasks involving higher mental functions requiring judgment and decisions during a continuous problem-solving situation, an individual may not be able to describe the strategies he or she used for solution (Broadbent, Fitzgerald, & Broadbent, 1986). Therefore, the assessment of planning behavior while the individual is solving a problem cannot always be facilitated by examining overt verbalization.

The use of a symbolic system such as inner speech to regulate behavior can persuade us to argue that planning cannot occur in very young children, before the age of 4 or 5, as the self-regulatory role of speech is not developed at that time. This will be consistent with Luria's view. This does not mean that the behavior of young children is disorganized or random or that they do not have the neurophysiological structure for planful behavior. What they do not have is the metacognitive activity, knowing about what they not only do, but what they know. The hallmark of planning is flexibility and evaluation of not only others' action but one's own action, of one's errors and successes. Examples of the breakdown of planning behavior, which occur as a consequence of frontal lobe damage, are found in failures of regulation of activities and evaluation of errors, as we shall see when we discuss the neuropsychological aspects of planning. However, from a cognitive view of planning, it is not clear at what age planning begins except to reiterate that speech must regulate action as a prerequisite for planning. In cases of impulsive actions of children and adults alike, the regulatory role of speech is obviously absent.

We present first the neuropsychological aspects of planning and then the history and conceptualization of planning, selected from cognitive psychology. The two aspects are by no means separate.

NEUROPSYCHOLOGICAL ASPECTS OF PLANNING

Luria's Legacy

As Shallice (1982, 1988) has stated, the executive functions and their disorders provide a meeting ground for neuropsychology and cognitive psychology. He goes on to say, "Within neuropsychology, Luria's (1966) concept of a system specialized for the programming, regulation and verification of activity is widely used clinically to explain certain types of specific disorder" (Shallice, 1982, p. 199). Disorders arise from lesions in the frontal lobes. According to the influential book *Human Neuropsychology* (Hecaen & Albert, 1978), the tasks of the frontal lobes include the regulation of the active state of the individual, control of intentions, programming complex activities, and monitoring them. Luria (1969) observed that the frontal lobes "regulate the 'active state' of the organism, control the essential elements of the subject's intentions, program complex forms of activity and constantly monitor all aspects of activity" (Hecaen & Albert, 1978, p. 376). Luria (1969) further observed that injury to the frontal lobes disturbs impulse control, regulation of voluntary action, and perception as in visual search. It has an adverse effect on memory that requires the adoption of strategies. Above all, symbolic functions are badly affected because frontal lobe damage leads to incorrect choice of programs and results in an inability to restrain premature operations.

There seems to be good neurophysiological reason to justify the important role which the frontal lobes play in planning. We quote Luria to give a firsthand account of his conceptualization of the physical base of planning.

> *The frontal lobes of the brain are the last acquisition of the evolutionary process and occupy nearly one third of the human hemispheres. . . . They are intimately related to the reticular formation of the brain stem, being densely supplied with ascending and descending fibers. . . . They have intimate connections with the motor cortex and with the structures of the second block . . . their structures become mature only during the fourth to fifth year of life, and their development makes a rapid leap during the period which is of decisive significance for the first forms of conscious control of behavior. (In Sapir & Nitzburg, 1973, p. 118)*

Consciousness and the Verbal Regulation of Motor Behavior

Planning may be the most complex human activity, but is it always a *conscious* activity? How are plans and consciousness related in the neuropsychological writings of Luria? Consciousness, according to Luria (1969), is the ability to assess sensory information, to respond to it with critical thought and actions, and to retain memory traces in order that such traces or actions can be used in the future. While fulfilling all of these functions, consciousness is closely related to speech. It is on the basis of speech that complex processes of regulation of one's own actions are formed. This complex form of brain activity that is consciousness entails the analysis of incoming information, the evaluation and selection of its significant elements, the use of memory traces, control over the course of goal activity, and, finally, the evaluation of the consequences of its own activity. Luria emphasizes the *role of speech* in the formation of conscious activity. By means of speech, a person can analyze a situation, distinguish its important components, and formulate programs of action. In forming images and plans, speech too has an extremely important role. Planned behavior is goal directed, and speech plays a major role in the maintenance of goal direction.

Luria lists three characteristics of goal directed activity: (1) recoding of information, (2) the formation of action programs with selection of appropriate responses and inhibition of interfering ones, and (3) a comparison of the effect of action with the original intention. These are the three characteristic features of conscious activity. To reiterate, conscious activities that are under the control of the individual and are carried out with the intimate participation of speech processes.

The recognition of the role of internal speech in planning controlled (as opposed to automatic) motor activity is the salient link between cognition and action. The link was first suggested by Vygotsky (1934, 1965) in his concept of *extracerebral connections,* the inputs from an individual's social-psychological milieu. These shape an individual's speech, cognition, and actions. Their origin is outside the brain, and yet these higher psychological processes are interiorized as the child develops, and become interiorized mental activities. Inner speech is the best representative of the interiorized mental functions. It also represents the uniquely human part of the functional organization in the brain, and transforms the brain into an "organ of Man's Conscious Life" (p. 386). Luria (1969) utilized the notion of a uniquely human function in interpreting the essential features of the entire human brain. He wrote:

> *We can fully agree with the assumption that the human CNS is really a Conceptual Nervous System and that its basic task consists in elaborating some inner codes which result in the execution of certain plans and programs in the regulation and control of Man's own behavior. This really makes the human brain an Organ of Freedom. (Luria, 1969, p. 19)*

Activities of the Prefrontal Cortex: The Organ of Planning

Planning is an expression of interiorized, or inner, codes that is adversely affected by injury to the frontal lobes. The specific frontal region is the prefrontal cortex, by consensus (Perecman, 1987; Fuster, 1989). (See Figure 5-1.) We shall simply summarize the functions of the prefrontal cortex as

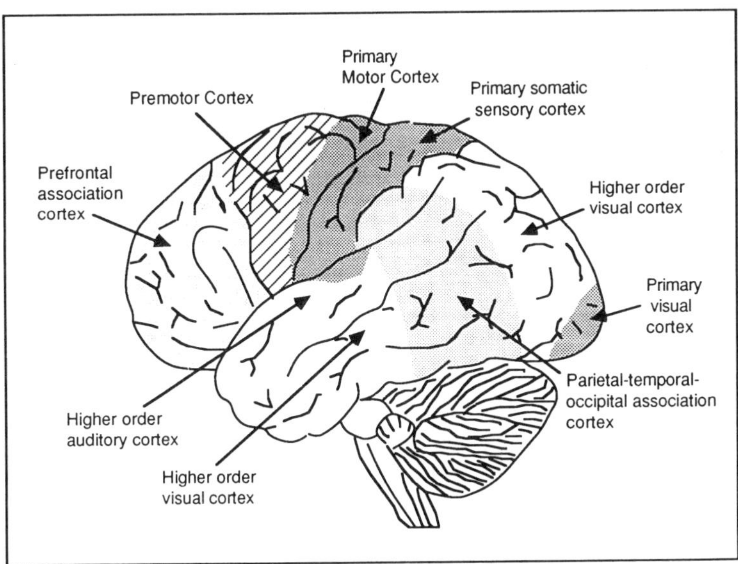

FIGURE 5-1 Prefrontal Cortex

Illustration by Jack A. Naglieri.

these relate to planning, and only later discussing the relevance of these functions for constructing tasks for the assessment of planning. We provide the summary mainly from Fuster (1989).

1. The functions of the prefrontal cortex can be included within a superordinate function organizing a wide range of cognitive and motor activities.
2. Its superordinate function consists of the formation of temporal structures of behavior with a purpose or a goal; it structures goal-directed behavior.
3. The development of this part of the brain enables us to form and perform novel, complex behavior.
4. It binds different activities; that is, activities spread over time can be brought together under one behavioral structure.
5. Assuming that planful behavior is arranged hierarchically in temporally structured units (one step at a time) and defined by a purpose, it is not terminated until the goal is reached. To support this hierarchical structure, the prefrontal area has a corresponding hierarchy of neural structure.
6. Its basic function is the anticipation and realization of future events.

7. It is the active force behind planful actions, deriving its neural energy from the arousal system.
8. Its critical role can be simply put as the temporal organization of behavior.
9. A dissociation between thought and action is the significant consequence of damage to this area. The patient can recall the thought, as well as the action, although failing to regulate his or her behavior.
10. Lack of inhibitory control is a prominent consequence of damage to this area. Damage results in the lack of inhibitory protection against internal interference, which is a disruption of temporal organization of behavior; an untimely behavior appears or an untimely impulse is allowed by the individual.
11. A smooth execution of voluntary motor acts is controlled by the prefrontal region, ensuring (a) the retention of information about prior events, (b) the anticipatory preparation of the motor system, and, finally, (c) the inhibition of inappropriate motor impulses. We wish to point out these three elements are all important of for understanding hyperactivity and attentional disorders.

The cognitive functions of the prefrontal cortex have been stated in nonphysiological terms. These appear to be directly applicable to assessment of planning functions. Upon rereading the preceding summary of functions, a few stand out as the salient features to be included in assessment. The planning task should be novel and complex, requiring the formation of a temporally integrated gestalt, and, above all, be goal directed. These tasks depend on attitudes and motivations, as well as the knowledge base of the planner. These are the components that determine the functional organization of planning processes in the brain. Planning is preeminently a product of social-cultural conditions that provide us with uniquely human tools such as language. Are these views of Vygotsky, Luria, and the contemporary researchers in neuropsychology far from those of cognitive psychologists who discuss planning?

THE VIEW FROM COGNITIVE PSYCHOLOGY

Purpose is the central determinant of behavior in rats and humans alike! Tolman (1948), a purposive behaviorist, observed anticipation, goal-directed behavior, and even the use of cognitive maps in rats. The arrival of information processing ideas in communication—the ideas of input, noise, channel capacity, output, and uncertainty (Shannon, 1948; Broadbent, 1958)—opened the way for treating cognition as a proper subject matter to be studied scientifically. The subject matter of inquiry into mental functions such as planning dealt with the following questions: How do people take in information, recode, store, and remember it, transform their internal knowledge states, make decisions, and translate the decisions to actions (Lachman, Lachman, & Butterfield, 1979)? The transition to a computer analogy for mental functions followed these attempts at explaining cognitive functions (Newell & Simon, 1961). The landmark publication on planning, *Plans and the Structure of Behavior* (Miller, Galanter & Pribram, 1960) defined the cognitive approach. We shall discuss the two pairs of influential concepts in this book, images and plans, and search and prediction. Then we pass on to a discussion of problem solving, as conceptualized by Simon (1981), and the decision-making experiments of Broadbent, Fitzgerald, and Broadbent (1986). These pioneers are still active researchers in the field of planning and problem solving. It is not surprising, as we shall see in this chapter and the following one, that their research and that of the neuropsychologists should give direction to the construction of planning measures. We summarize first the central concepts of Miller, Galanter, and Pribram (1960).

Image and Plan

Image

The *image* is all the accumulated, organized knowledge that the organism has about itself and its world. The image consists of a great deal more than imagery. What we have in mind when we use this term is essentially the same kind of private representation that other cognitive theorists have demanded. It includes everything the individual has learned—values as well as facts that have been organized by the concepts, images, or relations that have been acquired. These make up the knowledge base for cognitive processing.

Plan

Any complete description of behavior should be adequate to serve as a set of instructions: that is, it should have the characteristics of a plan that can guide the action described. *Plan* refers to a *hierarchy* of instructions. *A plan is any hierarchical process in the organism that can control the order in which a sequence of operations is to be performed.*

Search and Prediction

Related but broader concepts are search and prediction. *Searching* provides a model for all processes involved in problem solving. Searching involves discrimination or discernment; it involves selection and is concerned with exploring alternatives, although such explorations need not always be exhaustive or systematic. But Miller, Galanter, and Pribram (1960) ask if all problem solving could be modeled after search. They support the distinction between *problems to find* and *problems to prove.* The problem to prove is concerned with testing the veracity of a statement that could be either true or false. It is the problem to prove that may not apparently fit in with a search model.

An example of a problem to prove can be found in syllogistic reasoning. The manner in which we prove a three-term syllogism of the type "if *a* is greater than *b* and if *b* is greater than *c,* which is greatest?" can be reduced to *finding a path* to connect two things, *a* and *c,* that have not been related. As such, it involves a search. But how does the searching for a path differ from searching for a target in a visual display as in the Visual Search task (described later in this chapter)? Miller, Galanter, and Pribram (1960) suggest that the former involves the generation of an operating plan; that is, this search relates to a plan by which the inference between *a* and *c* can be made. There is a special way of searching. This involves the making up of hypotheses, that is, predicting that *a* will follow *b,* and then verifying whether or not this can be proved. It is a familiar technique in problems or games that involve strategies. Problems to prove require prediction.

An example of a game based on prediction is *Mastermind,* in which the subject is asked to break a code that the experimenter has set by choosing different combinations of items involved in the code (see Das and Heemsbergen [1983]). Miller, Galanter, and Pribram (1960) give predicting a special status within the broad paradigm of searching and suggest that while setting up a hypothesis that would predict an outcome we are engaged in building up an appropriate image, rather than executing a plan. This appears to be a very important distinction. They make the additional point that construction of a better image is involved in evaluations and judgments, whereas execution of plans, which prompt some overt activity, are separate from image building.

Recent Ideas on Planning

Most of the preceding ideas are consistent with more recent research on planning. To give one example (Hayes-Roth & Hayes-Roth, 1979), planning is defined as the predetermination of a course of action aimed at achieving some goal. Also compare Miller, Galanter, and Pribram with the conception of problem solving posited by Simon (1981): When individuals are faced with problems they may do three things: (1) They formulate the problem as a problem of searching through an abstract space using certain operators to move from one point in the space to another. This operation is very close to the Miller, Galanter, and Pribram (1960) search paradigm. (2) The individuals perform a means-end analysis. That is, given a goal and situation, find the difference between them and retrieve from the knowledge base an operator that is relevant to reducing the difference. Repeat this process until the present situation is identical with the goal. (3) Individuals do not pursue multiple solutions at the same time. Instead, they usually pursue a single lead in some depth. Only when the search is unsuccessful do they back up to another lead and then explore it.

Metacognition

A key component of planning is *metacognition,* the awareness of and knowledge about cognitive processes. Metacognition was introduced as a concept by Flavell (1970) and has become a powerful explanatory construct in developmental and educational psychology (Brown, 1977; Borkowski & Cavanaugh, 1979). As we have seen earlier in this chapter, much of the concept of planning requires that subjects be aware of the relationships between tasks and strategies, monitor the success of their strategies, and make decisions about new strategies to adopt. Metacognition is relevant to all of these aspects of planning.

One ambiguity in the literature on metacognition is whether *metacognition* should refer to only the knowledge and awareness aspects, or to the executive control aspects as well (e.g., Lawson, 1980, 1984). While it is certainly possible to distinguish between these aspects (Kirby, 1984; Kirby & Ashman, 1984), it seems clear that both are aspects of the broader construct of planning; perhaps metacognitive "knowledge" should be seen as the knowledge base from which planning operates.

Metacognition (or its absence) is often invoked as the explanation for the failure of instruction. Students are commonly taught content (knowledge, particularly declarative knowledge) and how to do things (skills and strategies, or procedural knowledge); what they often fail to acquire is an understanding of why that knowledge is important, how it should be employed, and when. In short, they lack the metacognitive awareness to use their knowledge effectively, and thus they are unlikely to see the value of that knowledge or be able to retain it. Paris, Newman, and McVey (1982) have provided a good example of this. They taught 7- and 8-year-old children a strategy for remembering numbers, which improved their immediate performance in the task. Four days later the children were tested again; those who had been taught only the strategy reverted to their previous approach, with resulting poor performance, similar to a control group who had not been taught the strategy. The third group—children who had been taught the strategy and been given an explanation of its usefulness—was the only group to use the strategy (and maintain a high level of performance).

Two aspects of metacognition should be mentioned to strengthen the links with planning. The first, alluded to previously, is that metacognition is fundamentally related to motivation: Strategies only become effective when combined with a purpose and a need. This recalls the connections between the frontal lobes and the limbic system described earlier. The second aspect concerns cognitive development. Metacognition seems to make at least two large jumps in its development (cf. Kirby & Moore, 1987). The first comes around age 5, when children begin to take conscious control of their strategies or thinking; and the second comes around age 12, when children begin to take a more abstract, analytic, and systematic approach to controlling their thinking. Not surprisingly, these two jumps correspond to major transitions in Piaget's view of cognitive development, from preoperations to concrete operations, and from concrete to formal operations. The first also corresponds to the period of rapid growth in the frontal lobes that Luria (1969) observed when verbal self-control becomes possible.

The Usefulness of Verbal Reports in Studying Individual Differences in Strategies

We study the planning behavior of individuals in comparison with other individuals. The individual differences may be obtained by observing the strategies used while the problem is being solved. Although it is possible to observe the overt behavior of the individual, it is not always informative simply because strategies and plans are not explicit in behavior. Asking the individual for a verbal report is sometimes informative, but there are two difficulties that are commonly recognized: The process of eliciting verbal report interferes with the accurate description of the strategies which were used; for instance, the individual may become aware of a strategy at the time of giving the verbal report but might not have used it during the task. A more serious difficulty is that the strategies or plans may be "opaque" to introspection. This point becomes clear when we discuss Broadbent, Fitzgerald, and Broadbent's (1986) experiment which demonstrating the dissociation between verbal report and action.

Simon presents a third approach, the collection of thinking-aloud protocols, and their examination for the purpose of detecting individual differences (see Simon [1990] for a recent discussion). The protocols themselves are the behaviors; whether or not they can accurately reflect the process of planning and problem solving is uncertain. However, Simon recommends it as a method for studying individual differences much superior to the psychometric method of examining means and deviations from the mean. Unfortunately, the possibility of dissociation between verbal knowledge and action is still in the protocol analysis, and this diminishes its value and the value of verbal reports, as explained in the following paragraphs.

In the experiment by Broadbent, Fitzgerald, Broadbent (1986), adult subjects were asked to do decision making tasks, one of which was as follows: Subjects were asked to achieve a particular load on the buses in a city in terms of passengers per 100 buses, and a given amount of utilization of empty spaces in parking lots. They were asked to do this by determining the time interval between buses and the parking fee. They had to achieve the best balance between load, parking space, fee, and the interval between buses. They received feedback as they manipulated these four factors and learned to get the best solution. A dissociation between verbal report and action was noticed frequently; under certain conditions, the verbal report changed, but had no effect on action.

The research raises doubt about what we assume from common sense—that a person has knowledge, and this knowledge guides his or her action as well as making him or her answer questions about the action. Dissociation occurs when there are so many interrelationships that the person cannot describe how the elements in the task are related and how they interact with each other, and, furthermore, when there are many conditions that guide action, making it difficult for the person to know which is the salient one. Verbal knowledge may not help in planning ahead a course of action. This may happen when the person has so many possible actions that it is difficult to predict the one that will be the best combination of all the factors involved. Therefore, verbal knowledge is separate from efficient performance in planning tasks, and only under certain conditions can verbal knowledge reflect the action performed by the person. We give examples of some of our planning tasks later in this chapter.

In spite of the limitations of introspective reports and thinking-aloud protocols, they are useful supplements to the direct observation of strategies during the performance of some planning tasks. However, for some other tasks, verbal reports are uninformative. Consider, for example, Visual Search (described in detail in the next chapter) for a number embedded in a field of other numbers. The search process is carried out correctly, but the verbal report of the process is mostly uninformative. When asked how the target was located, the subject may answer evasively—"I just found it! It just appeared." Searching seems to be a well-learned behavior by middle childhood, and it has been learned through several exposures to search situations in everyday life as well as in schoolwork. Searching involves many variables. It fits in with the type of task that is likely to show a dissociation between verbal report and action. Broadbent (personal communication, 1986) describes tasks that show dissociation as having a very large number of variables; the tasks are best learned by storing information equally about contingencies between them rather than selecting a few variables, and then concentrating on learning the relationship between them.

For another task, Matching Numbers, verbal report may be informative for identifying strategies. In this task, six strings of digits appear in a row; one of the strings appears twice. The subject is required to find the two identical strings in the row. The strings may have three, four, five, or six numbers. Subjects who solve the tasks correctly use a number-by-number comparison for longer strings. Some report that they compared the first two numbers in a string of four numbers, then the last two numbers; then changed the strategy for longer strings, comparing the first three rather than two numbers, which is more economical. These verbal reports are mostly accurate reflections of their plan of action. Therefore, in assessment of planning, the usefulness of verbal report must depend on the task and the strategy used by the subjects.

Automatic and Controlled Processes in Planning

We may not be aware of the process of planning in solving a problem, but that does not mean that no effort was expended in solving it. The planning process was simply unavailable for conscious verbalization. Such is the case in many acts that we can describe as creative. A painting, when begun, does not follow a conscious and deliberate plan. Every brush stroke is not predetermined at the beginning. The artist is simply unable to tell us how the finished work of art happened. The reason perhaps lies in the many improvisations made during the painting. In any case, creative work is free from preconceived notions and set procedures; otherwise, machines could produce creative work. Planning processes overlap with creativity to a certain extent in that they are improvised; although they are not completely undetermined, plans are opportunistic, taking advantage of what is available at the moment when one is faced with a novel situation. In creative work we start with a plan or a course of action, but everything from then on is flexible. Creative work is an event whose beginning is determined, but the activity then proceeds unpredictably, and the end product is unpredictable. This does not mean that creative activity is unplanned, but only that its progress and culmination are not predetermined.

Automatic acts are unavailable for conscious verbalization as well, but they differ from controlled acts and processes in a fundamental way—they do not require much effort and are not under the control of the subject. Controlled processes or acts, on the other hand, are limited by capacity, usually serial, and under the deliberate control of the subject (Estes, 1982). Acts can be naturally automatic, such as the perception of an ink blot on white paper, or, as has been claimed by some psychologists, the perception of frequency of an event. These do not engage central processing resources; we do not have to think about them. We just do them. An example of an automatic search task is a field of numbers in which one picture is embedded. The embedded picture just pops out (see Figure 5-2). There are many instances in nature of automatic search and loca-

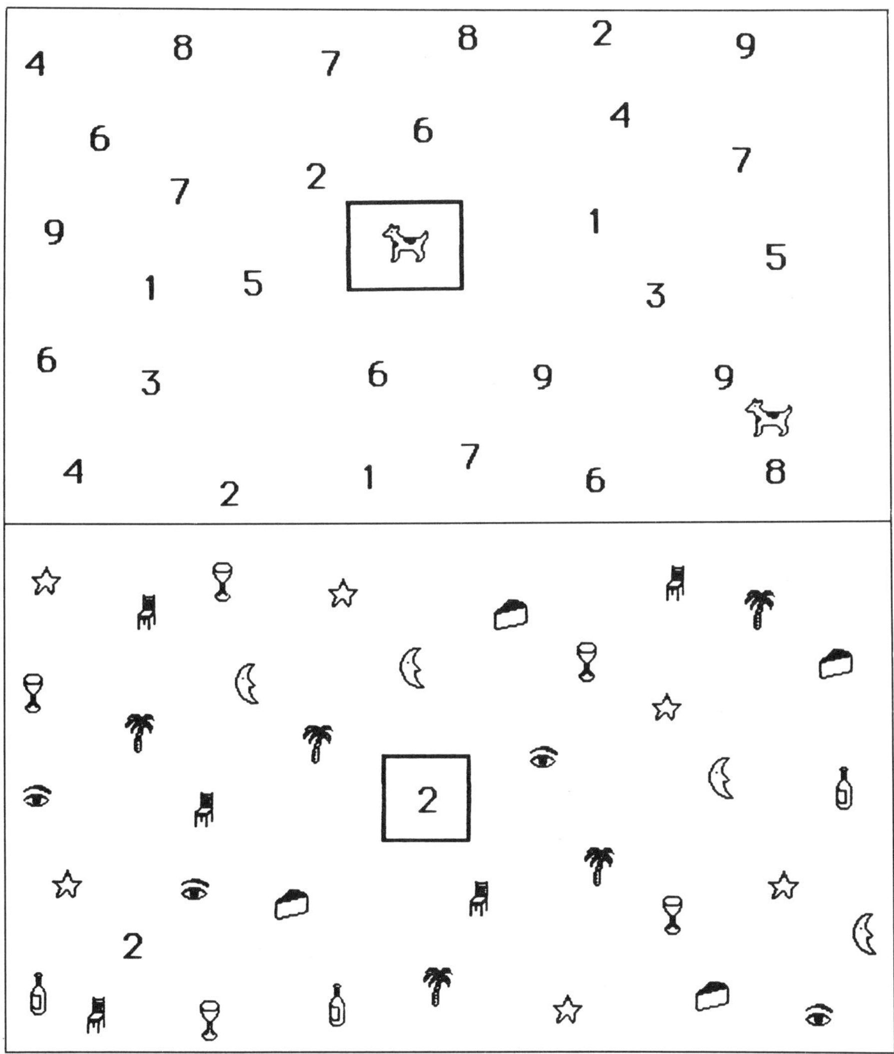

FIGURE 5-2 Example of Automatic Search

tion—the appearance of a pool of blue water in a dried up riverbed, or the presence of a barnhouse when one is lost in a snow field.

Controlled search is exemplified by the search for a number among other numbers, or, in real life, search for your blue flight bag among other flight bags (which are usually blue). But controlled search may become automatic with extensive practice (Schneider & Shiffrin, 1977). It is this kind of extensive practice that makes effortless the reading of a popular pulp novel for an educated adult, or the recitation of multiplication tables for many children in India by the end of elementary school. The contentious issue is: Is an automaticity all or none, or does it have degrees? Is letter recognition, for example, as automatic as reciting the multiplication tables, or more so? Some research has begun to suggest that it occurs in degrees, the processes being continuous rather than all or none, and therefore requiring different degrees of attention (Cohen, Dunbar, & McClelland, 1990). This is quite apparent in two tasks we present: One of them has a picture target among numbers (see 5.2) and the other, a number target embedded among pictures. Logically, both should be automatically detected. However, in fact, one of them (the first) invariably takes longer to detect than the other, and the pop-out phenomenon is absent in that figure.

The automaticity that is normal for the Figure 5.2 is not true for mentally retarded subjects in even the moderate range of ability. One procedure for testing for automaticity is to compare the time taken for target detection in two levels of density (as shown subsequently). If the search is automatic, increasing the density 100% does not slow down the detection of the target; whereas, if the search is controlled, it does slow it down significantly.

These search tasks, described again in the next chapter, are constructed to assess planning at a simple perceptual level. These are examples of how we have used the knowledge from both neuropsychology and cognitive psychology in their construction.

STUDIES OF PLANNING

It is obviously difficult to operationalize such a complex and uniquely human process as planning, yet the tests described here constitute an attempt to measure planning in general terms without being specific to certain areas of expertise such as physics, math, business management, or planning everyday activities. We wish to review several studies on planning. We first review the emergence of a factor of planning. This is consistent with the factor analytic evidence that has been provided in identifying tests that load on a particular process factor such as simultaneous or successive. Then we separate planning from the notion of speed. We present next some studies on visual search as a prototype for all planning, relate planning to scholastic ability and academic achievement, and, finally, review studies of enhanced planning through dynamic assessment.

In Ashman's (1978) doctoral study, a planning factor was first identified. It was defined by three tests, Visual Search, Trail Making, and Planned Composition, given to eighth-grade children. Subsequently, when adult mentally retarded sheltered workshop employees were given the tests, there was substantial agreement as to the identity of the planning factor. The one test that could not be administered properly to the retarded was the Planned Composition. Instead, Verbal Fluency ("say as many words as you can that begin with the letter *c*") had a substantial loading along with Visual Search and Trail Making. In a different study (Snart, O'Grady & Das, 1982) on mentally retarded adults whose IQs were lower (mean IQ = 50) than those of Ashman's subjects, it was observed that planning as measured by Visual Search and Trail Making separated itself from the factors of simultaneous and successive processing. Since mentally retarded subjects did demonstrate a separate factor of planning and their mental age was approximately 7–8 years, it was argued that third-grade children who had a similar mental age could also demonstrate a separate planning factor. These children from the regular class had been given simultaneous and successive tests, the planning tests of Visual Search and Trail Making, as well as the two Stroop cards that required reading as fast as possible the names of colors (the words *red, green, yellow, blue*) and color patches (the words *red, green, yellow, blue*). Four factors were expected: the simultaneous, successive, and planning, and a "speed" factor defined by the Stroop reading tests (not the interference condition used as a measure of attention). These were obtained with extremely high loadings (the highest was .89 and the lowest was .80). This study on third-grade children is important in that we could separate speed of response and planning. In other words, since Visual Search and Trail Making are measured in terms of speed of response, as the two Stroop tests are also measured, it might be argued that if the planning tests were nothing but measures of response speed, then the study should not yield planning and speed as two orthogonal factors. Obviously, that was not the case. These studies have been described in some detail by Das (1984).

Continuing with the idea of separating speed from planning, a stronger argument could be supported by the data on different speed tasks (Das, 1984a.) The speed measures used with the third-grade children were the two Stroop card reading times, Trail Making (form A and B; A involves joining consecutive numbers—1 to 2 to 3, etc.—and B involves joining numbers to letters of the alphabet in a sequence of 1 to A to 2 to B, etc.), two Visual Search times (number embedded in pictures and pictures embedded in pictures), and, finally, the reaction time for numbers in pictures and pictures in pictures. The reaction times represent movement time, that is, the time taken to hit the target after having located the target, whereas the Visual Search times traditionally represent decision time. Table 5.1 is presented here to clarify the point of the argument. The principal components analysis demonstrates a factor on which the two reaction times have high loadings, a factor on which the two Stroop Reading and Color Naming times have high loadings, and, finally, the planning factor, which has loadings from the two Trail Making and two Visual Search tasks. So planning retained its separate status, and speed as a unitary factor was not obtained.

It is obvious from the foregoing discussion that the two tests that have been used over and over again as planning tests are not merely measures of perceptual motor speed; instead, they are indices of planning strategies. Further support for the separation of planning from speed was later obtained by Naglieri, Prewett, and Bardos (1989) and Naglieri, Das, et al. (1991).

We demonstrate this further as follows: (1) by relating the two marker tests of planning to tasks that require obviously complex strategies and (2) by first selecting individuals who are good or poor in these marker tests and observing their behavior in tasks that require problem-solving strategies. These points will become clear in the following descriptions of the studies.

Reviewing the measures of planning, one will find several tasks that require complex strategies. Planned Composition and Crack-the-Code can

TABLE 5-1 Principal Components Analysis of Measures of Speed of Reaction (Varimax Rotation)[a]

Variable	1	2	3	h^2
Color Reading		837		708
Color Naming		799		656
Trail Making (A)	346	339	563	551
Trail Making (B)	369	359	470	486
Visual Search time (number-picture)			736	603
Visual Search time (picture-picture)			649	452
Reaction time (number-picture)	916			840
Reaction time (picture-picture)	926			872
Variance	2.0	1.6	1.5	
Percentage of total variance	25.3	20.5	18.9	

[a]Decimals omitted in loadings. Loadings below 300 have been omitted. High scores represent poor performance for all variables.

be easily identified as strategy tasks, along with the "pharmaceutical problem solving" task, which we have not used in our planning studies as yet. These tasks are described in Appendix 1 at the end of the chapter. In a study on adult college students (Das & Heemsbergen, 1983), four tests of planning were used—Planned Composition, Syllogistic Reasoning Solving Time, Visual Search, and Trail Making. In the Syllogistic Reasoning tasks, subjects were given three sets of syllogisms consisting of major premise, minor premise, and a conclusion required to be given by the subject (e.g., Susan is taller than Ann, Jane is taller than Susan, Ann is taller than Jane, true or false?). Other sets were of the type "Alice is smaller than Sally, Sally is smaller than Ann," then a set such as "Ann is taller than Alice, Susan is shorter than Alice." Each set consisted of eight syllogisms that were homogeneous and required the same kind of logical thinking for the syllogisms in the set. The solution time should be faster as the subject recognizes the similarity of the syllogisms within each set. The faster the subject can do the syllogisms, the better would be his or her planning—this was the assumption that guided us in including syllogistic reasoning speed as a test of planning. As mentioned before, the other tests of planning included Planned Composition and the two marker tests. Factor analysis of these tests, along with simultaneous and successive tests, yielded the three expected factors of planning, simultaneous and successive. The correlations between the planning tests were quite high as well. Planned Composition correlated highly with Syllogistic Reasoning. This could be expected from our assumption that both were tasks involving strategy. But it also correlated significantly with Trail Making and Visual Search.

Continuing our effort to relate strategy tasks to the so-called perceptual-motor tasks such as Visual Search, Das and Heemsbergen (1983) divided adult students into those whose Visual Search was fast (mean 8.86 sec) and slow (17.35 sec), and gave them a game of strategies, *Mastermind*, to play. They recorded the number of rows (or prompts) that were needed to complete the problem in *Mastermind*. In general, it was found that not only did the slow students require significantly greater number of prompts to solve the problem, but they also demonstrated superstitious behavior and inadequate use of feedback.

As final evidence for an independent planning factor that can be defined by Visual Search and Trail Making, we would like to refer to a study on hierarchical factor solution of coding and planning processes (Das & Dash, 1983). The simultaneous-successive and planning tasks, as well as the speed tasks involved Figure Copying and Memory-for-Design, Serial Recall and Digit Span, Visual Search and Trail Making, and Stroop Word Reading and Color Naming, respectively. A Schmid-Leiman hierarchical factor solution clearly demonstrated two second order factors, one of them involving the simultaneous-successive and the Stroop speed tests, and the other involving the two planning tests.

We are convinced that planning emerges as a separate factor as operationally defined by the tests we have used. Some of the tests appear to be similar to perceptual-motor tasks, whereas others appear to involve higher-order strategies; yet both come together in a planning factor. Recently, attention tasks have been added to the planning, simultaneous-successive tasks and it has been possible to show four separate factors, each representing one process (Naglieri, Prewett, & Bardos, 1989; Naglieri, Das, et al., 1990). In these recent studies the marker tests of planning were Visual Search and Trail Making.

ACADEMIC ACHIEVEMENT AND PLANNING

The relation of planning to scholastic achievement among normal children is much weaker than the relationship of simultaneous and successive processing tasks to school achievement. For example, in the review given in Das (1984c), the simultaneous-successive tasks on the one hand and reading-decoding on the other show correlations of .31 and above, whereas with planning the correlation was .24. However, the remarkable finding was the relationship of planning to ability tests measuring verbal, quantitative, and nonverbal abilities from the Canadian Cognitive Abilities Test battery (CCAT). The correlation between planning and these abilities was close to zero. Consider that CCAT lacks planning so the correlation is zero, whereas the correlations between simultaneous processing or successive processing and the three abilities were substantial. However, it does not mean that scholastic abilities such as reading comprehension have very little relationship to the planning process, because high proficiency in comprehension ought to involve some degree of planning. This was proved in an interesting research study by Ramey (1985), who studied 15 high school students who were very good on Visual Search and 15 who were poor in Visual Search (there was no apparent difference in their IQ) and gave them several kinds of reading tasks. The activity that is of interest to us is the reading and recall of literary passages. Recall was scored in terms of the number of sentences recalled. It was found that the fast visual search group recalled more sentences, made more inferential statements, questioned and evaluated the responses they made, tended to encapsulate the central message in the text, and were likely to modify their hypotheses about the content of the passage as they went on reading. The slow visual searchers, in contrast, recalled fewer sentences, made fewer inferential statements, tended to be impulsive, were easily frustrated, and stuck to incorrect hunches.

DYNAMIC ASSESSMENT AND PLANNING

In the final part of our review, empirical studies relating to planning, we wish to show the effect of dynamic assessment. The type of dynamic assessment used in the two studies discussed next involved simply overt verbalization by the subjects in regard to the problem at hand. In the first study (Cormier, Carlson, & Das, 1990), it was assumed that poor planners would benefit better from an opportunity to verbalize and reflect on what they were doing, compared to good planners who would perhaps spontaneously engage in these activities. The marker tests for planning were Visual Search and Trail Making. The subjects were children from fourth-grade classes; the subjects were divided in to good or poor planners on the basis of a median split on both tests. Those who scored below the median on both were poor planners and those who scored above were the good planners. The task on which enhancement of performance was assessed was Raven's Progressive Matrices. The results fulfilled the expectations in that the poor planners indeed gained significantly in their performance on the Matrices under the verbalization condition, whereas the good planners did not show any significant improvement in performance under standard instruction and the verbalization condition that involved dynamic testing.

In the next study (Kar, Dash, Das, & Carlson, 1993), the criterion task for classifying children (in fifth-grade) was Visual Search, and the test on which improvement was to be observed was similar to the Number Matching task. Subjects were classified as high and low planners by taking the top and bottom 15 children in Visual Search. They were then given the number matching tasks under two conditions, standard instruction and verbalization. The high planners, as expected, displayed a faster rate of number matching than the low planners, and although the speed of matching improved as a result of verbalization for both groups, the high planners did not improve as much as the low planners. The implications of the studies using dynamic assessment are clearly twofold. First, they validate the use of simple perceptual-motor planning tasks as basically reliable and useful markers for planning. Second, they extend the validity of laboratory-type planning tasks as predictors of efficiency in strategy use in game situations such as *Mastermind* or in the amount of gain from verbalization in dynamic assessment procedures.

SUMMARY

Planning is the overarching process that seems to unite attention-arousal and simultaneous and successive processes. The importance of the neurophysiological base of planning has been merely suggested in this chapter. Similarly, connections of planning with activities in the everyday world and decision making in business and industry have been alluded to but not discussed in depth. Yet, there is enough material here to help us understand planning as a concept based in neuropsychology as well as in cognitive psychology. The discussion of planning is also linked to its operationalization in terms of tests. Empirical studies using some of these tests have yielded interesting and meaningful results. We are confident that we have made a beginning by using the process of planning as a construct for understanding higher mental activities.

APPENDIX 1. Planned Composition: A picture, such as Thematic Apperception Test (see Ashman & Das, 1980) is given to the Subject who must write a one-page story, describing what was happening in the picture. The story is judged by 2-3 raters on the following scale.

Planned Composition Rating Scale

	1 2	3 4 5	6 7
EXPRESSION	Appears that thought has been given to the story; writer says what is meant; points relate to the topic; no padding.	Impression given that the writer does not fully understand what is meant; does not relate clearly; some padding & irrelevant material.	Hard to tell what the writer is saying; makes little sense; gives the impression of trying to get something on paper.
ORGANIZATION	Good starting point; has a sense of directed movement in story; appears to have an underlying plan; seems logically arranged.	Organization is standard and conventional; some trivial points given more importance than deserved; logic in progression is not always clear.	Starts anywhere and never gets anywhere; ideas are presented randomly with no apparent forethought.
WORDING	Use of uncommon words or words in unusual combinations which shows imagination; word experiments need not be successful 100% of time.	Uses common phrases or expressions; no apparent concern with the use of words.	Uses words carelessly; many mistakes in usage; unclear wording or childish vocabulary.
MECHANICS	No serious errors in sentence structure; punctuation correct; spelling consistent & appropriate for grade.	Some errors in structure but does not obscure meaning; violations in punctuation and spelling.	Serious errors in sentence structure making story difficult to understand; many punctuation errors makes story fragmented; many spelling mistakes.

INDIVIDUALITY	1 2	3 4 5	6 7
	Unique or creative approach to material; unusual or original ideas; gives story a "twist".	Some originality shown; few interesting or unique aspects.	Not original at all; ideas are mundane, not creative and uninteresting.

Crack the Code: Crack the Code is a Planning test. In this test the student's task is to determine the correct sequence of a number of colored chips when given a limited amount of information. The subject is given two to five trials with feedback to determine the one correct order of chips for each of the 7 items. The subtest is organized into 7 items with 2 or 3 trials per item and a 3 minute limit per item. An example of one of the problems is given below.

5 colour chips are used in this problem which are: White, Black, Orange, Yellow and Blue. The colours are arranged in rows, against each row is the number of chips correctly placed. These are the feedbacks which the subject should use to get the correct answer.

White	Blue	Black	Orange	Yellow	3 correct
White	Black	Orange	Yellow	Blue	Zero
Black	Orange	Yellow	Blue	White	Zero
Blue	Orange	Black	White	Yellow	3 correct
Orange	Yellow	Blue	White	Black	Zero
(not shown to *S*:					
Blue	White	Black	Orange	Yellow	Answer)

A TEST OF STRATEGIC PLANNING INVOLVING TACIT AND FORMAL KNOWLEDGE

Suppose in a pharmaceutical company you are the Chief Executive Officer. The company can have the following overall strategies in order to prosper: (a) be innovative, (b) achieve a good share of the market, (c) be known for its economical price—low cost of products (d) produce high quality goods.

Cautionary Notes for Each Strategy: (a) Requires an outlay of capital in research and development. But the world record shows that in the last 5 years, research and development money has increased five fold, but the number of new products launched has remained the same. (b) Requires aggressive advertisement, but the company's star product (i.e., Bayer

Aspirin) is about to be replaced by a new break-through medication for fever. (c) Requires getting the components of the products, from manufacturing to packaging, from developing countries where labour is cheap. But this has a disastrous effect on employment at home. (d) The product of high quality may cost so much more as to make it uneconomical.

In the 50 year past history of the company, the following weights had been given to the strategies with results indicated. Your job is to achieve a 100% growth by rearranging the strategies; but you must take into account the information from the past results.

A past manager gave 1st place to C, 2nd place to D, 3rd place to A, and 4th place to B. None of CDAB are in the correct position. The profit dropped to 0% because not even one of the strategies was in the correct place.

Another manager gave 1st place to D, 2nd place to A, 3rd place to B, and 4th place to C. 2 of DABC are in the correct position. The profit was 50%, because only two of the strategies were in the correct place. You do not know which two.

Another manager gave 1st place to B, 2nd place to C, 3rd place to Î, and 4th place to A. BCDA—2 in correction position. The profit was was also 50% because, again, only two of the strategies were in the correct place.

How will you assign the priorities so that the right strategy will have the right place to give a 100% outcome. Having found the solution (DCBA or BADC), write an essay in one page justifying how the plan produced the best results when the solution is DCBA, and another essay when it is BADC.

Experimenter rates the essay for organization and individuality (unique and original).

PART III

MECHANISMS OF MEASUREMENT

6

OPERATIONALIZATION OF PASS

The purpose of this chapter is to summarize some of the tasks used by researchers when measuring planning, attention, simultaneous, and successive processes. Our aim in this chapter is to provide examples of the types of tasks used, rather than an exhaustive list of all those included in the many relevant papers published on this topic. After the tasks have been summarized, their attributes will be discussed.

INTRODUCTION TO PASS MODEL OPERATIONALIZATION

The main goal behind the development of tasks following the PASS model has been to provide a more valid approach to the measurement of human cognitive functioning. To achieve this goal the decision was made to base the PASS model on the broad concepts of cognitive functioning proposed by A. R. Luria.

The decision to base the model on Luria's broad theoretical views has several important advantages. First, because test development efforts intended to operationalize theoretical constructs come directly from the model of cognitive processing, previous concepts of what intelligence may be do not limit the scope of tasks that are included. Second, by using a theoretical model with a base in neuropsychology, a link to the processes involved in human cognitive functioning, as discovered through the examination of brain function, can be achieved. Third, a theory-based approach to measurement and conceptualization of intelligence can provide the capability to define normal and exceptional individuals on the basis of their cognitive processing status, rather than on subtest patterns or discrepancy scores as has previously been done. Fourth, a theoretical approach to the conceptualization and measurement of intelligence allows for theory-based approaches to intervention. These points are further discussed in various sections of this book.

The operationalization of the PASS model was based on the identification of tests that are consistent with the process of interest. Tasks were selected on the basis of their correspondence to the theoretical framework. Because this method is not restrained by notions that the only abilities that should be included are those that have been previously used, the potential for increasing the validity of a new system may be realized. For example, attentional functioning has been an area of increasing interest and concern in recent years. Much has been written about attention deficit disorders of various types (e.g., Barkley, 1990), and researchers have stressed the importance of attention in cognition as well as education. Although attentional functioning is certainly an important aspect of cognitive functioning, no scale or subtest intended to measure it appears in tests such as the Wechsler or Stanford-Binet. Similarly, despite the fact that planning and organization of cognitive functioning play an important role in cognitive activities (Das, 1984; Naglieri & Das, 1987), tests such as the WISC-R and K-ABC do not include measures of executive function. These limitations can be overcome when a battery of experimental tasks is constructed if it is based on a sound theory such as the PASS model.

NEUROPSYCHOLOGICAL RELEVANCE

Conceptualization of intellectual functioning based on a neuropsychological understanding of how various regions of the brain may function is valuable, especially if the brain itself is considered responsible for intelligence in the first place. We believe that this approach offers the greatest hope for increased validity of intelligence tests because it provides a model of functioning that rests on components of the functioning brain. We do not, however, suggest that because a model of intelligence is based on a neuropsychological theory that an individual's performance on the PASS tasks should be interpreted as indicators of neurological status or brain integrity. Rather, we prefer to focus on the cognitive processes associated with the broad neuropsychological functions and their relationship to academic and real world achievement.

PASS TASKS AND THE PASS MODEL

The PASS model comprises four cognitive components that represent the three functional units described by Luria (1966, 1973, 1980). The first functional unit is represented by Attention, the second by the Simultaneous and Successive, and the third by Planning. Each of these cognitive functions is represented by experimental tasks designed to measure the particular process in a slightly different way, using a variety of tasks developed according to strict guidelines.

The tests used to measure planning, attention, simultaneous, and successive processes were selected because they meet several important criteria. First, their cognitive processing demands match the structural requirements for the particular processing, as discussed in Chapter 2. This is a very important consideration because consistency with the theoretical model is of paramount importance. Second, potential tests reported in the literature, as well as new tasks, should provide a variety of ways to measure each process. That is, tasks should vary by content (e.g., verbal or nonverbal), presentation format (e.g., one task might have a memory component and another a motor component), and modality (e.g., some are visual and others auditory). Third, the tests were considered appropriate for individual administration (considering the amount of time required to administer the test and general ease of administration) and, fourth, there should be variety in the kind of response required (e.g., written or oral). Issues like these have influenced the selection of PASS tasks used in many research studies from 1972 to the present. Some of these tests were incorporated in a trial edition (Das & Naglieri, 1989); the current edition of the battery of tests (Das & Naglieri, 1993) is in standardization. Sample PASS are described in the following sections of this chapter.

MEASURES OF PLANNING

Structural analysis of a planning task indicates that such a test should require an individual to develop some approach of solving the task in an efficient and effective manner. This is the case in all the planning tests, and typically the actual task requirement is minimal (i.e., every item can be completed), but what leads to individual differences is the requirement that some effective means of solving the task must be developed. Therefore, these tasks do not have the same kind of progression of items on the basis of difficulty as those found in the simultaneous or successive scales. The hallmark of the planning tasks that have been used is that they require the development of an efficient system of completing a relatively simple task.

Visual Search and Trail Making (recently termed Planned Connections) have been the most often used measures of planning. These tasks were originally identified as appropriate measures of planning by Ashman (1978) and Ashman and Das (1980). Subsequently, Visual Search and Trail Making were consistently used by these and several other researchers studying the PASS model (e.g., Kirby & Ashman, 1984; Naglieri & Das, 1987, 1988; Naglieri, Das, et al. 1991). In addition to these tests, Planned Composition (writing a story) was used as a measure of planning (Das, Snart, & Mulcahy, 1982; Das, 1980; Ashman & Das, 1980; Das & Heemsbergen, 1983). More recently, tasks such as Matching Numbers and Planned Codes have been included with Visual Search and Trail Making.

Visual Search

The Visual Search task requires the individual to develop an efficient approach to finding a particular stimulus on a page. The subject is typically instructed to point to a picture, number, or letter located in a field around the target in a stimulus box. Items have been composed of one (e.g., Ashman, 1978) or two searches (to facilitate more accurate timing of the item) (e.g., Naglieri & Das, 1987) per page. Items are timed from the point the page is exposed to the moment the second target is found. The test raw score has been the amount of time it took to complete all the items. The items illustrated in Figure 6-1 show the arrangement of targets and fields for items involving letter and number searches. Other types of items have involved searches for objects, objects embedded in letters, and letters embedded in objects. The kinds of search strategies used in

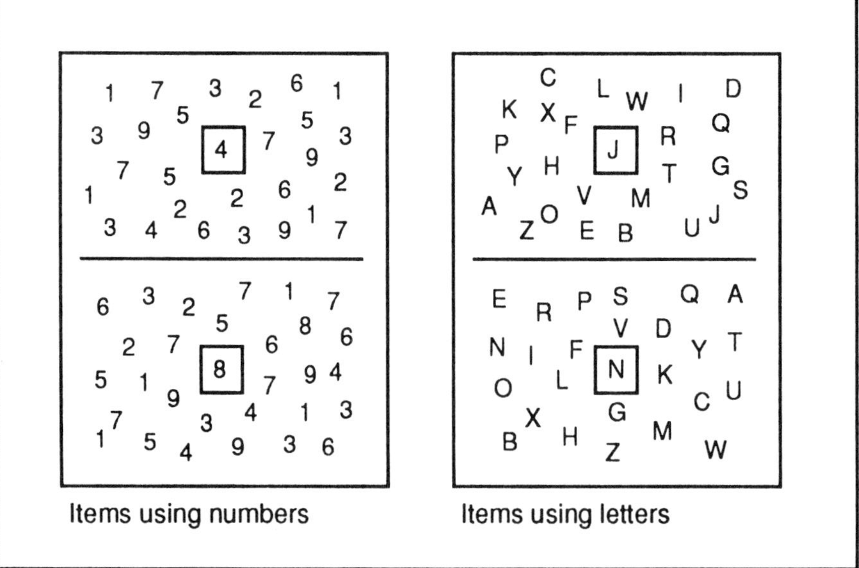

FIGURE 6-1 Visual Search Items

this test include, for example, looking left to right, top to bottom, or upper left–upper right–lower left–lower right.

Planned Connections

The Planned Connections test, illustrated in Figure 6-2, requires the individual to develop some effective way of connecting sequential stimuli (e.g., the numbers 1-2-3-4-5 etc.) that appear on a page. The easy items usually require the child to connect a series of numbers in their proper numerical sequence (1 to 2, 2 to 3, etc.), while harder items require the subject to alternately connect numbers and letters in their proper sequence (1 to A, A to 2, 2 to B, B to 3, and so on). Some of the strategies used in a test like this involve scanning the page for the next number or letter, looking back to the last number or letter to determine what comes next, looking at only a portion of the page that is most likely to have the next number or letter first, and repeating the alphabet/number series aloud as the task is completed. The best measure of the degree of efficiency of connecting these points is the time needed to complete the sequence. The test score is the total amount of time in seconds used to complete all the items. The illustration of the test items in Figure 6-2 shows that completion of this relatively simple task requires some kind of systematic approach.

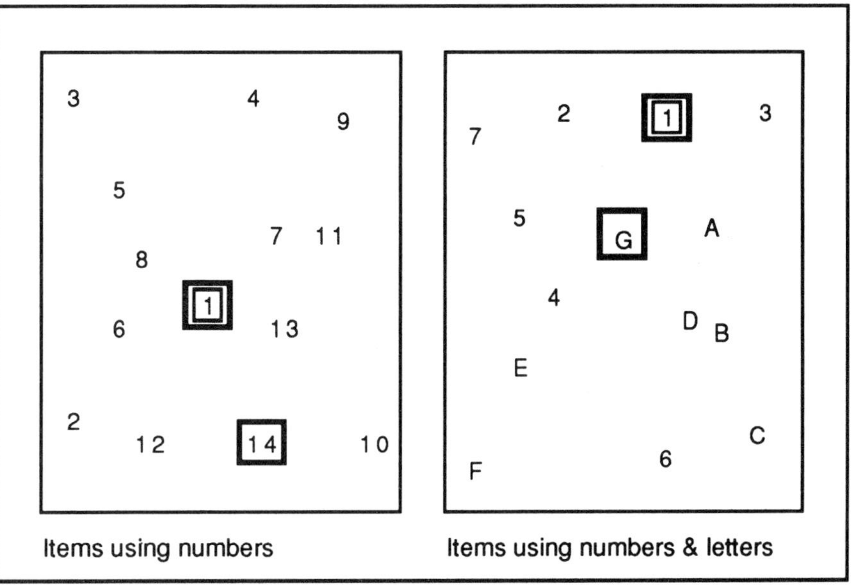

FIGURE 6-2 Planned Connections Examples

Planned Composition

The Planned Composition task was first used by Ashman (1978). The task requires the child to compose a short essay, which is evaluated according to five criteria. A three-point rating (high, medium, low) system has been used to evaluate written compositions on the basis of five categories: Ideas, Usage and Structure, Organization and Analysis, Wording and Phrasing, and Individuality. These categories were used to evaluate one-page stories written about a picture presented to the students over a 20-minute time interval (see page 95.).

Matching Numbers

The Matching Numbers task requires the individual to use an efficient system of finding which of two numbers on a row are the same (see Figure 6-3). The subject must find and circle the two identical numbers on each of eight rows on a page. There are six numbers of the same length per row, and the numbers increase in length from one to seven digits over the four pages. Subjects often use strategies such as looking at the first two numbers in each string of digits, looking at the last then the first and middle digits, and scanning the row for a match. As with the other planning tests, since the measure of efficiency is the time it takes the individual to find and circle the identical numbers, the test score is the total time used to compete

19	23	26	18	23
34	51	17	34	37
365	356	366	635	365
549	459	495	459	594
1793	7193	7139	7193	1739
8247	8724	8427	8274	8427

FIGURE 6-3 Matching Numbers Example

the items. As can be seen from examination of the example in Figure 6-3, the strategies used may involve approaches such as looking at the first, or the last, numbers in each group of digits and evaluation of the string of digits as a whole. This test is sensitive to planning processes because it reflects the degree to which an efficient system of searching the row is used.

MEASURES OF ATTENTION

Attentional tasks require the individual to selectively attend to one and ignore the other aspect of a two-dimensional stimulus. Structural analysis of these tasks always yields the procedure of examination, detection of the dimensions of the stimulus, and the decision to respond to one and not to the other competing dimension. These tasks always involve a competing stimulus that is as salient or more salient than the target stimulus.

Expressive Attention

A task called Expressive Attention that is similar to the Stroop test (Stroop, 1935) has been recently used with measures of planning, simultaneous, and successive processes (Naglieri, Braden, & Warrick, 1991). This task involves three conditions, although only the last page is used as a measure of selective attention. The first and second pages contain the words *red, blue,* and *green* (page 1) or colored rectangles of these same colors in varying order arranged in eight rows, five to a row. The child is first required to read all of the words on page 1 or say the names of the colors on page 2 as fast as possible. The selective attention component in this task is apparent on page 3 through the use of an interference paradigm. Here the words *red, blue,* and *green* are printed in colors different than the word. The subject is instructed to name the color used to print the word, rather than read the word, as fast as possible. In each condition the child's score is the time needed to complete each page.

Number Finding

Number Finding, like the Expressive Attention task, presents the individual with a number of stimuli and requires selective responding based on the instruction to identify a number when it appears in one form rather than another. The individual is instructed to circle the numbers 1, 2, and 3 when they appear in bold-(i.e., **1, 2, 3**) rather than regular-face (i.e., 1, 2, 3) type. Thus, the aspect of selective attention lies at the point of determining if the stimulus is bold-(respond) or regular-(do not respond) face type, as

Find the numbers that look like this: **1 2 3**

1	3	5	2	6	1	4	6	3
5	2	2	3	4	3	5	2	1
1	6	5	5	3	1	4	2	6
3	5	1	4	2	5	3	4	2
4	1	3	1	5	4	2	5	6

FIGURE 6-4 Number Finding Example

illustrated in Figure 6-4. This test usually involves the examination of many numbers arranged in rows on one page.

Auditory Selective Attention

The Auditory Selective Attention task is very much like Number Finding, only it uses auditory rather than visual stimuli and the individual is required to respond when a particular class of words is said by a male voice. For example, the color words *red, blue, green, yellow,* and *purple* and the fruit words *apple, pear, cherry, plum,* and *grape* are said one after the other for several minutes. Sometimes the words are said by a man and sometimes by a woman. The subject is instructed to tap his or her hand on the table when the man says the fruit word *apple, pear, cherry, plum,* or *grape.*

Receptive Attention

The Receptive Attention task, as recently used by Naglieri, Das, et al. (1991) consists of two pages containing rows of letter pairs. On the first page the child circles, row by row, all of the pairs of letters that are physically the same (e.g., *HH* but not *HN*). The second condition is similar except that here the child circles all the pairs of letters that have the same name (e.g., Aa but not Ba). For younger ages a pictorial version of this task has been used that contains pictures of a bird, face, tree, flower, and fruit instead of letters. In the first condition, identical picture targets have been used, while in the second condition, pictures from the same category, in this case fruits, were the targets.

MEASURES OF SIMULTANEOUS PROCESSING

The structural analysis of a test requiring simultaneous processing indicates that the subject must interrelate the component parts of the particular item to arrive at the correct answer. The need to appreciate the relationships among all components of the item is the hallmark of a simultaneous task. For successful completion of simultaneous tasks, therefore, the entire stimulus array has to be incorporated into some complete pattern or idea. The simultaneous tasks range in difficulty from very easy to very difficult as a function of the complexity and number of the interrelationships.

Copying a geometric design, drawing a geometric design from memory, and progressive matrices have often been used as tests of simultaneous processing. In addition to these, other simultaneous measures have included a concrete paired associate learning task (Das, Kirby, & Jarman, 1975); Wachs & Harris, 1984), WISC-R Block Design or a very similar type of task (Das, Mensink, & Janzen, 1991; Wachs & Harris, 1986; Naglieri, Das, et al., 1991), Children's Embedded Figures test, paper folding (Cummins, 1976), a task requiring comprehension of ambiguous sentences (Kirby, 1982; Cummins & Das, 1978), and one requiring comprehension of logical grammatical statements (Naglieri, Braden, & Warrick, 1991). Some of these tests are discussed here.

Figure Memory

Copying a geometric design from a model or after having seen a model has long been used as a marker for simultaneous processing. In the copying version a recognizable geometric design is reproduced by the subject. In the memory condition the subject looks at a geometric design such as a square or a triangle for 5 seconds; then the design is removed and the subject is asked to trace the original stimulus within a more complex design that includes the original figure (see Figure 6-5). For a response to be scored correct, all lines of the design have to be indicated without any additions or omissions. The requirement that the design be reproduced in its entirety and incorporated into memory as a whole so that all the parts of the figure are interrelated makes this task congruent with the simultaneous paradigm.

Matrices

The completion of figural analogies using designs that form a progressive matrix has also been considered a marker simultaneous task. The subject is required to choose one of six options that best completes the abstract

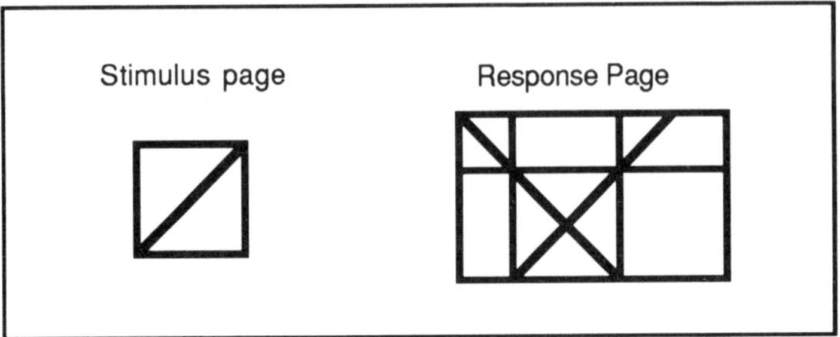

FIGURE 6-5 Figure Memory Example

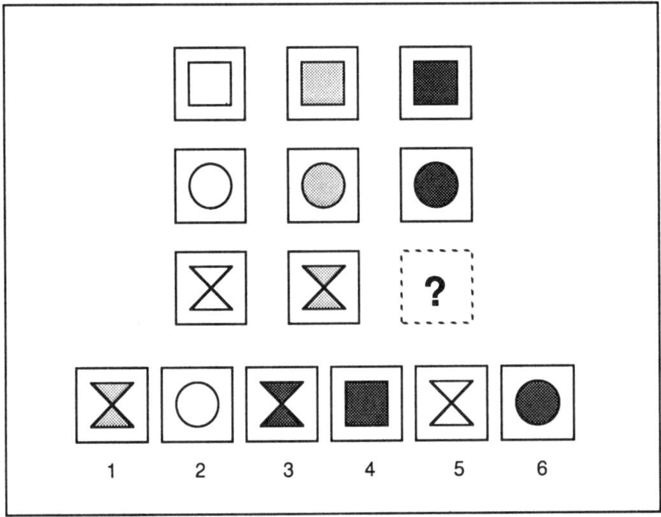

FIGURE 6-6 Matrices Example

analogy (see Figure 6-6). The requirement that each component of the matrix must be interrelated to the others makes this task congruent with the simultaneous paradigm. The score for this test is the total number of correct figures identified.

Simultaneous Verbal

The evaluation of logical grammatical relationships has been frequently presented as an example of a simultaneous task involving verbal content. This test exemplifies such an approach because it presents the subject with a question that must be answered through the interrelation of the parts. The subject is shown six illustrations and asked to point to the picture that, for example, shows "the ball in a basket on the table" or "the woman pointing to the ruler with a pencil." This test is scored for the total number correct.

MEASURES OF SUCCESSIVE PROCESSING

The structural analysis of a task of successive processing should indicate that the individual is required to appreciate the serial nature of stimuli that range in difficulty from very easy (spans of two) to very difficult (spans of nine). All the successive tasks require the individual to either reproduce a particular sequence of events or answer some questions that require correct interpretation of the linearity of events. Successive measures have included free and/or serial recall of lists of words, recall of numbers in order (see Das, Kirby, & Jarman, 1979) as well as measures of underlying structural ambiguities in sentences (Kirby, 1982) and, similarly, comprehension of the syntactic relationships within sentences (Naglieri, Braden, & Warrick, 1991). Some of these tasks are described in the following sections.

Sentence Repetition and Sentence Questions

Sentence questions and repetitions tasks both involve reading to the child sentences that use color words in place of nouns, verbs, and so on (e.g., The blue is graying). Color words are used to provide statements with minimal meaning. Sentence Repetition requires the child to repeat the sentence exactly as presented including word endings as well as word reversals, omissions, or any other inaccuracy. Sentence Questions requires the subject to answer a question about the statement (e.g., "The blue is graying. Who is graying?" Answer: "The blue."). These tasks demand appreciation of the syntax in the sentences for successful completion.

Word Recall

The recall of words has been shown to load on a successive factor in many studies and has been considered a marker for successive processing. This task usually consists of nine single-syllable words presented in series ranging in length from two to nine words. This task has long been used as a measure of successive processing because it clearly fits the linearity requirement of the successive processing paradigm.

INFERENCES FROM PASS TASKS

Planning and Speed

Inspection of the way the PASS tasks are typically scored sometimes gives the impression that planning tasks may also be measuring speed of processing, perceptual speed, or simply how fast a person can do something. There are two compelling reasons to reject this interpretation: One, there are differences in the cognitive processing requirements of planning versus speed tasks, and, second, there is ample experimental evidence that does *not* support this hypothesis.

Analysis of tasks that are sensitive to planning processes clearly shows that what is required is a complex analysis or generation of a method to solve the problem, execution of the solution, monitoring of the solution, modification as needed, and so on (see diagrams in Chapter 2). Time is the best estimate of the *efficiency* with which these activities are applied to solving planning tasks because disorganized execution, false starts, inadequate monitoring, and generation of bad plans consume much time. Our experience in administering these tasks has shown this as well. Children who are poor planners solve Visual Search items by looking at the page in a disorganized manner, they choose incorrect targets impulsively and make many errors, and they are remarkably resistant to changing this inefficient method of solving these problems. Time is an excellent measure of planning in these tasks because it is sensitive to the inefficiencies and efficiencies of plans that subjects use.

For another reason, the use of time as a measure should not lead to the conclusion that speed is being measured. Time has been used to measure performance on tasks such as WISC-R Object Assembly and Block Design. In fact, fast performance is necessary to obtain enough credit on these tasks to earn average scores at the upper ages. In studies involving PASS planning tasks and the WISC-R Block Design, these tasks have not emerged on the same factor, indicating that even though they are both timed, the scores do not reflect speed (Naglieri, Das, et al., 1991; Stutzman, 1986). Thus, scores are not measures of speed simply because they are timed; neither do planning test scores reflect speed simply because they are timed.

The hypothesis that planning and speed are separate has been examined in several investigations. Das and Dash (1983) and Naglieri, Prewett, and Bardos (1989) found clear factorial evidence that planning and speed tasks do not load on the same factor. These authors used a direct measure of speed—the time it took subjects to read four color words (*red, yellow, green,* and *blue*) and tell the color of objects (red, yellow, green, and blue *X*'s). When these speed scores were entered into the factorial analyses, they formed a distinct group from the planning tasks (Visual Search and Trail Making). Naglieri, Das, et al. (1991) tested this hypothesis differently. In this study the PASS model was compared to a Verbal-Spatial-Speed (VSS) model using the LISREL confirmatory factor analytic approach. Again, no support for the VSS model was found, but the PASS model was supported. Simply put, when planning and speed tasks are experimentally examined, support for an interpretation of planning as speed is not found.

PASS and Modality

It is clear that the PASS tasks are presented using a variety of modalities. Visual stimuli are used for planning, simultaneous, and attention tasks, and auditory stimuli are used with successive tasks. The possibility that the modality of the tasks is more important than the processes required to solve them has also been tested empirically. Again using LISREL confirmatory factor analysis, Naglieri, Das, et al. (1991) showed that the PASS model was significantly better than a visual/auditory organization of the same tasks. This does not, however, diminish our recognition that simultaneous tasks are typically visual and successive tasks are typically auditory. This is logical given that simultaneous processes are associated with the occipital (visual) and parietal (somatosensory) areas, while successive processes are associated with the temporal (auditory) area. At the secondary and tertiary levels within the second functional unit, however, the degree to which modality is related to process is considerably reduced. The involvement of the processes is determined by the requirement of the tasks, but there is a likelihood that most simultaneous tasks will be visual and successive tasks will be auditory. This is especially probable with tasks that are simple and do not require involvement of other processes.

CONCLUSION

In this chapter we have shown that Luria's conceputilization of human cognitive processing could be used to operationalize intelligence. We have suggested that the PASS model is a useful way to measure Luria's theory and build a measure of ability that goes beyond traditional tests. The illustrative experimental tests we have developed fit the theoretical definition of each of the respective PASS processes and therefore have validity on that basis. We have also provided evidence that alternative interpretations of these tests, such as planning as speed, or successive processing as verbal have not been supported. Finally, it becomes clear that although some new theories of intelligence have been recently proposed, this is the first to have made a successful transformation of theoretical concepts to methods appropriate for intellectual assessment.

7

PASS AND CURRENT IQ TESTS

In this chapter we evaluate current IQ tests from the perspective of the PASS model. This task can be accomplished now only through speculation and extrapolation because no studies of the PASS model with current IQ tests has been conducted, although some subtests from the WISC-R and K-ABC have been used with some PASS processing tasks. To evaluate current IQ tests, we use the little data that is available, analyze how current tests may relate to one another, and provide content analysis of the subtests to determine similarities and differences.

CONTENT ANALYSIS OF CURRENT IQ TESTS

Nonverbal Tests

The Wechsler, Binet: 4, K-ABC, and McCarthy scales measure intelligence using very similar tasks. Each of these tests has a group of nonverbal spatial tasks that resemble the WISC-III Block Design. On the Binet:Four it is called Pattern Analysis and in the K-ABC, Triangles. Similarly, a task similar to the WISC-III Object Assembly appears in the McCarthy, called Puzzle Solving, and progressive matrices subtests are used in the K-ABC and Binet: Four. Despite the fact that the different authors of these tests give different names to the scales in which they are included, such as Performance (WISC-III), Perceptual-Performance (McCarthy), Simultaneous (K-ABC), and Abstract/Visual Reasoning (Binet), they are essentially measuring the same cognitive function in the same way.

There is evidence that the Performance, Abstract/Visual, Perceptual-Performance, and Simultaneous scales included in these IQ tests could be viewed as involving simultaneous processing. WISC-R Block Design and a similar task developed by Das and Naglieri (1989) have been used in studies involving the PASS model. Hurt and Naglieri (1991) found WISC-R Block Design to be highly related to the PASS simultaneous tasks Figure Memory (r = .56) and Matrices (r = .48), as did Stutzman (1986). Naglieri, Das, et al. (1991) found similar results in a LISREL confirmatory factor analytic study using a task called Pattern Completion.

The results of these studies are consistent with the expectation that construction of a design to match a standard involves simultaneous processing because the component parts of the design must be interrelated in order to arrive at the correct solution. The requirement of surveyability dominates the task, as do its spatial requirements. These are the same processing demands placed on tasks such as Matrices and Figure Memory, which also demand spatial conceptualization of a geometric figure. Therefore, functional analysis of the cognitive processing demands of Block Design, along with some experimental evidence of the relationships between Block Design with Matrices and Figure Memory supports the view that this is a task that demands simultaneous processes. Because Block Design, or a very similar subtest (e.g., Triangles on the K-ABC), often dominates a Performance scale on current IQ tests, it is logical to assume that these scales could also be reinterpreted as measuring simultaneous processing.

Verbal Tests

In addition to nonverbal tasks, current IQ tests also have a large number of measures that involve verbal content, or verbal achievement, and numerical knowledge. This is evidenced by the Wechsler Vocabulary subtest and Word Knowledge on the McCarthy, Verbal Relations on the Binet, and Expressive Vocabulary on the K-ABC. Similarly, Arithmetic subtests appear on the Wechsler and the K-ABC, Number Questions and Quantitative scales appear on the McCarthy and Binet. These verbal and quantitative subtests, either included in one overall scale (such as the WISC-R Verbal IQ or the K-ABC Achievement Scale) or subdivided into Verbal and Quantitative scales as in the McCarthy and Binet: 4, all essentially measure counting and/or oral arithmetic problem solving. From the PASS model we view these tasks as a collection that cannot be represented by a single process. That is, some math tests, such as math computation, can be influenced by planning processes (Garofalo, 1986), but others, such as those in the Metropolitan Achievement Test, have been shown to require all PASS processes (Warrick, 1990). Therefore, to describe the verbal/achievement scales in current IQ tests in terms of one PASS process does not seem warranted. We suggest, instead, that they should be conceptualized as measuring verbal/academic achievement.

Memory and Sequential Tests

Measures of memory or sequencing have been included as separate scales on some tests (McCarthy and Binet) or integrated into the Verbal Scale (WISC-III Digit Span) or constitute an entire scale (e.g., Sequential Scale on K-ABC). These tests typically involve the repetition of some order of events for credit. In general, the repetition of events in order likely involves successive processing. It cannot, however, be uniformly accepted that successive processing alone is involved if a serial task requires repetition.

It should not be assumed that any task involving repetition in some order will require successive processes. For example, the WISC-R Digit Span score is not a pure measure of successive processing for two reasons. First, Digit Span comprises Digits Forward and Backward. Schofield and Ashman (1986) showed that forward span was significantly related to successive processing but backward span was related equally to *both* successive and planning processes. Similarly, the K-ABC subtest Hand Movements has consistently been shown to be related to *both* K-ABC Simultaneous and Sequential scales (Kaufman & Kaufman, 1983), and, therefore, this task cannot be assumed to reflect successive processing from the PASS model. Thus, careful analysis of any task involving the serial repetition of events is needed when making decisions about the underlying processes involved. Of all the tasks included in memory scales or sequential scales on the various tests, only those that are limited in their format (e.g., WISC-III Digit Span Forward, K-ABC Number Recall, Binet:Four Memory for Digits Forward, and McCarthy Numerical Memory I) have potential to reflect successive processes.

Processing Speed

With the introduction of the WISC-III a new Wechsler scale, Processing Speed, has been added. This scale, composed of the Symbol Search and Coding subtests, is based on factor analytic findings of the WISC-III. However, its theoretical fit and validity (beyond factorial) is only minimally described in the test manual (Wechsler, 1991). This has led some to caution (e.g., Naglieri, 1993) that there is a need for validity evidence to support the "processing speed" label. Although there is some limited evidence that the WISC-R Coding subtest may be related to the Woodcock-Johnson-Revised G (Processing Speed) factor (Woodcock, 1990), no evidence is currently available on the relationship of the WISC-III Processing Speed factor to other measures of speed.

The measurement of speed has been examined by researchers investigating the PASS model, especially as it relates to a possible alternative explanation of the Planning component. Because planning tests are timed, some have asked if these measures are better described as processing speed. The distinction between planning and speed has been examined in two factorial studies, one by Das and Dash (1983) and one by Naglieri, Prewett, and Bardos (1989). These researchers found that pure measures of processing speed (the time taken to read the same four familiar words over and over again and tell the color of a page of rectangles printed in four colors) did not load on the same factor as measures of planning even though planning tests were timed. These studies showed that although a test may be timed, it does not necessarily mean it is a measure of speed. If timing alone was sufficient to label a subtest as speed, then many other tests, such as Block Design and Object Assembly on the Wechsler scales, for example, would also have to be called speed. The importance of the PASS research in this area is that speed of processing is not a unitary concept, and hence appears to be external to the PASS model, as will be processing speed scales from other IQ tests.

Our analysis of the form of current IQ tests lead us to conclude that Performance scales can be considered to have some simultaneous processing demands, successive processes likely underlie tasks such as Digit Span Forward and the K-ABC Sequential Scale, and verbal and quantitative scales are best described as verbal/achievement. Figure 7-1 categorizes the contents of the Wechsler scales (WISC, WAIS, WPPSI), Binet:Four, McCarthy, and K-ABC and our analysis of the processes demanded by these groups of tests. It is important to consider this figure in light of the fact that we are attempting to see beyond names used by test authors and examine the content and processes involved in the tasks. Additionally, this first level of analysis is based more on the content of the tests than on their

	Constructs Measured			
IQ Tests	*Achievement*	*Simultaneous Processes*	*Successive Processes*	*Quantitative*
Wechsler	Verbal Scale	Performance Scale	Digit Span Forward	Arithmetic Subtest
K-ABC	Riddles & Faces and Places Subtests	Simultaneous Scale	Sequential Scale	Arithmetic Subtest
McCarthy	Verbal Scale	Perceptual Performance & Motor Scales	Numerical Memory I	Quantitative Scale
Binet: Four	Verbal Reasoning Scale	Abstract/Visual Reasoning Scale	Memory for Digits	Quantitative Reasoning Scale

FIGURE 7-1 PASS Constructs Measured by Various IQ Tests

factorial structures. This is, of course, a difficult and risky method, which can be more fully explicated by empirical evidence.

EMPIRICALLY GUIDED ANALYSES—EVIDENCE OF OVERLAP

WISC-R and K-ABC

The similarity of current IQ tests based on a logical analysis is also apparent through the results of studies that have compared them using correlational analyses. The close relationship between the WISC-R and K-ABC was clearly illustrated by Naglieri and Das (1990), who summarized the results of three studies that involved joint factor analytic examinations of the two tests (Kaufman & McLean, 1987; Keith & Novak, 1987; Naglieri & Jensen, 1987). The results (Table 7-1) clearly showed that the WISC-R Verbal factor (Information, Similarities, Vocabulary, and Comprehension) loaded with the K-ABC Achievement subtests; the Performance and Simultaneous scales formed a second factor; and a third factor was composed of K-ABC Sequential subtests with Arithmetic and Digit Span. These results can be interpreted to mean that the Wechsler Verbal factor and K-ABC Achievement subtests could be called verbal achievement and the Performance and Simultaneous subtests simultaneous, and the Sequential subtests plus Digit Span and Arithmetic likely involve successive processing to some extent.

The WISC-R Verbal Expression and Comprehension factor (Information, Similarities, Vocabulary, and Comprehension) and the K-ABC Achievement Scale subtests obviously measure knowledge of information across a number of areas (general facts, reading, and arithmetic) and therefore can be considered as verbal/achievement. This interpretation is consistent with Kaufman's view (1979) of the WISC-R and is obvious if one considers that the K-ABC Achievement subtests obviously measure achievement even though they do not have as much of a verbal expression requirement as the WISC-R Verbal subtests. What these two sets of WISC-R and K-ABC subtests share is a dependency on accumulated knowledge measured through tests of general information (WISC-R Information, Comprehension, and K-ABC Riddles, Faces & Places), word knowledge (WISC-R Vocabulary, Similarities, and K-ABC Expressive Vocabulary, Reading Decoding, and Comprehension), and arithmetic (Arithmetic subtests on both instruments). These tests represent the child's base of knowledge, which is influenced by all of the PASS processes, and do not represent any one type of process.

Simultaneous processing, however, is represented in several subtests of the two scales. The WISC-R Perceptual Organization subtests (Picture

TABLE 7-1 Mean Factor Loadings of WISC-R and K-ABC Subtests from Three Studies

Subtest	Factor 1	Factor 2	Factor 3
Gestalt Closure	16	45*	09
Triangles	19	60*	19
Matrix Analogies	25	38*	26
Spatial Memory	12	49*	22
Photo Series	20	50*	21
Hand Movements	10	22	44*
Number Recall	16	07	69*
Word Order	21	08	58*
Faces & Places	65*	17	16
Arithmetic	47*	26	36*
Riddles	65*	20	12
Reading/Decoding	56*	10	31
Reading/Understanding	65*	12	22
Information	68*	21	18
Similarities	63*	18	14
Arithmetic	35*	25	42*
Vocabulary	73*	13	19
Comprehension	60*	22	14
Digit Span	17	09	65*
Picture Completion	24	49*	09
Picture Arrangement	18	50*	09
Block Design	19	63*	14
Object Assembly	13	65*	10
Coding	05	31	23

Reprinted from Naglieri & Das (1990), *Journal of Psychoeducational Assessment,* with permission.
* = average Fisher z loadings > .35

Completion, Picture Arrangement, Block Design, Object Assembly, and to a minimal extent Coding) and the K-ABC Simultaneous Scale subtests (Triangles, Matrix Analogies, Spatial Memory, Photo Series, and Gestalt Closure) clearly load together. This is logical given that the tasks on each test are very similar—Block Design and Triangles are essentially the same test as are Picture Arrangement and Photo Series. These tests all require that the parts of each item be interrelated for success at the task. For example, in Object Assembly each puzzle piece needs to be examined in relation to the others to determine where the particular piece belongs, for example, a portion of the automobile door for the car item. Similarly, the correct sequence of cards cannot be determined in Picture Arrangement and Photo Series unless each frame of the entire event is interrelated to the others. Therefore, the Perceptual Organization factor, along with similar tests Kaufman included in the K-ABC, can be understood as involving simultaneous processing. This is further supported by Naglieri, Das, et al. (1991), Hurt and Naglieri (1991), and Stutzman (1986), who found that Block Design loaded with Matrices and Figure Copying (simultaneous tasks from a DN:CAS experimental version) to form a simultaneous factor.

The K-ABC Sequential subtests (Number Recall, Word Order, Hand Movements) and some WISC-R subtests were strongly related. However, a close examination reveals that the WISC-R Arithmetic subtest had similar moderate loadings on each of the three factors and therefore is not seen as clearly with this group of tests. This collection of tests mainly consists of Kaufman's Sequential Scale subtests and the Wechsler Digit Span, although it is confounded in two ways. First, the Arithmetic subtests from Wechsler and Kaufman's tests loaded on nearly all the factors and clearly did not load decisively on any one factor. Second, the WISC-R Digit Span is not as unidimensional as the K-ABC Number Recall: as already noted, Schofield and Ashman (1986) found that Digit Span Forward involves successive processing although Digit Span Backward requires successive and planning processes. The K-ABC Sequential subtests and WISC-R Digit Span are the basic subtests of this factor and fit the structural architecture for successive processing. Although the various tests involve different content (Digit Span and Number Recall use numbers, Word Order involves words and pictures, and Hand Movements is nonverbal), they all have the requirement of linearity without the requirement of interrelating the parts.

Stanford-Binet IV, WISC-R, and K-ABC

Like the WISC-R/K-ABC results showing the similarities of these two tests, Thorndike, Hagen, and Sattler (1986) report that the Binet:Four is also similar to the three Wechsler scales. The data they report is summarized in Table 7-2. These results show that the Wechsler FSIQ and Binet:Four Composite scores are indeed very similar, correlating .83 (WISC-R), .80 (WPPSI), and .91 (WAIS-R). Interestingly, the WISC-R Performance correlated about the same with all four of the Binet:Four scales and highest with the Abstract/Visual scales for the WISC-R and WAIS-R. The Binet:Four Verbal Reasoning Scale was the only one that showed a clear pattern of highest correlations with the Wechsler Verbal Scale, even though it also correlated highly with all the other Binet:Four scales. Thus, the overall strong interrelationships among *all* the Wechsler and Binet:Four scales is the basis for the high intercorrelations of the two tests' composite scores and illustrates the high degree of overlap between the tests.

TABLE 7-2 Correlations between the Wechsler Scales and Binet:Four

	Binet:Four Scales			
Wechsler Scales	Verbal Reasoning	Abstract/Visual	Quantitative	Short-Term Memory
WISC-R				
VIQ	.72	.68	.64	.64
PIQ	.60	.67	.63	.63
WPPSI				
VIQ	.80	.46	.70	.71
PIQ	.63	.56	.66	.59
WAIS-R				
VIQ	.86	.68	.85	.82
PIQ	.79	.81	.80	.65
Average *r*				
Verbal	.80	.62	.75	.73
Performance	.68	.69	.71	.62

Average *r* values were computed using Fisher *z* transformations of the correlations reported by Thorndike, Hagen, and Sattler (1986, pp. 62–66).

Data provided by Thorndike, Hagen, and Sattler (1986) shows that the Binet:Four also correlated highly with the K-ABC Mental Processing (.89) and Achievement (.89) composites. Like the WISC-R Verbal/K-ABC Achievement correlations, the Binet:Four Verbal Reasoning Scale correlated highest with the K-ABC Achievement Scale (.87) owing to the similarity in academic and verbal content of the two scales. Similarly, the Binet: Four Abstract Visual Reasoning Scale correlated highest with the K-ABC Simultaneous Scale (.78) because both tests have similar underlying processing requirements (simultaneous processing). Finally, the Binet:Four Short-Term Memory Scale correlated highest with the K-ABC Sequential Scale (.82) because of the successive processing demands of these two groups of subtests. Therefore, like the WISC-R/K-ABC analysis, the Binet: Four scales align as would be expected using the PASS model as a guide.

IQ TESTS AND PASS—PUTTING IT ALL TOGETHER

The content analysis and empirical findings lead to the conclusion that the field of intellectual assessment as represented by the Binet, Wechsler, and K-ABC essentially represents a limited view of intelligence. From the PASS model, these tests mainly measure simultaneous processes through tests such as Block Design and Object Assembly that appear on the WISC-R Performance, Binet:Four Abstract Visual, and K-ABC Simultaneous scales. Successive processes are involved in tests such as WISC-R Digit Span Forward, Binet:Four Memory for Digits, McCarthy Scales Numerical Memory, and most, but not all, of the K-ABC Sequential Scale subtests. The verbal subtests on all these tests can best be described as verbal/ achievement measures that are related to general academic achievement and, to varying extents and combinations, each of the PASS processes. The alignment of current tests with the PASS model, described in Figure 7-1, illustrates the limited scope of current instrumentation.

FURTHER ANALYSIS OF IQ TESTS

The WISC-R Third Factor as Planning

The WISC-R subtests Arithmetic, Digit Span, and Coding form a third factor in the traditional factorial analyses of the test (Kaufman, 1979) that has been the focus of much discussion but little empirical research. Over the years, many researchers and practitioners have speculated on what this factor measures, and practitioners in particular have struggled with its influence on the Verbal and Performance IQ scores and the apparent incongruity with the Wechsler verbal/nonverbal model. The third factor has been described as many things, such as Freedom from Distractibility, a reflection of behavioral rather than cognitive ability, anxiety, sequencing problems, memory, motor performance, problem solving, concentration problems, attention, hyperactivity, facility with numbers (Kaufman, 1979), personality factors, emotional disturbance, and executive processes (Wielkiewicz, 1990). Clearly, it does not seem reasonable that this group of three subtests can be measuring *all* these diverse abilities and behavioral or personality characteristics.

A recent hypothesis about the third factor of the WISC-R is that it does not exist at all. This has recently been suggested because of confirmatory factor analytic evidence provided by O'Grady (1989). Following his analysis of the WISC-R standardization sample data, O'Grady concluded that the "practice of interpreting a Freedom from Distractibility score for children, as advocated by Kaufman (1979) and discussed by Sattler (1982) seems to be ill-founded" because support for a three-(as well as a two-) factor solution was not found. The interpretation of the WISC-R third factor as any specific ability or variable has also been questioned by some recent experimental evidence.

Some researchers have found that the WISC-R third factor may not be cohesive. For example, Stewart and Moely (1983) examined the relationship between the Arithmetic, Digit Span, and Coding subtests with measures of comprehension monitoring, memory span, strategy use, achievement, and IQ test scores. They found Arithmetic was predicted by the Key Math subtest Missing Elements and math achievement test scores, Digit Span by a memory span measure, and Coding by rehearsal strategy and math achievement. They concluded that "no single cognitive construct . . . appears to underlie all of the subtests" (p. 941).

An investigation by Ownby and Mathews (1985) has been cited as providing evidence that the WISC-R third factor could be interpreted as a measure of executive processes (Wielkiewicz, 1990). The data and conclusions provided by Ownby and Mathews, however, are neither strong nor conclusive, which led them to conclude: "Although our argument and data suggest that the term executive processes might reasonably be applied to this factor, an interim more modest proposal until additional research is completed would be simply to refer to it as 'Factor 3', rather than the potentially misleading label Freedom from Distractibility" (1985, p. 534). Clearly, the studies by Ownby and Mathews, like Stewart and Moely's, have done more to refute the "Freedom from Distractibility" label (Kaufman, 1975, 1979) than to provide ample evidence that the third factor subtests measure executive processes. The more conservative conclusion suggested by the Ownby and Mathews, as well as the Stewart and Moely, investigation is that the Arithmetic-Digit Span-Coding triad may not represent any unitary variable at all. Moreover, we can only conclude that the interpretation of the WISC-R third factor as executive processing, which would be similar to the Planning component of the PASS model, is unsupported.

The K-ABC and the PASS Model

The relationship between the PASS model and the K-ABC warrants further consideration due to the association the authors of that test have made with the work of Das, Kirby, and Jarman (1979). Although there is no doubt that the position taken by the Kaufmans when they developed the K-ABC is *not* consistent with the PASS model, the early work on simultaneous and successive processing did influence the K-ABC. This is apparent in their statement describing the Sequential-Simultaneous Dichotomy model they choose based on the idea that a variety of research trends within cognitive psychology, neuropsychology, and related disciplines support two basic types of information processing: sequential versus parallel or serial versus multiple, successive versus simultaneous, and other dichotomies associated with Freud, Pavlov, Maslow, and James (paraphrased from Kafman & Kaufman [1983]).

The concept that many divergent theories of intelligence converge on the dichotomous model proposed by the Kaufmans is the essence of the view of ability they advocated during the development of the K-ABC. Note that no one of the theories in particular is emphasized, but rather they are conglomerated into the Sequential-Simultaneous dichotomy. That is, although the work of Das, Kirby, and Jarman (1975, 1979) on simultaneous and successive processing was one of many models that *influenced* the Kaufmans, their test was not designed to reflect any particular model. The limited use of the PASS model (that is, the exclusion of planning and attention) has been made evident by the recent research.

In a recent investigation by Das, Mensink, and Janzen (1990), a sample of 198 Elementary school students from grades one, three, and five were administered both the K-ABC and four planning tasks. The K-ABC and planning tasks were analyzed by principal components analyses with orthogonal varimax rotation and using LISREL confirmatory analyses performed to determine if the results fit the hypothesized model (i.e., that planning is a separate cognitive process from K-ABC sequential and simultaneous).

Both the principal components analysis (see Table 7-3) and the LISREL confirmatory analyses yielded the same answer—that the planning tasks (Planned Connections and Visual Search) loaded on a factor separate from simultaneous and sequential processing. The three variables of Simultaneous, Sequential, and Planning were also confirmed by LISREL analyses (Joreskog & Sorbom, 1986). The fit between the hypothesized model and the data from the 10 subtests was good. Other analyses also suggest that the cognitive processes of simultaneous-sequential and planning exist apart from a general or common factor of intelligence. This data clearly showed the distinction of the K-ABC Sequential and Simultaneous scales subtests from the planning component of the PASS model. This is, of course, logical given the nature of the tasks involved, and is consistent with Luria's view of the cognitive requirements of the tests.

In the interpretative manual of the K-ABC, Kaufman and Kaufman (1983) cite a correlational study between K-ABC scores and factor scores on the successive and simultaneous battery that Das, Kirby, and Jarman (1979) used in research reported in their book. The results Kaufman and Kaufman provide are presented in their table 4.18 (1983, p. 110). The two studies involved samples of trainable mentally handicapped (n = 37) and learning-disabled children (n = 53). The results suggest that the K-ABC Simultaneous and Sequential subtests correlated as would be expected with the simultaneous and successive tasks described by Das, Kirby, and Jarman. That is, the sequential and successive tasks correlated highly (.69 for the retarded and .50), as did the two groups of simultaneous tasks (.50 for the learning disabled and .54). Therefore, the Simultaneous and Sequential scales of the K-ABC can be viewed as having similarity with the Simulta-

TABLE 7-3 Principal Components K-ABC and DN:CAS Experimental Test Battery Planning (n = 198)

	Planning	Simultaneous	Sequential
Gestalt Closure	.125	.788*	–.095
Number Recall	.053	.119	.807*
Triangles	–.307	.623*	.110
Word Order	–.044	.149	.810*
Matrix Analogies	–.294	.537*	.206
Spatial Memory	–.506*	.428*	.265
Tokens	–.374	.426*	.202
Planned Connections	.792*	–.106	.085
Visual Search	.622*	–.189	–.001
Crack the Code	–.431*	–.173	.433*
% of Total Variance	18.0	17.7	16.7

* = loading ≥ .40

The negative loadings are an artifact of the scoring of Planning Connections and Visual Search as latency; the higher the score, the poorer the performance on the two tests.

neous and Successive components of the PASS model even though the K-ABC scales have some important limitations (see Das, Mensink, & Janzen, 1990; Das, 1983; Naglieri & Das, 1990).

One of the major limitations not discussed so far is that the K-ABC battery does not have a verbal simultaneous task. An attempt was made (Das, Mensink & Janzen 1990) to address this limitation by including Tokens in the set of simultaneous tests chosen from the K-ABC. This additional task has a large factor loading (.64) on the K-ABC simultaneous factor as described in the previous section. Das, Mensink & Janzen (1990) examined how Tokens improved the prediction of achievement when it was added to the K-ABC.

Tokens as developed by Das and Naglieri (1987) in their experimental test battery requires the child to use the concepts of shape and color in various combinations and is somewhat similar to the test described by Lezak (1976). It is used to measure simultaneous verbal functions that require the use of simultaneous relations, such as categories, above-under, and left-right. In the present task, eight tokens are presented to the children. The tokens vary in shape (square and circle) and color (blue, yellow, white, and black). An example of a test item is, "Put, under the black round one, all the squares that are not blue."

The K-ABC subtests and the additional test, Tokens, were used as predictors of reading and math. The results showed that both reading decoding and comprehension were found to be best predicted by Tokens,

TABLE 7-4 Prediction of Achievement in Reading and Mathematics

The following are the results of stepwise multiple regression analysis using the K-ABC plus Tokens to predict achievement in reading and mathematics:

1. Prediction of achievement in reading decoding on the basis of Gestalt, Number, Triangles, Word, Matrix, Spatial, and Tokens.
   Step 1: Tokens (r = .50)
   Step 2: Tokens, Spatial (r = .55)
   Step 3: Tokens, Spatial, Matrix (r = .58, f = 13.1, p < .002).

2. Prediction of achievement in reading comprehension on the basis of Gestalt, Number, Triangles, Word, Matrix, Spatial, and Tokens.
   Step 1: Tokens (r = .50)
   Step 2: Tokens, Matrix (r = .55, f = 17.5, p < .001)

3. Prediction of achievement in mathematics on the basis of Gestalt, Number, Triangles, Word, Matrix, Spatial, and Tokens.
   Step 1: Spatial (r = .45)
   Step 2: Spatial, Tokens (r = .52)
   Step 3: Spatial, Tokens, Gestalt (r = .56, f = 11.8, p < .001)

and to a lesser extent by other simultaneous tests (see Table 7-4). Tokens, being verbal and simultaneous, was expected to contribute most to the variance in reading achievement, and it did: r = .50 for decoding as well as for comprehension. In contrast, math achievement was best predicted by K-ABC Spatial (r = .45), followed by Tokens and K-ABC Gestalt, which increased the value to only r = .56. All three are simultaneous tests.

The results of the study in terms of the relationship between processing and achievement are clear: The K-ABC Simultaneous Scale relationship to achievement can be improved through the use of a verbal subtest. Results of multiple regression showed that Spatial Memory and, to a lesser extent, Matrices from the K-ABC added to the prediction of reading decoding, and Matrices to the prediction of comprehension. But Tokens emerged as the best predictor; the K-ABC subtests contributed to the prediction only minimally. These results show that the addition of a verbal simultaneous test is needed to assess simultaneous processes, especially when predicting reading achievement.

Woodcock-Johnson, Wechsler, Binet:Four, and K-ABC

The relationship between traditional IQ tests and the Woodcock-Johnson–Revised (WJ-R) was examined by Woodcock (1990). His analyses were based on a series of investigations involving the relationships between the eight WJ-R factors and the Wechsler, Binet:Four, and K-ABC scales. The results of these analyses showed that (1) the Wechsler Verbal, Binet:Four Verbal Reasoning, and K-ABC Achievement subtests loaded on the WJ-R Comprehension-Knowledge (Gc) factor; (2) Wechsler Performance, Binet: Four Abstract/Visual Reasoning, and K-ABC Simultaneous subtests loaded on the WJ-R Visual (Gv) factor; and (3) the Wechsler subtest Digit Span, Binet:Four Short-Term Memory, and K-ABC Sequential subtests loaded on the WJ-R Short-Term Memory (Gsm) factor. These results are quite consistent with the findings that traditional IQ tests published by Wechsler, Binet, and Kaufman evidence considerable redundancy and that there is some overlap between these tests and the WJ-R. Because no investigations of the WJ-R and the PASS model have been conducted, we can only suggest that the WJ-R Visual (Gv) factor will likely be similar to our simultaneous factor and the successive component may relate to a limited extent with WJ-R Short-Term Memory (Gsm), but the relationship between the WJ-R, as well as the WISC-III and Binet:Four, and the planning and attention constructs needs to be examined empirically.

Postscript—A CASE STUDY

The evidence presented in this chapter provides a view of the Binet, Wechsler, and other IQ tests from the PASS model. In simplest terms, all intelligence tests in use today measure a limited number of the PASS processes. They measure verbal/achievement (verbal and achievement scales), contain mediocre measures of simultaneous processing (nonverbal/performance scales), and poor measures of successive processing (Sequential scale on K-ABC). From our perspective, this is a very limited view of intelligence because only two of the four cognitive processes we consider important to represent human functioning are assessed. Unless the four processes are evaluated in tests of intelligence, an abbreviated view of human functioning will continue to misinform psychologists. In order to illustrate this in concrete terms, a case study will be presented.

The case of Tony L. is presented because it illustrates the problems current IQ tests pose when evaluating students whose difficulties lie outside of what is measured using the Wechsler. This case is an actual one, not a fabricated illustration, that was conducted through The Ohio State University Psychoeducational Clinic.

Tony, age 9 years 10 months, was evaluated to determine his current level of intellectual, emotional, and academic functioning because of recent difficulties in school and at home. His third- and fourth-grade teachers described him as a boy who was constantly in a state of disarray. He had much difficulty staying on task and was easily distracted, very immature, very disorganized, and generally at a loss in the class. He had many social problems involving fighting and aggressive outbursts and failed to conform to the rules. Because of these problems, he was not well liked by the other students and was seated in a separate area of the room.

Tony had a tendency to give up quickly on difficult questions, especially the less structured tasks, and yet he was at times able to perform at or above grade level. Tony's difficulty keeping track of his books and assignments interfered with his participation in class discussion, and his academic difficulty was largely influenced by his disorganization and inability to complete assignments and projects.

Analysis of Tony's school records indicated that he earned one *B*, two *C*'s, and five *D*'s (average grade of 1.5) in fourth grade. His group achievement test scores for grade three are consistent with the grades. He earned scores in reading and math that were average or below on the Comprehensive Tests of Basic Skills Form V Level E, which was administered in April. His Total Reading and Total Math standard scores (mean of 100, SD of 15) were 109 (74th percentile) and 87 (19th percentile), but his Math Concepts and Applications score of 101 was considerably higher than his Math Computation score of 78 (these are aggregated in the Math total). The group achievement scores, in conjunction with his earned grades and teacher reports, clearly indicated problems in behavior, completion of classroom assignments, and and some academic areas.

Tony earned scores on the various measures of intelligence and achievement that varied considerably. He earned scores that fall in the high average range of functioning on those measures of intellectual performance that measure ability using verbal and nonverbal content. His WISC-R Full Scale IQ score of 116 ±5 falls in the high average range of intelligence and is ranked at the 86th percentile.

Tony earned average and above average scores on measures of intelligence that involve nonverbal content such as spatial reasoning (e.g., building a design with blocks or completing a visual analogy). He earned a WISC-R Performance IQ of 115 ±8 (84th percentile), an MAT-EF standard score of 111±7 (53rd percentile), and a Draw A Person: Quantitative Scoring System standard score of 117±9, which fall in the high average and average ranges. There was no significant variation among these various nonverbal measures or subtests within the WISC-R Performance Scale.

Tony performed similarly well on measures of intelligence that are verbal. He obtained a Verbal IQ of 113± 6, which falls in the high average range and is ranked at the 81st percentile. Tests in this area involve verbal expression and verbal comprehension, such as defining words and explaining how words are alike. Within the verbal scale, Tony performed significantly poorly on Digit Span (repeating digits forward and backward), Arithmetic, and Information. This trio of subtests suggests a weakness in memory (Kaufman, 1979). However, further analysis revealed that no memory problem existed.

Tony's low score on WISC-R Digit Span was not a function of a memory problem because his recall of digits forward is good. He earned a score ranked at the 75th percentile on the K-ABC Number Recall subtest, which is in sharp contrast to (and significantly higher than) his 25th-percentile score on the WISC-R Digit Span. Although his span of memory for forward digits was the same on both tests (that is, five digits were correctly recalled), the WISC-R Backward portion of the test depressed his score considerably (he only had a span of 2.5 digits). Recall of digits backward is sensitive to organization and planning ability because it requires the individual to develop some method of solving the task (Schofield & Ashman, 1986).

Another task requiring planning processes is math computation (Garofalo, 1986). Although Tony earned good scores in Reading Decoding (126±4) and Reading Comprehension (107 ±6), he earned a Mathematics Composite score of 96± 5, with significantly poor performance in Math Computation (82± 6). Tony's Math Computation score is ranked at the 12th percentile and is consistent with his low CTBS Match Computation score of 78. Math computation is an academic activity that requires systematic execution of rules, checking of one's work, and organization of the activities, which is regulated by planning processes.

Tony also performed poorly on the PASS cognitive processing tasks specifically designed to measure planning processes. These measures are sensitive to planning because they require the child to develop and use a systematic approach to solving problems. On the Visual Search and Planned Connections tests of the DN:CAS, Tony earned low scores that were consistent with his level of performance on Math Computation and Digits Backward (about 2 standard deviations below normal). He had considerable difficulty with these tests because they required him to develop and use some systematic method of solving the problems. Additionally, he evidenced difficulty with tasks involving control of attention and effort to respond to particular aspects of a complex stimulus.

In summary, Tony consistently earned low scores on tasks that required a systematic organization and control of intellectual activity regardless of the content of the task (auditory memory task as in recall of digits backward, visual tasks, and achievement in math computation). There is, therefore, considerable evidence of a deficit in planning processes that is related to Tony's academic difficulty as well as his social and behavior problems. Tony's difficulty with planning processes also extends to personal and interpersonal areas. His current difficulties in school and at home involve problems with self-control that are related to his cognitive deficit in planning. Tony's difficulties maintaining proper behavior, following rules, controlling his impulses, disorganization in class, and failure to complete less structured activities are all related to his cognitive processing deficiency. This difficulty was also reflected by scores on the Achenbach Child Behavior Profile that indicate concern in the areas of behavioral difficulties.

Tony's case illustrates the limitations of current technology in identification of those with problems and reflects what we typically find in such instances. That is, in Tony's case, the child is seen as having average or better IQ scores, mostly average achievement, but is failing in school and in some specific academic area. Tony's planning disability causes personal and academic problems that warrant attention, but under current technology he would be identified as a learning-disabled, or perhaps behavior-disordered, student, without knowledge of his real cognitive deficiency. He and his parents would be told that there is no intellectual reason for his school failure, an inaccurate statement.

Treatment of Tony would, if based on WISC-R results and behavioral problems, center on memory exercises and some kind of therapy to gain control of his behavior. We recommend, instead, remedial training based on the PASS model (see Chapter 9.)

SUMMARY

In this chapter we have attempted to show that curent IQ tests are quite limited in scope, in relation to the PASS model. The limited scope of current technology has had a significant influence on how psychologists understand the difficulties experienced by children and adolescents, as well as adults. The case study presented illustrates how misleading current IQ tests can be. We suggest that the PASS model may provide a more accurate view of the difficulties experienced by many students, especially those who are identified as learning disabled.

PART IV

DISCOVERY AND AMELIORATION OF DEFICITS

8

EXCEPTIONAL CHILDREN

The four PASS cognitive processes are used in this chapter to understand some common categories of special populations including the reading-disabled, the mentally handicapped, and individuals with attentional disorders. Our knowledge of these special populations is currently limited, especially because of the heterogeneity of these populations. Therefore, our goal is to reduce the chaos by defining the special groups in terms of the PASS cognitive processes. This will replace the traditional definitions based on general ability or a theoretical collection of psychometric and achievement tests. A process-based approach should be an improvement over IQ- or achievement-based grouping. We shall show the value of this progressive approach by considering each of the special groups of children.

LEARNING DISABILITY

Learning disability (LD) includes a large number of disabilities associated with reading, arithmetic, writing, listening, and speaking. In this chapter (and, in fact, in the book), however, we focus only on reading and arithmetic, demonstrating the relationship between PASS and these two disabilities that occur frequently among young schoolchildren. First we discuss the relevant research on reading disability and then on arithmetic disability.

Reading disability is itself a broad category, which includes decoding, spelling, and comprehension. Of these, the cognitive functions associated with reading and word recognition have been an engaging research topic.

Children with reading difficulties are divided into those who are true dyslexics and those who have been called "garden variety" dyslexics (Stanovich, 1988). The defective cognitive functions of the dyslexics are specific and therefore less pervasive than those of the "garden variety" type (Torgesen, 1989). The dyslexic with specific cognitive deficit, it is argued, can be easily found among children with high scores on traditional IQ tests who have severe problems in acquiring reading (decoding) in elementary school. The specific deficits in the majority of dyslexics are in phonological coding (Stanovich, 1988), although visual-spatial problems can be found in a minority of these poor readers. It has been suggested by Siegel (1988) that the phonological deficit occurs in all reading disabled, irrespective of IQ. In word recognition, as well as pseudoword reading, poor readers of low to high IQ have the same low scores, whereas average readers show better performance as IQ increases (Siegel, 1989).

Siegel's position blurs the distinction between the two types of poor readers in terms of their difference in performance on cognitive tasks not directly related to phonological coding. "Pervasive" cognitive deficits include those found in general ability. We expect, following Torgesen and others, that the low IQ reading disabled will be inferior to those with high IQs in several cognitive tests not directly related to reading. In regard to test performances related to phonological coding, one can reasonably expect no difference between the two groups (Siegel, 1988; Siegel & Ryan, 1989). In the review of PASS research in this chapter, a link between poor reading and the four cognitive processes will be clearly observed.

How do we distinguish between decoding and comprehension? Decoding disability can be measured by the failure to orally read pseudowords. Comprehension of a written passage requires an efficient decoding of the words and therefore may be adversely influenced in cases of decoding failure. Reading comprehension has been conceptualized as a multiplicative function of decoding and listening comprehension. If listening comprehension alone is defective and decoding is not, it is doubtful that the diagnosis will be "dyslexia", especially when we apply the further constraint that a deficit is to be found in only a limited number of cognitive functions. Anyone with significantly poor listening comprehension but adequate decoding skills is not likely to be a dyslexic. Thus, a decoding deficit should be ruled out before a comprehension deficit can be established.

Decoding

A printed word has visual characteristics that are perceived and received by the eye. Proceeding from this stage, the word is either visually coded as a pattern or phonologically coded as speech sounds. Traveling through one of these routes, the word reaches the next stage, which is pronunciation of the word. Once the required pronunciation is available, the final stage, oral reading of the word, is reached. (See Figure 8-1.)

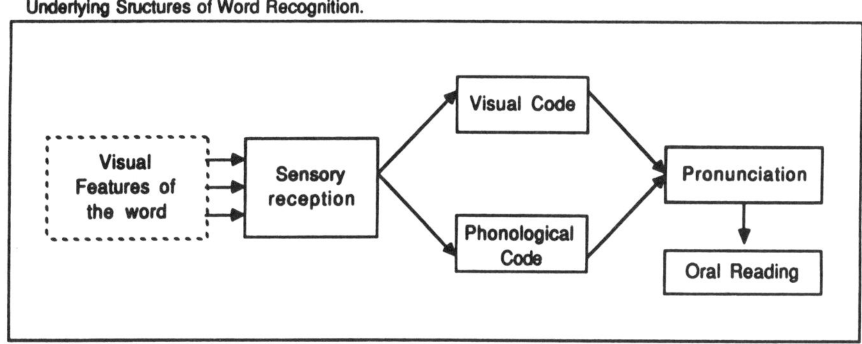

FIGURE 8-1 Decoding

Most dyslexics are assumed to show a breakdown in the phonological coding route. They use direct visual access. As they advance through elementary school, word reading becomes increasingly dependent on the meaning of the word and the context in which it appears. Even when they have become adults, they make many mistakes in recognizing words, especially when nonwords such as plit, culk, bipe, etc., are given for reading. Adult dyslexics were less accurate than sixth-grade children (Bruck, 1990) on such a task.

Phonological coding deficit is related to broader cognitive dysfunctions such as successive processing. Word recognition, however, uses both direct visual access and phonological coding—the direct route for familiar words and the phonological route for unfamiliar and especially multisyllable words. The first should relate to simultaneous processing and the second to successive processing. Pronunciation of the word predominantly requires successive processing. However, planning processes are also involved in assembling pronunciation and programming speech output. Thus, measures of all three processes show correlations with reading words. In a simplified view, word reading is related to the dominant processes of simultaneous and successive processing as shown in Figure 8-2.

Cognitive Processes in Decoding

Cognitive processes underlying decoding are shown in Figure 8-2, an elaboration of Figure 8-1. The emphasis is on simultaneous and successive processes because simultaneous processing is preeminent in visual coding, whereas successive processing plays a major role in phonological coding. Pronunciation of the word is assembled by organizing speech sounds corresponding to the printed word; this is predominantly a successive process requiring the motor program (articulations of the sounds) for oral reading.

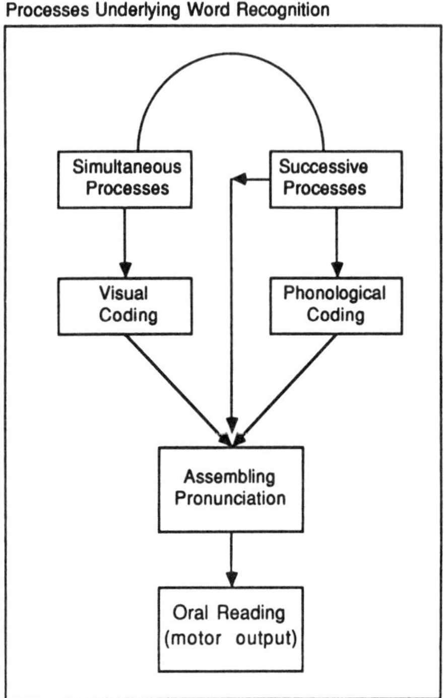

FIGURE 8-2 Cognitive Processes in Decoding

The key dysfunctions of dyslexics who are identified by a decoding deficit appear to be related to speech processes. Both Figures 8-1 and 8-2 would suggest this because pronunciation is a critical component. Frith (1986) comes to the conclusion that speech related development appears to have been obstructed in dyslexics. In a review of developmental reading disorders, she traces the normal development of reading through symbolic, logographic, alphabetical, and orthographic stages. In the symbolic stage, written words are considered as arbitrary symbols or designs, almost magical—the child scribbles some lines and pretends to have written. Next is the stage of whole-word reading by sight, in which the pattern of letters is considered as a whole to be read by sight. Then follows a stage in which the whole word is analyzed as a sequence of letters in the alphabet. This is the stage in which phonological decoding occurs; it aids reading and spelling. Lastly, the alphabetic reading changes into orthographic analysis. Words such as *rain* and *rein* differ orthographically but have the same pronunciation; the two words have to be differentiated by the reader. Dyslexics have a problem in the alphabetic stage; they do not seem to engage in alphabetical analysis of the word.

Is dyslexia an anomaly, or can it be understood as an extreme condition in an otherwise continuous development of an alphabetic approach to reading? The answer is not clear as far as current research is concerned. One of the prominent researchers, Stanovich (1988), distinguishes dyslexics by considering an arbitrary cut-off point in "phonological-core variable." He makes the following observations: Phonic and visual-orthographic reading skills can be separated as independent axes; the coordinates can define several clusters of dyslexics. The main clusters are the dysphonetic and dyseidetic following Boder's (1973) terms.

The first group, the dysphonetic, is much more frequent than the second. Clearly, the first group is expected to show a weakness in successive processing especially when verbal information is involved, whereas the dyseidetic may be weak in simultaneous processing. Decoding of words, particularly familiar ones, may be done directly as a visual pattern and only unfamiliar and pseudowords need phonological coding that requires successive processing, but even in the case of unfamiliar and pseudowords, some part is recognized as a whole or gestalt. Therefore, it is not uncommon to find that both processes need to be used while reading words.

Previous Research

Although the most recent studies of the PASS model have included all four of the PASS processes, early investigations usually involved only simultaneous and successive measures. In order to provide a concise discussion of these results, we will examine the relations between each of the PASS processes and reading. Our review contains studies whose results do not always agree with each other. For instance, while some of the experiments show that only successive processing was weak in the LD children, others implicate mainly a weakness in planning (Naglieri & Das, 1990). Yet, some other research has shown both simultaneous and successive processes to be of critical importance; if one of these is weak, reading difficulties appear. This apparent inconsistency arises mainly because the subjects selected for different studies were not comparable. The samples of "LD" vary among themselves—some have poor reading achievement scores that do not specify the type of reading problem (decoding, comprehension, both, and/or related problems such as attention disorder), whereas in some other studies, subjects have been selected only for word reading or comprehension problems.

Reading Disabilities and Attention

Do reading disabled children perform poorly on sustained attention compared to normal children? This was investigated by Das (1988), who compared children in fifth-grade who were reading at third-grade level with normal readers in grades 3 and 5. The control groups provided a reading age control and a chronological age control, respectively. The tasks included a measure of vigilance, or sustained attention, presented on tape (see Melnyk, 1988). It included eight familiar, one-syllable names: four boys' and four girls' names, which were presented randomly every 1.5 seconds for 10 minutes. The child was to indicate the presence of each signal (a boy's name followed by a girl's name, then another boy's name) that occurred randomly, four times every 90 seconds.

No differences between the groups were obtained. The reading disabled students did not show any "deficit" in vigilance (sustained attention). Neither were the fifth-grade subjects significantly superior to the third-grade subjects. If there is any attentional deficit, either it may show up in a prolonged vigilance task of more than 30 minutes duration or in a vigilance task transformed to measure selective rather than sustained attention. The selective attention differences also examined are discussed in a subsequent section.

The relevance of this investigation to other research is helpful to determine if reading disabled children have a sustained attention deficit. For example, perhaps the best among the studies concerning vigilance is an experiment by Swanson (1983). He used a vigilance task commonly referred to as the *continuous performance task (CPT)* (see Rosvold et al., 1956). It involved presentation of 12 letters from the English alphabet including *A* and *X*. The letters were presented visually or auditorially in two separate conditions for a duration of .5 second, and an interval of 1 second separating the letters. The signal was *X* preceded by *A*. The difference between this task and the one used by Das and Melnyk (1989) is that in Swanson's study the signals occurred 48 times in each 5-minute block compared to 15 in Das's task. Such high frequencies are not typical in vigilance tasks, which are modeled after the original Mackworth task (watching a clock face with a moving pointer that skipped infrequently). The results of Swanson's study show that (1) when decoding of printed letters is involved, reading-disabled children may show a spatial handicap, and (2) when event rate is high, reading-disabled children cannot keep pace with the detection task.

Reading-disabled children are not assumed to have any deficit in arousal itself, although they cannot cope with attending to the target letter when event rate is high. They have difficulty in discrimination. Discrimination requires allocation of attentional resources or effort, as we have mentioned before (Chapter 3). A higher event rate puts stress on the subject and therefore requires a greater effort to be invested. Another factor, memory load, makes the vigilance task harder. When dyslexics show poor vigilance, one of these two causes or both could be implicated. In teaching poor readers, the good teacher does not talk quickly. The teacher repeats the theme in many different ways. Consequently, "event rate" is slow and memory is not stressed.

Attention and Distractibility

Learning-disabled children have been studied for attentional deficit by many investigators who have tested the hypothesis that distractibility, or the failure to attend selectively, is a major cause of reading failure (Ross, 1976; Copeland & Reiner, 1984). However, the evidence linking selective attention disorder to reading disability has been inconclusive (Samuels & Miller, 1985).

Fleisher, Sodak, and Jelin (1984) mention a number of problems in the theories and methodologies relating to studies of selective attention in the literature; these problems contribute to the inconclusive evidence. For example, using a specific task such as central-incidental learning in order to study selective attention has been a major drawback; it is not clear theoretically how the task relates to attention, because in the central-incidental learning task, memory and attention are confounded. Ford, Pelham, and Ross (1984) tried to separate the two and conclude that for reading-disabled children, defective rehearsal rather than deficiencies in selective attention may be the problem.

Posner's physical and name matching task has been used as a measure of selective attention that requires processing at the time of receiving the stimulus, as described in Chapter 3. In this research, reading-disabled children were by no means slower in physical match, but they were on the name matching task. Das (1993). The reading-disabled are not generally deficient in letter matching, except when they have to engage in name matching.

The implication of the studies on attention are as follows:

1. Reading-disabled individuals are not deficient in sustaining attention; they are as good as normal readers.
2. Reading-disabled individuals take a longer time in matching upper to lowercase letters. Thus, in selecting the appropriate response and in encoding letters as same or different, they are less efficient.

A Planning Deficiency Possibility

Does a planning deficiency make sense? Certainly it would be an overgeneralization to state that a planning deficiency alone can account for all types of learning disabilities. On the other hand, could a processing deficit in one or more of the four areas exist individually, as a group, or in various combinations, and be related to different types of learning disabilities? Might a planning deficit be the major deficit through its interactions with the remaining processes? Could a planning deficiency provide some explanation of the disproportionate numbers of males identified as learning disabled? Let us review the evidence.

Deficits in various combinations of PASS processes can be the underlying determinants of different types of academic underachievement. A planning deficiency could lead to difficulty with computation (Garofalo, 1986) and complex word problems in mathematics (Luria, 1966), while a simultaneous deficiency could lead to difficulty with less complex word problems and use of quantitative concepts (Garofalo, 1986; Luria, 1966). Such a view is consistent with Luria's (1966) observation that tasks such as arithmetic (as well as reading and other academic areas) may be affected by difficulty in the "occipital, temporal, and frontal" areas (p. 12). Because of the interdependence of their functions in relation to performance in complex tasks such as mathematics, the specific deficiency in one type of process can influence performance across a wide range of activities. One broken link in a net weakens the whole net.

Using this conceptualization as a model, the seven areas of learning disability from the federal definition could be considered for their processing requirements. For example, oral language is one area for which a child can be identified as learning disabled (Interagency Committee on Learning Disabilities, 1987). According to Luria (1982), oral language involves basic speech production (i.e., articulation of the appropriate sounds of speech) as well as conversational and narrative (communication of a particular event) aspects. Speech production involves the conversion of an idea into a sequentially organized speech utterance (Luria, 1982), which involves successive processing, especially during the early stages of development. At a later stage, by adolescence, it becomes automatized to a large extent. Production of more complex statements requires knowledge of the appropriate rules of syntax (related to successive processes) and grammar (related to simultaneous processes), as well as analysis of the intent, structure of the statements, and assessment of the production for effectiveness and completeness (planning processes). Attention to speech sounds is obviously critical for acquiring oral language.

Some Experiments Using Planning Tasks

Although in previous studies by Das, Kirby, and their associates (see Kirby & Das, 1990) some planning and attention tasks had been used, the experiment reported here is the first one to use a good number of tasks from all four functions and to compare their relative contributions to reading disability. Bardos (1988) administered measures of PASS to normal and reading-disabled fourth- and fifth-grade students. The reading-disabled sample was of average intelligence based on their WISC-R IQs but was poor in achievement tests of reading, decoding, and comprehension. Thus, the sample was not comparable to those used by Kirby and Das. On the PASS tasks the reading disabled sample earned scores equal to the normal sample in simultaneous, successive, and attention but was significantly lower than the control group in planning. These results support previous research that detected a planning deficit as well as a successive deficit (Das, Bisanz, & Mancini, 1985; Kirby & Ashman, 1984; Kirby & Robinson, 1987).

The relationships between the cognitive processing variables and specific reading disability in decoding were examined, with particular emphasis on individual and group differences in planning. In a study by Das, Snart, and Mulcahy (1982), four planning tasks were included along with simultaneous and successive tasks. Two of the four tasks were verbal (Planned Composition and Syllogistic Reasoning), and hence a strong relationship with reading was expected. The other two tests, however, were visual-perceptual (Visual Search and Planned Connections). The subjects included normal and reading-disabled children from grades four and six. The results of the study indicated that reading decoding showed a significant correlation with successive as well as planning processing for the fourth-graders only. At grade six, significant correlations between decoding and simultaneous processes as well were found in addition to the other two processes. In contrast, reading comprehension correlated significantly with simultaneous and planning processes at both fourth and sixth grades.

Other researchers have also found the PASS processes to be meaningfully related to individual differences in word reading (Das, Bisanz, & Mancini, 1985). These authors found that reading performance in a simple word recognition task can be predicted by performance in simultaneous, successive, and planning tasks. In complex reading tasks such as comprehension and memory for text, the important role of planning was clearly demonstrated by a qualitative analysis of products of reading by Ramey (1985). He found that the planning scores based on the test Visual Search distinguished between children who were good and poor in comprehension. The top planners made more inferential statements, questioned and evaluated the responses they made, and were more often able to see the author's message in the text. In contrast, poor planners made fewer inferential statements, did not question or evaluate their responses, and tended to be impulsive, easily frustrated, and unlikely to modify their ideas (also see Chapter 5 for discussion of Ramey). Incidentally, the groups were comparable on IQ.

These kinds of qualitative analyses suggest that it may be profitable to carry out studies to examine the unique styles of high and low planners in learning and recall of text. In this regard it is consistent with the following conclusion reached by Das and Cummins (1982): "The matter can be looked at broadly as a weakness *in control processes* . . . the RD (reading disabled) children had adequate vocabulary and comprehension . . . and coding skills, but they apparently need to adopt efficient *strategies for utilizing these optimally*." (p. 20)

The results on decoding and comprehension support the following conclusions: (1) Decoding at the lower grades requires successive processing; (2) comprehension in both lower and upper grades requires simultaneous processing—however, if the results can be replicated, we have to entertain the possibility that decoding, even at a higher grade, may also need simultaneous processing; and (3) planning as an underlying process contributes significantly to reading achievement in general.

Reading Disability and High IQ

The relationship between the coding processes of simultaneous and successive processing and reading has been summarized in Das, Kirby, and Jarman (1979) and in subsequent papers as mentioned in this and other chapters. Snart, Das, and Mensink (1988) examined the relationship between reading and components of the PASS model, but using subjects with reading decoding problems who scored high above the average on traditional IQ tests. In this study using the sequential and simultaneous processing scales of K-ABC, as well as the PASS tests of selective attention (Posner tasks) and planning (Visual Search and Planned Connections), it was found that the reading-disabled subjects performed poorly on the sequential scale, as expected, compared to the simultaneous scale.

The high-IQ reading-disabled (RD) group was almost equal to the low-IQ RD group in the sequential scale, but maintained its superiority in the simultaneous scale performance. On attention and planning tasks, RDs, irrespective of IQ, performed poorly in name matching tasks that required lexical access of the letter names from long-term memory. The RD group was equal to the normal readers as expected in physical match, which does not involve lexical access. Similarly, the RD groups were poorer in planning task performance.

Thus, having a superior IQ score on traditional tests does not give any advantage to the children with RD in the selective attention task requiring lexical access, a process related to reading, nor does it make them good at planning tasks. Traditional IQ does not provide a good description of the cognitive competence of RD children. What then are the cognitive functions that are related to IQ and what are the functions that are unrelated to traditional IQ among reading disabled children?

Separating traditional IQ and poor reading is the topic of a study by Das, Mensink, and Mishra (1990), who attempted to identify the PASS processes that discriminate between poor and good readers when intelligence, defined by the Lorge-Thorndike test, is controlled. The tests that emerged as discriminators between good and poor readers were three measures of successive processing (Sequence Repetition, Naming Time, and Speech Rate), and a measure of selective attention (the Stroop Color-Word test). All four of these tests involve the use of articulatory representation, confirming the important role that speech-related processes play in reading (decoding). The results also support the assumption that deficient speech-related processes may be the central problem of the majority of poor readers. Phonological coding and articulation, which represent successive processes, therefore could have a causal link to decoding deficit.

PASS AND MENTAL RETARDATION

A Proposed Model

The definition of mental retardation typically used, as illustrated in Figure 8-3, stems from four possible combinations of IQ and adaptive behavior. There are certain characteristics that describe the level of adaptive functioning of a child or a retarded individual, such as social skills and good work habits, but adaptive behavior itself is a combination of a person's competence and adjustment. *Competence* is another name for cognitive functioning or ability, and adjustment is a part of personality. As Figure 8-4 shows, both cognitive functioning and personality lead to an important

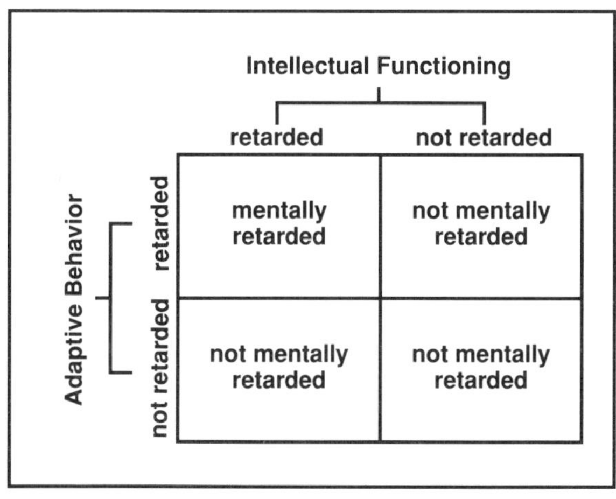

FIGURE 8-3 Definition of Mental Retardation

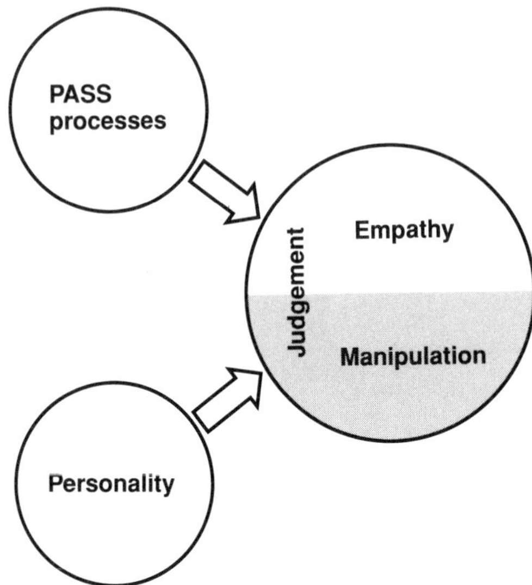

FIGURE 8-4 A Simple Model of Adaptive Behavior

component of adaptive behavior, *judgment*. That is, a person with excellent adaptive behavior is a good judge of his or her environment and can discriminate what is appropriate and what is inappropriate. The person takes into account both the social situation as well as personal biases and goals before acting. Retarded individuals who have not adequately acquired good social judgment must be taught to be friendly to strangers (with greetings such as "hello" or "how are you?"). They may have difficulty in a novel situation where they must evaluate the situation (noticing that a person is sad, sulky, or seriously immersed in thought) because social judgments such as these require cognitive competence, especially planning processes.

The model given in Figure 8-4 is an attempt to picture adaptive behavior theoretically. Empathy and manipulation are presented as the two aspects of adaptive function. *Empathy* is the appreciation of the other person's thoughts, feelings, and reactions in a given situation. It requires placing oneself in the conditions of another person and realizing how that person may react to the condition. A retarded individual does not show empathy to the same extent as does a nonretarded individual. Lack of empathy can be apparent even in very simple behaviors of the severely retarded. For example, a severely retarded man who cannot feed himself must be able to appreciate the intention of a caregiver who is about to provide a spoonful of food so that he can open his mouth and hold his head in an appropriate posture.

Manipulation is the interaction with the environment and people in the environment of the individual to achieve a specific goal. This is the other aspect of adaptive function. We influence others in order to have our wishes fulfilled; in that sense we manipulate the environment. Making others respond to your needs and be instrumental in achieving your goal requires manipulation. Retarded individuals are less able to manipulate, and the more severely retarded are almost helpless; they cannot manipulate their environment.

Both empathy and manipulation serve their purpose only when they are backed by good judgment. Planning, including judgment, may be the most important function that distinguishes the retarded from the nonretarded population, even though all other functional units have an important role as well.

PASS Processes and Mental Retardation

Let us consider arousal and attention (see Chapter 3). The first study we wish to report involved mentally handicapped subjects of mild to moderate level. Two vigilance tasks were given, a simple and a complex one. We describe these because they have not been given before. The simple task consisted of presenting via a tape recorder a series of 11 familiar nouns in a random order, one noun per second. The signal was the word *man,* the 10 other words being *box, bell, bat, boy, baby, cat, door, girl, key, and knife.* There were five signals in every 5-minute period. The ratio of signal words to nonsignal words was 1:20 per minute. The complex vigilance task was a random series of six words and six numbers; the words were *baby, boy, hand, food, table, and chair,* and the numbers were 1, 3, 5, 6, 7, and 9. Subjects were to press a button in both the simple and the complex task when they detected a signal. The signal for the complex task was any of the words, baby, hand, and table, whereas, as mentioned before, the signal for the simple task was just one word, man. Obviously the complex task required a higher memory load and more discrimination. In spite of this, the results showed no difference in vigilance between the mildly and moderately handicapped groups in the simple or complex tasks. Thus, the mildly and moderately retarded are equally good and do not show substantial deficit in attention-arousal. Information load in a complex vigilance task has to be increased if we were to contrast the groups again.

We compare next two attention-arousal tasks that offer a greater contrast in information load. Melnyk (1988) observed mildly mentally handicapped adolescents as they performed sustained and selective attention tasks. The adolescent mentally handicapped students were divided into those who showed attentional deficit and those who did not according to their ratings by their teachers on the Conners Scale (Conners, 1969) and on

TABLE 8-1 Das Attention Checklist with Factor Loadings

Observation	Factor 1
1. Does the student have a short attention span?	.90
2. Does the student appear detached from class activities?	.74
3. Does the student accurately heed directions?	.72
4. Does the student daydream in class?	.72
5. Does the student have trouble concentrating?	.89
6. Does the student stay with one activity long enough to complete it?	.87
7. Does the student work independently?	.87
8. Is the student easily distracted?	.86
9. Is the student able to concentrate on a task until completed?	.88
10. Does the student listen attentively?	.90
11. Does the student become easily engrossed in an activity?	.85
12. Does the student disregard some or all directions?	.84

an attention checklist developed by Das (Melnyk & Das, 1992). Those selected as demonstrating attentional deficit scored high on both the Das and the Conners scales. After classifying the two groups of adolescents as poor in attention or good in attention on the basis of these scales, Melnyk gave them a vigilance task (sustained) and a selective attention task, picture matching, which was an analogous variation of Posner's physical and name matching task.

The vigilance task was of comparable difficulty to the complex vigilance task used by Das (1970), reported in the previous section. Melnyk's study demonstrated that subjects who are rated as showing attentional deficits in the class do almost as well in sustained vigilance performance as those who do not show such deficit. However, in selective attention, the first group is lower in performance than the second. Again, this happens because sustained attention in contrast to selective attention has a low cognitive load. See Table 8-1 for a factored list of components of attention deficit.

Successive Processes: Naming, Recall, and Memory Span

Digit span is a specific instance of memory span that includes at least two separate components: the memory for items and the memory for the temporal order in which the items are presented. The first reflects speed of accessing from long-term memory the name or label for the presented stimulus, whereas the second requires a successive processing of the stimulus items (Das, 1984, 1985).

Individual differences in digit span, as in any memory span task, can be attributed to item identification speed (naming time) and memory for order. In naming time, subjects are asked to read 50 single digits as fast as they can. The relationship between the two was examined in an experiment (Das, 1985) with educable mentally retarded (EMR) and nonretarded children. Order memory and digit span had significant correlations for both groups. Naming time was found to determine span only for EMR subjects: Digit span was a linear function of the number of digits named in 2.89 seconds. To explain, spans could be determined as a multiple of naming time. For nonretarded subjects no relationship between the two was observed. This was likely due to the extremely easy task of naming digits by nonretarded subjects—the task is automatic and therefore does not require a deliberate effort either for phonological coding or for articulation.

An important subgroup among the retarded is Down's syndrome persons. Individuals with Down's experience problems in both phonological coding and articulation. Since both processes are involved in successive tasks such as word recall, we expect that those with Down's syndrome will be particularly poor in successive processing. This was indeed shown in the next two studies.

One of the measures of successive processing is the speed of accessing names of letters, digits, or words. In the Naming time test, the subject is asked to name some 30 to 50 letters, digits, or words rapidly (Denckla & Rudel, 1976; Das, 1984, 1985). Naming time predicts short-term memory span for letters, digits, and words. In the next three studies, we explore the intricate working of successive processing. In the first one, we try to understand digit span and why the speed of naming digits should determine the span. In the next two, we separate the individuals with Down's from other trainable mentally retarded individuals on successive processing tasks.

Factor analysis of simultaneous and successive tests on data from mentally retarded subjects has shown that the same two factors are found in this group. Snart, O'Grady, and Das (1982) added planning tasks and factor analyzed the performance data from 64 trainable mentally retarded students (mean IQ 51). Three factors were found, which could be easily recognized as simultaneous, successive, and planning. In the two successive tests, which were serial word recall and digit span, the individuals with Down's were significantly behind the other mentally retarded students. Their successive processing was relatively poor.

What is involved in the two tasks of successive processing? We suggest that speed of access to names and articulation are involved in causing individuals to differ in successive processing. Therefore, there is a strong suspicion that Down's individuals are weak in successive processing because they are particularly deficient in both. The next study, in fact, supports this suggestion.

Varnhagen, Das, and Varnhagen (1987) tested a group of adult Down's and other retarded individuals matched on intelligence, giving them Posner letter matching tasks, visual and auditory letter span tasks, as well as serial word recall tasks. Results showed that among the Down's individuals there was a strong correlation between the speed of letter matching and visual span, and not so strong a correlation with auditory span. A deficit in accessing names in long-term memory for those with Down's was suspected.

The other important result was obtained from serial recall; in the list of words, one-half were acoustically confusable (*mad, mat, man* . . .) and the other half was not (*cow, wall, hot* . . .). Recall of the confusable words is usually much worse than for the nonconfusable; this common finding relates to the use of the articulatory loop (Baddeley & Hitch, 1974) as discussed in Chapter 3. The results suggest that the Down's individuals do not use the articulatory loop and therefore they will be almost as good or bad in recalling the confusable as the nonconfusable words. In contrast, the nonDown's, who like normal individuals utilize the articulatory loop, are much worse in recalling the confusable words. This, indeed, was the case in this experiment.

We describe next a study on planning involving mildly retarded children. If planning processes are responsible for the effective utilization of simultaneous, successive, and attentional process and the application of prior knowledge to function on a daily basis in academic or social areas, then the retarded must be viewed as substantially disadvantaged. This view was examined by Bardos (1988). The mildly mentally retarded sample's WISC-R scores of 72 (Verbal), 76 (Performance), and 71 (Full Scale) were similar to their achievement test scores of 63 (Reading), 68 (Spelling), and 70 (Arithmetic) on the Wide Range Achievement Test. The results of the PASS tasks based on the local norm sample were (using a mean of 100 and SD of 15) as follows: Planning = 70.1; Attention = 78.0; Simultaneous = 75.0; and Successive = 80.6. Thus, these data tentatively support the hypothesis that the retarded have a greater deficiency in planning.

The retarded appear to be a heterogeneous group so far as deficiencies in cognitive functions are concerned. Although we have considered only these with Down's as a separate diagnostic group, other kinds of retardation are found among children—for example, retardation due to alcohol or other substance abuse by parents. The retarded, in a simplistic view of PASS, must be below average in all four processes. Perhaps a criterion of 2 standard deviations below in each processing area would be the simplest to propose. However, this would have to be empirically tested. Most probably a uniform retardation in all four areas cannot be found in all mentally retarded individuals. We can anticipate that the retarded must be subaverage in the four process areas, but the extent of retardation in each area may vary. For example, planning will be the overarching deficit of many individuals with mental retardation who lack rehearsal strategies and the ability for social judgment.

ATTENTION DEFICIT DISORDER

Deficits of attention in children can be due to many causes. Attention deficit hyperactivity disorder—AD-HD—is a developmental disability of behavior in which attentional deficits appear to be primary symptoms, as do hyperactivity, impulsivity, and noncompliance. Although the name for this behavior disorder has varied over the years, there is considerable consensus among researchers and clinicians regarding primary and secondary symptomatology and exclusionary criteria (Ross & Ross, 1982). The description of AD-HD–like children goes back to at least 1960, but even long before that the diagnosis was masterfully summarized by Still (1902). Still identified are deficits of attention, moral consciousness, responsibility to discipline, emotional maturity, and social conduct as the characteristics of some children, despite apparently adequate child rearing and environmental stimulation. These children were distinguished from those with established brain damage and those with neurological signs suggestive of brain damage. AD-HD–like children were viewed, nevertheless, as medical problems, though it should be emphasized that this was as much by necessity as by design since other forms of child mental health services were either in their infancy or nonexistent.

In part, because AD-HD–like children were seen as medical problems and had certain characteristics in common with brain-injured children, this disorder came to be associated with neurological damage (Strauss & Lehtinen, 1947). Since brain-damaged children could be restless, inattentive, impulsive, noncompliant, and so on, the children who showed these behaviors were thought to be brain damaged. The tautological nature of this argument was exposed by Sarason (1949), but treatment and in particular educational practices were formulated and in some places maintained into the 1980s according to a brain injury model. The minimal stimulation classroom and its more "integrative" equivalent, the individual study carrel, became the means to deal with supposed distractibility. Teachers were advised to wear plain clothing and no jewelry. Classroom walls were grey or beige and part of an austere environment. Although some brain-injured children may need such unstimulating environs, it has repeatedly been demonstrated that AD-HD children do not. In fact, these children are not distractible in the same sense as brain-injured children.

Because hyperactivity, i.e., a high level of activity inappropriate to situations and not readily inhibited by command, is one of the most common behaviors of AD-HD children, this symptom has been a major focus for naming this disorder (e.g., hyperkinetic syndrome). However, through the collaborative research of Douglas and associates at McGill University and Ackerman, Clements, Dykman, and Peters at the University of Arkansas (Douglas & Peters, 1979), *impaired attention* has become a central diagnostic concept. This shift in focus was reflected in accepting hyperactivity and impaired attention as inseparable facets of Hyperkinetic Reaction of Childhood *(DSM-II),* which is separated into Attention Deficit Disorder with and without hyperactivity in *DSM-III* (1980). The fact that hyperactivity is a very common feature of this behavioral disturbance has been reaffirmed in the revised *DSM-III* (1987) category of Attention Deficit-Hyperactive Disorder. But whereas the overactivity symptom usually subsides by adolescence, a fact which was initially misinterpreted to mean that children grew out of the disorder, it is now recognized that the attentional difficulties continue throughout adolescence and adult life (Wender, 1987). The primary focus of research of AD-HD has consequently become an understanding of the attentional deficits of these children and how these deficits can influence their social behavior as well as cognitive development.

Assessment of Cognitive Characteristics of Children with ADD

Identifying the cognitive characteristics of individuals with an attention deficit disorder (ADD) has been a difficult task. Several methods of assessing this syndrome have been employed with varying degrees of success. For example, while research involving extraneous, peripheral distractors has not provided convincing evidence that hyperactive children are more distractible than normals, investigations using measures of sustained attention, impulsivity, and planning provide evidence that they have cognitive deficits in these areas (Douglas & Peters, 1979; Hallahan & Reeve, 1980; Whalen, 1983; Douglas, 1980).

What are these deficits and the tests that measure them? Rosenthal and Allen (1978) stated that ADD children are reported by teachers, parents, and clinicians to be distractible and to exhibit short attention spans, low frustration tolerance, and impulsive behavioral patterns. Other researchers state that the failure to invest, organize, and maintain attention and effort and the inability to modulate arousal levels to meet task demands are the pervasive cognitive deficits that characterize the ADD syndrome (Douglas, 1980; Keogh & Margolis, 1976).

Studies involving instruments that measure attention, impulsivity, and planning have been marginally effective in differentiating between normal and AD-HD groups. For instance, while the Stroop Color-Word test (Stroop, 1935) has been used as a measure of selective attention, it has not successfully differentiated between hyperactive and normal subjects, nor has it been sensitive to drug therapy (Cohen, Weiss, & Minde, 1972). Cohen Weiss, and Minde (1972) note, however, that hyperactive children do make more errors of commission and fewer self-corrections while engaged in the task.

The test quotient (*t* quotient) of the Porteus Maze task, which is presumed to be a measure of planning and attention, has accurately discriminated between hyperactive and nonhyperactive groups. However, the qualitative score, which is considered a measure of impulsivity, has not demonstrated significant between-group differences (Sprague & Sleator, 1976; Kuehne, Kehle, & McMahon, 1987).

The Continuous Performance Test (CPT) (Rosvold et al., 1956), and Kagan's Matching Familiar Figures Test (MFFT) (Kagan, 1965) have for a long time differentiated between hyperactive and normal children. These tasks are viewed as measures of sustained attention (Rosvold et al., 1956) and reflectivity-impulsivity (Kagan, 1965). Sykes et al. (1971), Sykes, Douglas, and Morgenstern (1972, 1973), and others (Doyle, Anderson & Halcomb, 1976; Dykman, et al., 1971) have shown that, when compared to normal children, hyperactive children identify fewer target stimuli and respond more frequently to incorrect stimulus sequences while completing the CPT. Their performance also deteriorates more severely over time (15 minutes) than does that of normal children. The performance of hyperactive children on the MFFT is characterized by fewer eye fixations, fewer stimulus pair comparisons, and more rapid response production than that of normals (Nelson, 1969; Seigelman, 1969). Typically, ADD children approach the MFFT in a disorganized manner, they tend to have shorter response latencies, give less consideration to alternative solutions, and make more errors in judgment than do normal subjects (Campbell & Werry, 1986; Cohen, Weiss, & Minde, 1972).

Although many instruments have been utilized as measures of sustained and selective attention (CPT, Stroop), impulsivity (MFFT), planning (Porteus Maze), inconsistent findings and the lack of a theoretical base from which to understand and interpret processes measured by the tests diminish their diagnostic value. Because constructs such as distractibility, selectivity, impulsivity, and planning have been operationalized and measured in a variety of ways, there exists considerable confusion and inconsistency in the conceptualization of attentional capacities and related disorders (Douglas & Peters, 1979; Krupski, 1980; Rosenthal & Allen, 1978).

LD and ADD Children

The possibility that learning-disabled children have an attention deficit has been studied by many investigators who considered that reading failure was related to distractibility, or the failure to attend selectively (Ross, 1976;

Copeland & Reiner, 1984). However, there has been little evidence that distractibility can explain low WISC-R third factor scores (i.e., Digit Span, Arithmetic, and Coding) (Stewart & Moely, 1983). The evidence in favor of linking selective attention disorder to reading disability has been inconclusive (Samuels & Miller, 1985). The equivocal findings in this area appear to be due to a number of problems in the theories and methodology (Fleisher, Sodak, & Jelin, 1984).

Krupski (1986) objected to regarding distractibility as a general trait and criticized many studies that try to show that learning-disabled individuals are distractible. Similarly, Ford, Pelham, and Ross (1984) have shown that memory and attention are often confounded in tasks used to test the selective attention capacity of the learning disabled. These authors have concluded that reading-disabled children evidence defective *rehearsal strategies* rather than deficiencies in selective attention. This indicates that the attention tasks used by some researchers who have separated learning-disabled from nondisabled children using measures involving discrimination, selectivity, and complex stimulus analysis (e.g., Ford, Pelham, & Ross, 1984; Copeland & Reiner, 1984) may be confounded with planning. If the learning disabled are weak in planning, then their separation from normals on the basis of tasks intended to measure attention may need to be attributed to planning. The difficulty with these studies, therefore, may have been the result of confounded tasks and the interrelationship between planning and attention. The learning disabled appear to be deficient in planning, while the attention deficit individual's primary difficulty is with attention.

The difference between the ADD and LD populations is, conceptually, related to the specific process deficiency as well as the breadth of the deficiency. The ADD individual would be expected to be deficient in several processes, with a marked deficiency in attention, while the LD individual is more likely to be deficient in one of planning, simultaneous or successive processing. In general, planning deficiency influences attentional functioning more than simultaneous or successive processes because of the close relationship between the first and third functional units. This close relationship is found in the results of factor analysis as well (see Naglieri, Prewett, & Bardos, 1989).

PASS Tasks and ADD Children

Reardon and Naglieri (1991) investigated the utility of planning, attention, simultaneous and successive cognitive processing tasks with a sample of students identified as having an attention deficit disorder. The ADD subjects were matched with a sample of normal subjects on the basis of age (from 7 to 12 years), sex, race, and socioeconomic status. The experimental subjects were diagnosed as Attention-Deficit/Hyperactivity disorder (AD-HD Code 314.01, *DSM-III-R,* 1987) by the supervising psychiatrist at a university child psychiatric clinic. The assessment procedures comprised parent and child interviews, clinical observations, behavioral rating scales (e.g., Achenbach & Edelbrock, 1983), and measures of cognitive vigilance and selective attention (Gordon's Diagnostic Battery [Gordon, 1983]). The results showed that the ADD group earned significantly lower scores than the normals in the areas of planning, attention, and successive processing, but no significant difference was found on the simultaneous processing tests.

These results differ from those reported here for the learning disabled in two important ways. First, the ADD group investigated by Reardon and Naglieri evidenced deficiencies on attention tasks as well as planning and successive processes. Only on simultaneous tasks did this group perform like the control group. Thus, the ADD group evidenced significant and substantial cognitive deficits in three out of the four processes.

SUMMARY

The nature of exceptional children from the perspective of the PASS model of cognitive processing is still emerging and therefore no firm conclusions can be made at this time. We suggest, however, that on the basis of current information, that there are important cognitive processing patterns that may distinguish between different types of learning disabled (reading-disabled, math-disabled, etc.), as well as different types of retarded individuals (e.g., Down's versus non-Down's samples). Additionally, those with ADD are also likely to show a different pattern of PASS cognitive processes than others without this dysfunction. We strongly encourage researchers to examine distinct groups of exceptional individuals to gain an understanding of their cognitive processing profiles and to determine the extent to which initial research may be clarified by their efforts.

9

FROM ASSESSMENT TO REMEDIATION

We assess to place the child in an appropriate instructional environment; this was in fact the aim of Binet. The objective of cognitive assessment is to facilitate the education of children. Unfortunately, traditionally assessment has been employed in the past as an instrument for selection that has frequently led to denying quality education and preferred jobs. We should assess children in order to help them. The overall aim of assessment is not to label the deficiencies, but to observe and monitor them and, where possible, help those whom we assess.

Children's approach to a task is demonstrated during assessment. Therefore, a necessary by-product of assessment is the opportunity to observe how the individual approaches a test, especially when such individuals have handicaps in learning, thinking, or adaptive behavior. Thus, test taking provides an occasion for the psychologist to understand the individual's cognitive functions. A related outcome of assessment is the construction of training and remedial programs for the amelioration of the individual's handicap. In fact, many argue that this should be the sole reason for assessment—that its only legitimate purpose should be to facilitate the design of remediation.

In the background of such assumptions, let us examine the literature on remedial training, especially as it relates to an improvement of learning and thinking. The terms *learning* and *thinking* are purposefully used in a loose sense to include a wide range of remedial programs that focus on improvement of mild mental handicaps and learning disabilities. The disabilities can be either idiopathic (due to unknown causes) or caused by neurological impairment. A quick review of attempts at remediation reveals that there is inconclusive evidence in support of their efficacy. Although this is true for both idiopathic and organic conditions that promote learning disabilities, we shall concentrate on the unexplained variety of learning disabilities in this chapter.

REMEDIATION AND DIRECT TEACHING OF PHONOLOGICAL SKILLS

A quick overview of the psychoeducational research since 1986 relating to remediation of reading disability will show that most of the remedial programs are not supported by either hard or consistent evidence in regard to their efficacy, and the majority of them are based on no theory at all or on poorly conceived theories. We would like to think that our remediation research is an exception. It is effective within the range of average general abilities and it is obviously based on a theoretical model.

More specifically, we are concentrating on remediation of reading and to a lesser extent on arithmetic skills. But in doing so we are not suggesting a teaching of the curriculum in reading and arithmetic. For, as we shall show in reviewing the existing studies, the teaching of curriculum has not succeeded. Teachers teach curriculum all the time, and the good teachers do it well. In spite of this, a fair number of children cannot acquire reading adequately, even though they are of normal or superior intelligence. They have an unexplained deficit in reading. In the previous chapters we have tried to explain their deficit in terms of the PASS model. Now we discuss remedial training as a sequel to the identification of their processing deficits. We should state at the beginning that a review of the remedial training research published in recent years clearly shows the limited efficacy of direct curriculum teaching; where substantial gains and transfer have been found, some general strategies have been taught as well.

More Teaching of Curriculum

Extensive examples of direct curriculum teaching are found in textbooks. We cite three instances to illustrate the practice of direct teaching of word recognition and phonic skills. We consider first a popular book by Harris and Sipay (1980) in its seventh edition, entitled How to Increase Reading Ability. The portion relevant for the present chapter is teaching of decoding skills. These include the teaching of grapheme-phoneme association mainly for consonants, morphemic analysis and structural analysis (breaking a word down to syllables and subsyllables). What is the best method of teaching these skills? The authors state that the evidence is inconclusive. No critical review of the evidence in terms of well-conducted experimental studies is given, probably because it does not exist in the literature.

The next example is a publication that is research oriented (Miller, 1988). Miller's book provides guidelines for direct teaching for remedial purposes. After recommending that remediation should be specifically based on diagnosis, the method for remediation becomes a teaching of phonics if the diagnosis reveals a deficit in phonics. More specifically, if the child has difficulty in short vowel sounds, teach that as the skill to be acquired. "Follow the methods of teaching in elementary classrooms" is the advice given by the author. We see nothing wrong in this except that the specific reading disability manifested in decoding deficiency can be the consequence of a cognitive deficit not involving reading at all, as we argue in this chapter.

Our last example is from a recent and popular textbook (Ekwall & Shanker, 1988) that does refer to cognitive functions, but only in the context of cognitive styles; field dependence/independence and impulsivity/reflectivity are considered briefly. However, remedial teaching is not thought to be practical if attention is given to these stylistic differences. Ekwall and Shanker's recommendations for remedial teaching of phonics and structural analyses are similar to those of Harris and Sipay; they emphasize the need for direct instruction in these skills.

Efficacy of remedial training can be established only by an adequate research design. By this we mean that (1) the criteria for selection of children as reading disabled should be objective and valid, and (2) a proper statistical design involving treated and untreated groups of reading disabled children who meet the criteria must be adopted. To our knowledge, the direct teaching of reading as exemplified in the textbooks has not been properly evaluated for their efficacy.

The *conclusions* that emerge from reviewing remediation research are given in Lovett, Ransby, et al. (1989). Citing several previous reviews, they conclude as follows: (1) Word recognition is a pervasive problem with reading disabled children. This is now widely accepted. (2) Not many studies have used adequate designs to support the efficacy of a remedial method. Rather, most studies lack specific information in this regard. (3) The treatment research literature is full of opinionated and unscientific studies.

Problems of Phonemic Training

There is a need not only for specifying the designs and basing them on some theoretical rationale, but also to define the group of children receiving remediation. Do the treated children show decoding difficulties without any deficiency in listening comprehension, or do they show deficient performance in both? Phonemic training as used by Lovett, Ransby, et al.

(1989) and reported in detail (Lovett, Benson, & Olds, 1990) does not aim at improvement in comprehension, unless of course, reading rather than listening comprehension is tested. On the other hand, if improvement in comprehension is to be the aim of remediation, then other methods instead of phonemic training should be used.

A second concern is transfer and maintenance. If the effect of phonemic training, for example, does not transfer to new words and pseudowords, then word recognition difficulty has not been remediated. Similarly, if comprehension of new passages is not demonstrated without frequent prompting of the strategies taught to the disabled reader, then the remedial training is of course not successful. We shall discuss transfer in a later section of this chapter; however, unless the cognitive processes underlying decoding or comprehension are the focus of remediation, then remediation will not work. The simple teaching of phonetic skills or atheoretical strategies and tricks does not constitute adequate remediation.

Consider Lovett and her group's attempt at remediation of word recognition and spelling (Lovett, Warren-Chaplin, et al., 1990; Lovett, Benson, & Olds, 1990; Lovett, Ransby, et al., 1989). The last two papers are based on the same empirical study. The remedial treatments were decoding skills contrasted with oral and written language skills. The researchers hoped that the decoding skill training group would be better at recognition of regular and exceptional words, whereas the others would show improvement in contextual reading and oral skills. Maintenance of the profit from remediation was not tested. The results show limited transfer of decoding skills for the first training group; although more new words were recognized, pseudowords were not, and the grapheme-phoneme correspondence principles, which were the object of remedial treatment, were not grasped. The researchers concluded that the children's word recognition improvements were not dependent on new knowledge about grapheme-phoneme rules, but may be attributed to learning specific to each individual word. In a subsequent experiment on decoding skills training, the children "again failed to show any post-test advantage on instructed vocabulary" (Lovett, Warren-Chaplin, et al., 1990, p. 777).

Another remediation study attempting to improve decoding used computer synthesized speech. Reading-disabled students read entire stories on the computer screen and "targeted" any word they could not pronounce. The computer can then give five different kinds of feedback: It utters the whole word that was targeted, utters the syllables, further breaks down the syllables to subsyllables, gives a combination of first the subsyllable followed by syllable feedback, and, lastly, gives no feedback (the control condition). Although the subjects improved in their speed of recognizing words when given the same stories to read, they did not improve in the word recognition test included in the Peabody Individualized Achievement Test (Dunn & Markwardt, 1970). Transfer effects marked by a permanent improvement in reading new words were therefore not clear. The purpose of discussing these carefully carried out investigations on remedial training is of course not so much to critique them, but to suggest that decoding training itself without training the underlying processes may not work.

Information Processing Training—An Alternative

Inability to engage spontaneously in phonological analysis while reading words may itself be a symptom of cognitive deficit. Within the context of our theoretical framework (see Chapter 4), decoding at the initial stages requires successive processing, although both successive and simultaneous processing are involved beyond the initial stage of decoding. Such discoveries have provided compelling reasons to look beyond reading training itself, including phonological aspects of decoding, and to remediate the information processing deficit. That has been our approach to remediation, as we shall describe in later sections of this chapter.

The persons who have done most of the research noted for its orientation toward information processing (outside the PASS model) are LaBerge and Samuels (1974). In a recent study, for instance, Samuels and Miller (1985) discussed the role of attention, visual memory, phonological memory, and semantic memory in reading difficulties. They suggested that absence of automaticity in decoding is the main deficit. Because of this lack of automaticity, the attentional system is overloaded, heavy demands are placed on memory, and comprehension is adversely affected. Following from this premise, therefore, a remedial program should be focused on developing automatic decoding. Rapid sequential naming exercises have been prescribed. This is the strategy that should be worked out for the classroom, according to Samuels and Miller. However, the emphasis on decoding without comprehension during the training program must have a limited effect as it would not take into account the roles of context and inferencing when words occur in a text. It also does not consider the deficit in cognitive processes of which decoding failure may be a symptom.

TOWARD A THEORY OF REMEDIATION

In constructing materials for remediation and devising techniques for using those materials, expediency and practical concerns have played a larger role than theories. Attempts at remediation including cognitive intervention have perhaps continued since the beginning of literacy; a relatively recent landmark is Itard's wild boy of Aveyron. Not going as far back as

Itard, and considering more recent research on remediation relating to the cognitive deficits of mildly mentally handicapped and learning disabled individuals, can we impose a conceptual framework? What are the sources that have influenced research on remediation? What are the theoretical roots we can reasonably delineate?

We can find in remediation research four theoretical roots. These are: (1) the research into memory, especially into its structure and control processes; (2) early experience and intellectual development, the research that was pioneered by Hebb; (3) learning styles and teaching strategies in the tradition of aptitude-treatment interaction; and, finally, (4) Vygotsky's views on learning, maturation, and the role of instruction. Let us consider each one separately.

The first root is in a model of memory, its structure and control processes. Atkinson and Shiffrin (1968) proposed a box model of long- and short-term memory which has since become quite influential (see Chapters 3 and 4). It had a great influence on researchers in the field of mental retardation who saw a possibility of improvement in memory of the retarded through the control processes suggested in the Atkinson-Shiffrin model (Belmont & Butterfield, 1971). The control processes serve a number of functions such as the maintenance of information in short-term memory and transfer of information from short- to long-term memory as well. Later research has begun to cast some doubt about the necessity of all information to first enter short-term memory before it can be transferred to long-term memory (see Chapter 4). The control processes, which include rehearsal and chunking, still survive as basic mechanisms for enhancing memory (see Chapter 5). These processes were fully utilized in techniques for teaching strategies for better learning and memory by a number of researchers since 1971 (Belmont & Butterfield, 1971). Among these techniques are simple instructions to use some strategies, presenting materials in a specific form that will require the use of a particular strategy, modeling techniques in which the experimenter demonstrates this strategy, fading, and prompting, which have all been described previously (Ellis,1979). How useful these techniques are, however, is doubtful. As several reviews, including Resnick's (1981), have pointed out, instructing individuals or letting them model strategies such as rehearsal has not resulted in a transfer of the learned skill. Therefore, the same group of researchers, joined by new ones such as Pellegrino and Glaser (1979) and Brown and Campione (1981), is formulating programs for future research that emphasize the development of general learning skills. As expected in the current spirit of the times, metacognition has crept into most of those new techniques. Current research, therefore, considers transfer as the primary aim for training in control processes, and there is much speculation concerning the teaching of strategies.

For example, consider Paris's suggestions for teaching strategies in reading. Paris and his colleagues (Jacobs & Paris, 1987; Paris, Cross, & Lipson, 1984; Paris, Lipson, & Wixson, 1983) have developed an experimental reading curriculum called Informed Strategies for Learning (ISL). They stress that children need to understand the need for and uses of reading strategies before those strategies can be properly learned and transferred. In other words, the children's strategy use must be "informed." Their program emphasizes these metacognitive goals in strategy instruction and has shown some success (Paris, Cross, & Lipson, 1984).

The second root that can be identified lies in the work of Hebb and his associates and students on sensory deprivation. Sensory deprivation has a deleterious effect on cognitive growth in animals and is the obverse of early stimulation, which has been shown to influence and accelerate cognitive development. Haywood and Tapp (1966) summarized this work. They mentioned three different kinds of deprivation conditions that have been tried on animals: (1) extreme sensory deprivations that involve giving no opportunity for sensory stimulation through vision, hearing, and so on; (2) social isolation and (3) unimodal deprivation by which the animal is made insensitive to a particular kind of sensory stimulation such as hearing or vision. They support early intervention based on the early work of McV. Hunt, who showed that not only rats but humans may profit from early stimulation. Following this review, Das (1973) has elaborated on the implications of cultural deprivation and its effect on cognitive competence and has critically examined the efficacy of early education and its relationship to sensory deprivation experiments. He concluded that the disadvantaged individuals we are likely to study have seldom been subjected to the extent of social and sensory deprivation that characterize studies on animals. However, education, early or late, as shown by Feuerstein (Feuerstein, 1979; Feuerstein & Hamburger, 1965) does improve cognitive abilities that might have been adversely affected by cultural deprivation. Compensatory education for disadvantaged children derives its impetus from the research on early experience.

The push for early stimulation as well as compensatory education has influenced the treatment of learning disabled children who are not culturally disadvantaged. Diagnosis of dyslexia at an early preschool age and treatment for the defective function have been widely recommended; Bradley and Bryant's (1983) work provides an instance of this prevalent trend. They noticed that potentially reading-disabled preschoolers were deficient in detecting rhyming, and they devised a program that strengthened the children's perception of rhyming words and increased their reading performance. Feuerstein (1979) attempted to remediate deficits in intentional learning by an interactive instructional procedure.

The third root of remedial training may lie in aptitude-treatment interactions. The matching of learning styles and teaching strategies has been quite popular for some time because of the common sense notion that the two should fit. Cronbach and Snow (1977) have written masterly reviews of aptitude-treatment interaction research. Most of the research offers mild support for the effectiveness of matching aptitudes to treatments. Reading requires many skills and can be performed in different ways; remediation could either try to overcome the weaknesses or work on the strengths (Kirby, 1980). On the other hand, it is not clear that qualitatively different approaches to reading, of equal merit, are possible (Kirby, 1988); this suggests remediation of weak processes may be required, if they are accurately identified.

The fourth root is the influential work of Vygotsky, specifically his contentions that learning is a collaborative effort and instruction need not always follow the level of intellectual maturity of children (see also Das & Conway, 1992). In fact, the purpose of education is to accelerate the cognitive development of the child. Children's existing level of cognitive competence may not indicate their potential; hence a teach-test-teach-test paradigm is recommended. "What children can do with assistance of others might be in some sense even more indicative of their mental development than what they can do alone" (Vygotsky, 1978, p. 85).

Through formal instruction, children acquire scientific concepts and are able to refine their experiential concepts. On the other hand, it is only through experience that scientific concepts acquire a broader base in the cognitive domain of the individual, which facilitates their application in new situations. Thus, the tradition of Vygotsky has influenced the mediated training and dynamic testing approaches of Feuerstein. At the same time it has begun to direct our attention toward the preconditions for transfer of training.

Vygotsky compares children to raw fruits in the field yet to mature fully, and thus their *potential for development* must be considered by any measure of ability. Such notions of Vygotsky have led to much talk and some research on the efficacy of "dynamic testing" and "instrumental enrichment" (Lidz, 1987). Instruction and mediated learning are the key concepts. Instruction may take place in formal or informal settings; the mediators can be peers or adults. But the central point is that learned skills have a social origin and, even more broadly stated, cognitive processes have a sociohistorical origin especially as these depend on a system of signs, which is commonly called language.

Following Vygotsky's leadership in the Soviet Union, new research and thinking on education have evolved, although the literature is almost entirely in Russian. As gleaned from the infrequent English articles of Vygotsky's intellectual successors such as Leontiev, Luria, Elkonin, and Davydov, research has shown that a psychologically based instruction could highly stimulate the mental development of the child, permitting younger children to acquire new forms of thinking (Leontiev & Luria, 1972).

VYGOTSKIAN CONCEPTS AND IMPLICATIONS FOR REMEDIATION

The concepts of Vygotsky and their applications to dynamic testing and intervention have been the topics of recent books (Lidz, 1987; Haywood & Tsuriel, 1992). Here we shall look particularly at his theories of internalization, mediation, and development.

Internalization and Mediation

Vygotsky's two major concepts relevant to mediation are internalization and sociocultural mediation. They determine, as well as characterize, mental activity.

Internalization can be found at many levels of children's activity; two of these are internalization of instruction and of language. Children learn through collaboration with others. Whenever children are given external instruction, either by another person or from reading books and manuals, they have to make the instructions their own. They have to know them and realize their meaning and feel thoroughly familiar with them so that the instructions become a part of their own thinking. In doing so, children transform the external to internal codes, changing and modifying the original, and thus stamping it with their unique cognitive character. The process of internalization takes long to develop (Wertsch & Stone, 1985). Internal speech is an excellent example of the process of internalization. It has its own code, it is a language system unique to an individual, and it is not isomorphic to external speech. The quality of internal speech—or, in common language, *ideas*—determines competence in thinking. Likewise, disturbances in the individual's inner speech are shown in thought disorders. Loss of internal speech codes is manifested as loss of language, or aphasia.

Signs and Their Role in Internalization and Mediation

The process of internalization of activity is assisted by language, both external and internal. Language itself is a sociocultural product. It is a system of signs, a mental tool. The meaning of signs is acquired, of course, through work and experience. Since an individual does not work alone, that is, in a vacuum without any context or purpose, or without using labor-saving tools and products of thought, all human activities have sociocultural roots (see Vygotsky [1978] and Wertsch [1985] for elaboration and critique). The point of interest for remedial instruction is the *quality* of internalization—not how *much* of internalization has taken place following instruction, but what is its quality. The ingredient that contributes most to a high quality is reflection on the material of instruction. Without reflection, rote learning of instruction does not qualify as internalization and does not facilitate transfer of learning.

We think internalization can be understood as a matrix of meanings that regulates the individual's activities. The pattern of interactions within this matrix changes qualitatively and characterizes stages of development. The factors that contribute to the matrix are ontological, entailing sociocultural and genetic influences; the latter may impose some limiting conditions, as in the case of the mentally retarded. Vygotsky recognized the existence of limiting conditions while accepting children's potential to improve their performance with the help of mediators such as their peers and instructors.

"An individual's activity assimilates the experience of humankind"—this statement by Leontiev (cited in Wertsch & Stone, 1985) is the essence of the theoretical context of Vygotsky and the other developmental psychologists after him who have improved his theory. To quote Vygotsky:

> *Any function in the child's cultural development appears on the scene twice or on two planes. It appears first on the social plane and only then on the psychological. It appears first between people as an intermental category and then within the child as an intramental category. This is equally true of voluntary attention, logical memory, concept formation, and the development of volition. (Minick, 1987)*

Mental functions have both a historical and a personal basis. They first appear in collaborative social interactions. Thus, *mediation* appears as a blending of two separate factors, which are integration (assimilation in Piaget's sense) and the history of the individual's experience; the individual is a member of a social-cultural group. Mediation can be activated from within the individual when formal and informal learning has been interiorized. Therefore, what is required for mediation to arise from within is a psychological tool. This is provided by internal speech, a system of signs or symbols that has evolved in the history of the culture. Signs, or the system of meanings they represent, mediate between stimuli and responses (Davydov & Radzikhovskii, 1985). Signs can be as simple as mnemonic devices for remembering a list of disconnected words or as complex as words and sentences that represent complex matrices of relationships.

The psychological tool of systems of meanings bears a strong resemblance to Pavlov's second signal system (Pavlov, 1942). A system of signals of primary signals is how Pavlov described the verbal system. Vygotsky's sign meaning is much more developed and refined, but the idea is essentially the same.

The foregoing discussion on internalization and the theoretical aspects of mediation can provoke a fresh look at the "verbal deficit" of learning-disabled children and a consideration of zones of proximal development as a key concept in remedial training.

Zones of Proximal Development

Zones of proximal development (ZPD) has become a central concept for understanding what remediation achieves and hence is a familiar topic in the remediation literature today. Rogoff and Wertsch (1984) offer a good description of the concept and its use in American research. Their book even offers a sociopolitical analysis of the concept by Bruner. Unfortunately, the original writings of Vygotsky on ZPD are not extensive. The concept could not be developed too well because, as the Russian researchers Davydov and Radzikhovskii (1985) observe, it had no theoretical superstructure. Vygotsky did not have much time to develop the concept because of his illness and premature death, although in spite of this, his writings run into six volumes in Russian. Most contemporary American researchers have not read Vygotsky's writings. Minick (1987), an American researcher, is translating them and has written a detailed review of the concept and its use by American researchers.

The ZPD literally translated should be *zone of nearest development* (Minick, 1987). It is described by Vygotsky (1978) as "the distance between the actual developmental level as determined by independent problem solving and the level of potential development as determined through problem solving under adult guidance or in collaboration with more capable peers" (pp. 85–86).

The earliest American research on ZPD was published by Budoff and Friedman in 1964; it used a test-train-test paradigm to obtain a quantitative measure of improvement or progress through ZPD. A recent book edited by Lidz (1987) contains many coherent treatments of ZPD. In this book, Brown and Campione report the use of a quantitative measure that is the number of prompts required for the learner to progress through the task. They do not claim to be measuring ZPD. Minick does not think that the essential characteristics of ZPD have survived the American attempt to quantify it; the concept does not lend itself to quantitative measurement. He is correct in pointing out that "[i]n outlining the concept of ZPD, Vygotsky was proposing a new theoretical framework for analyzing the child's current state of development and for predicting the next or the proximal level of development that the child might be expected to attain" (Minick, 1987, p. 3).

We would argue that the two important purposes for using ZPD are (1) studying cognitive development whithin a sociocultural context and (2) diagnosis.

Cognitive development can be seen as a product that is the consequence of the individual learning in collaboration with others. The context of learning is provided by the symbiotic relation between personal characteristics and social milieu. One is reminded here that in this relationship, the "natural" predispositions of the individual are confounded with sociocultural influences. ZPD cannot be measured: it has no baseline because it is not a characteristic of the learner. The product that is observable is cognitive activity. Cognitive activities are filtered through the prism of development (Luria, 1963) and thus have to be analyzed into basic components that may differ at different stages of development. We should remember that development is an integration of sociohistorical and genetic factors.

Diagnosis is the second purpose of considering ZPD. Budoff's early research was based on Luria's in which children who may have the same low score on a cognitive task at an initial testing may demonstrate small or large improvements after a period of intensive interaction with a mediator. Thus, ZPD "determines the domain of transitions that are accessible to the child" (cited in Minick, 1987). Luria was faced with the task of establishing a diagnosis of mental retardation for a large number of children whose initial intelligence scores were low. Some of these children improved substantially following what Feuerstein calls "mediated experience," whereas others showed little improvement. The truly retarded are of the last category; they have abnormal cognitive processing in addition to their failure to gain from mediated experience.

COGNITIVE INTERVENTION WITH THE LEARNING DISABLED AND MENTALLY RETARDED

The learning disabled are regarded as normal in Soviet psychology, but temporarily retarded. They do not benefit from normal instruction and may have specific disabilities in cognitive processing. But the assumption is that the specific disability can be circumvented with the help of appropriate collaborative effort. Learning-disabled children can use speech and language and can benefit from verbal instruction. In contrast, it is thought that the mentally retarded (1) cannot use knowledge obtained in the course of speech communication, (2) are unable to assimilate verbal instructions in a generalized form, and (3) have limited ability to use language as a means of independent thinking (Luria, 1963). The way to improve cognitive behavior of the mentally retarded is *not* through verbal instructions and "metacognitive" procedures because both rely heavily on a complex semantic system (sign meanings in Vygotsky's terms).

Verbal deficits associated with LD are not general as with the mentally retarded. They are specific and open to change. They are found in lexical access to phonology and semantics as well as in the knowledge of linguistic rules. But the deficits are not restricted to processing verbal material; they appear in nonverbal tasks such as Figure Copying as well (Das, Bisanz, & Mancini, 1985). A deficit when found frequently involves both verbal and nonverbal domains. It involves certain aspects of using signs.

We have explained the types of these difficulties by the coding processes in our PASS theory (Das, Kirby, & Jarman, 1979), relating the use of successive processing to learning of decoding skills and predominantly simultaneous processing to comprehension. "Whereas *both* processes are necessary at a lower level of competence in reading, it is *simultaneous* processing that makes for better comprehension rather than successive processing at higher levels where adequate vocabulary and decoding skills are required" (Das, 1984c, p. 39).

The question is, can these significant processing skills be taught (mediationally) and internalized sufficiently to be a part of the learning disabled child's own repertoire? Briefly, for the LD child, the answer is yes: Training in the use of successive and simultaneous processes, together with attention and planning, improves decoding and comprehension.

PERSPECTIVES ON TRANSFER

Developmental Considerations

Transfer is an integral part of not only learning, but development. When learning and development are considered to be inextricably blended together, transfer may become the essential ingredient for children's cognitive growth. "Development consists in part of going from the context-dependent state where resources are welded to the original learning situation to a *relatively* context-independent state where the learner extends the ways in which initially highly constrained knowledge and procedures are used" (Brown et al., 1983, p. 142).

Transfer need not be mediated by verbal instruction, nor does it need to be conceptualized by external speech, or even represented by inner speech. For if it were, animals could not be shown to transfer learning. Thus, the question is not whether mentally handicapped children or learning-disabled children can transfer what they learn, but what kind of learning are we targeting for transfer?

Brown and Campione (1986) have discussed the conditions of successful transfer in a number of papers. They emphasize principles as a target of transfer; these are based on inductive inferencing arising out of children's experience with the tasks rather than on the explicit teaching of principles. The children come up with the principle or the essential similarities between separate instantiations of the principle; even 3-year-old children can do this. Brown and Campione (1986) recommend, following Vygotsky, that learning take place in collaboration with peers and experts. A scaffold, an adjustable and temporary support, is to be provided to children for promoting their conceptual understanding of a set of similar problems; then transfer of learning becomes possible.

If both learning and transfer must be represented in a complex system of sign meanings, mentally retarded children cannot be successful in either of them. Luria's (1963) observation in regard to their weakness in the verbal system is basically correct: Mentally retarded children cannot use the information obtained through speech for generalization or transfer, and they have only a limited capacity for using language for thinking. Perhaps that is why in our research on process training (Conway, 1985), we observed that the retarded children failed to benefit from remediation.

The language deficit of mentally retarded individuals has reappeared in a new garb—mental retardation is being *defined* as failure of self-regulation (Whitman, 1990)! From Luria's original research on the role of speech in regulating activity and from the Vygotskian perspective, we can regard speech and language deficit not solely as an *individual* handicap, but in the social-historical context of the retarded individual. That is why the remedial program must be entrenched in that context, its efficacy cannot depend on teaching the retarded individual to regulate behavior by improving his or her language facility, although Whitman (1990) seems to think that it should.

Spontaneous transfer does not appear even for individuals who are adept at using the verbal system (mathematical symbols and inner speech included). Brown et al. (1983) note its absence in problem-solving situations such as in doing the Tower of Hanoi task. They recommend prompts and hints. The assumption is that individuals must be helped to see how a general principle may apply to a specific situation. Strategy teaching is not enough unless we also teach where to use what strategy. This task becomes formidable if IQ is in the retarded range. Such children need to be prompted frequently, which itself decreases the chances for transfer. The greater the number of prompts during training, the less the transfer.

We wish to suggest that in process training the behavior targeted for transfer is to be guided by principles or rules that have been learned. How that learning should take place, whether deductively by explicit step-by-step instruction or through inductive inferencing, will be discussed later. But let us distinguish between *three bases of transfer* following the ideas of E. L. Thorndike (Hilgard & Bower, 1956).

Basis of Transfer

Transfer of learning to a new situation may occur when the original and the new situations are (1) similar in content, (2) similar in procedure, or (3) share the same principle of learning. The greater the number of identical content elements in the old and the new situation, the stronger is the transfer. That has been shown in strategy training studies on mentally retarded subjects by Belmont and Butterfield (1977) and Borkowski and Cavanaugh (1979). Its application is limited because the transfer based on the number of identical elements is too narrow; hence pessimism surrounding the generalizability of strategy training with the mentally retarded has become widespread (Das, 1985).

The second type of transfer can occur if the procedure of learning is similar, even if the content is different. For instance, serial recall shows the typical bowing curve in spite of differences in content of learning; training that concentrates on the rehearsal of the middle items (which are involved in the 'bow') may elevate the subject's recall score. Other tasks with procedural similarities but which are far different in content are shown in common test-taking skills. Because of such similarities, subjects may improve in their test scores as they are exposed to more than one test, even if the tests are heterogeneous in content (e.g., memory and abstract reasoning). Feuerstein (1979) utilizes transfer of this type to a great extent in his instrumental enrichment procedures.

The third kind of transfer, of principle, is the aim of all "cognitive strategy" training because it should result in "far transfer." General strategy training aims at far transfer; the tacit assumption here is that we can teach an overarching set of principles that help the learner while traveling in a new land (Kirby, 1989).

The question of transfer in an educational context has been discussed (Salomon & Perkins, 1989) in terms of "low road" and "high road" to transfer. The low road is the first and second type of transfer discussed above. This is transfer brought about by varied and extensive practice. Its logical end is to ensure automaticity; the action has become so automatic that in a similar situation only minor adjustments in behavior are required, and these are handled with a minimal expenditure of attention. The high road entails abstraction and reflection. It uses forward anticipatory reflections as well as backward inferencing. It is, of course, a controlled rather than an automatic process. The authors give an example of teaching history that will facilitate far transfer. It deals with the French Revolution and the more recent Iranian revolution. "The teacher could decontextualize causal factors and important patterns in history, describing specific cases like the French Revolution, in terms of the general forces at work, and highlight how the same general forces figure in other periods of history as well" (Salomon & Perkins, 1989, p. 136). This type of teaching is conducive to transfer based on principle. The crucial question asked by the authors concerning facilitation of transfer is: What promotes reflection and abstraction? Our view is that strategy training will not necessarily result in reflection at the critical moment and does not necessarily lead to very far transfer. We discuss our reasons in the next section.

An Alternative to Strategy Training

As an alternative to general strategy training (cf. Borkowski & Cavanaugh, 1979; Glidden, 1979), it is proposed that transfer of principle can be facilitated only when the subject has acquired the principle through his or her own experience. Often the experiences have to be guided by an externally initiated structure. The procedure is identical to learning of new concepts as Vygotsky (1962) has discussed, passing through stages of imperfect and pseudoconcepts. But the learning is collaborative, that is, 'mediated,' and requires internal representation, which involves transitions from intermental to intramental representations. Such learning facilitates inductive rather than deductive inferencing.

Campione and Brown (1987) have conducted a series of exquisite studies on transfer of learning that, we think, facilitate inductive inferencing leading to the discovery of a rule or principle. They have shown that abstract principles can be transferred to new instances when the skill is acquired in a flexible rather than in a fixed context. A flexible use of strings—for example as a tool for measuring things, stuff for sewing, pulling people out of water—promotes transfer to a broader range of situations. In a fixed learning situation where children learn one general rule thoroughly, such creative uses of the tool are blocked; children develop a mind set. Their behavior becomes rigid and results in negative transfer.

Cognitive strategy training does not follow the inductive route (see the special issue of *Educational Psychologist* 1986 for a sampler). It comes in many forms, but essentially it is based on the *principle of deduction.* Some strategy is given to be applied in a set procedure. The learner has to identify the instance where the strategy is applicable, then follow the deductive procedure: All men are mortal. Is Jack an instance of a man? If so, he is mortal. The learner has not worked his or her way through experiences that lead to the education of the principle that "all men are mortal." The learner did not use the principles of induction.

It seems reasonable to consider structuring the remedial training program so that *inductive inference* will occur spontaneously. In deductive strategy training the students are given a principle or strategy that they have not produced themselves, and thus which they have not necessarily internalized. They have no sense of "ownership" over the strategy or principle and no comprehensive sense of its usefulness. The Vygotskian tradition argues instead for the importance of the students' ownership of the strategy or principle, acquired through the normal inductive process, generalizing from experience. This does not mean that a teacher should not guide the experiences encountered, nor that adults should not assist in the generalization process. The point is that the strategy or principle will only be used with insight and understanding when it is internalized by the students, and internalization requires induction on the students' part. The global-process training experience in our remedial program is intended to allow for this. The principle or strategy need not be verbalized in our training—indeed, it cannot be verbalized accurately. Learning is implicit rather than explicit. But the learner achieves a sense of where it should apply.

Training for cognitive processing has a better chance of leading to transfer in the mentally retarded when the inductive procedure through structured experience provided by the remedial tasks is followed. Even then the retarded may not show far transfer. An "inductive leap" is required to educe a common principle, to go from particular instances to a general rule. The extent to which the retarded children can do this is determined by a complex set of conditions. The major one seems to be the quality of sign meanings or inner speech. Even when the retarded are put through the structured remedial program for the enhancement of cognitive processing, they cannot conceptually represent and analyze the experience. Citing Campione and Brown again, young (3 to 5 years) children cannot understand complex explanations of the principle, although they have been able to derive it from their experience with a given set of problems. The limitation may be found in the elusive "quality of sign meanings." As Leontiev and Luria (1972) describe it,

> *[A]t each stage, the developing word meaning requires a different mental operation.* Thus, with a small child, a basic role is played by immediate impressions (partly emotional); with a school child this structure undergoes a deep change, and finally with an adult the mental operations required to process word meanings involve an extremely complex process of deep psychological changes. (Leontiev & Luria, 1972, p. 314) The retarded children, like 5-year-old children, have an immature sign meaning system.

So does the "inductive" training program relate to the Vygotskian perspective? We think it does, and also to the Piagetian notion that we learn by operating on reality. It is through *labor* that we learn, including the learning of symbolic tools such as language. And it is in collaboration with others that our cognitive development occurs. When a strategy or principle is articulated subsequent to experiences from which it is educed, it will have a better chance for application in "far" situations.

10

PASS REMEDIAL PROGRAM: PREP

An alternative to direct training of strategies for the remediation of reading skills was proposed in the previous chapter. We suggested that a strategy will be used by individuals with learning disabilities or mental retardation only when it is internalized. The process of internalization will emerge through induction when the individuals are taken through structured experience provided by training tasks. Direct training through rule learning and explanation of complex principles does not work for children with learning disabilities or mental retardation. We also suggested that an assessment of the cognitive difficulties of the child in terms of PASS would be the first step. After identifying the broad process or processes in which the child maybe deficient and the academic/vocational skill that is the target for improvement, remedial training can be planned. For instance, many children with reading disability are deficient in successive processing and lag behind specifically in word decoding. What are the processes involved in decoding? As we have explained in previous chapters, decoding words may primarily involve successive processing and to a lesser extent planning and simultaneous processing. The specific PASS tasks that pinpoint the children's deficiency are likely to be verbal successive tasks and the Stroop test. Armed with this knowledge, remedial training can be tailor-made, as it were, for each child.

The PASS remediation program, PREP, has been constructed to induce successive or simultaneous processing while involving the training of planning and promoting selective attention. This point will become clear as we describe the tasks. The repertoire includes 8 to 10 tasks to be selected for remedial training. Each task has a "global" process training form and a content-related "bridging" form. Each task has three levels of difficulty; passage from one level to the next is contingent upon at least an 80%

success rate in that level. The program is typically given for 15 to 20 hours, once or twice a week, spread over 12 weeks or more. Not too much time is spent on any one task lest it may result in overlearning that leads to "welding" of the skill and works against transfer.

Each session begins with establishing a base line of competence in performing a task and ends an hour or so later; improvement within the session can be objectively scored. Records are maintained for every session. No more than two children receive training in the same session, thus allowing each child to be helped. (A larger group might be tried and under the right supervisory conditions may gain as much from training as a two-person group.) Each child also takes a pretest for reading, spelling or comprehension that needs to be remediated and of course, a posttest. Selected PASS tests may be administered in the package of pre- and posttest, time permitting.

While improvement in PASS tasks will normally be attributed to "far transfer", improvement in reading/spelling/comprehension performance is the object of PREP. Such improvement when it occurs can be described as *very far transfer.*

Monitoring of session by session progress and qualitative observations of remedial instructors indicate the course of improvement, as do the pre- and posttests. We typically require a control group receiving minimal or no treatment in the program and an experimental, treated group receiving training. It may be adequate to show that the experimental group demonstrated statistically significant gain in reading tests. However, a rigorous criterion will be an interaction effect that shows significantly better gains in the experimental group compared to the control group. Frequently, however, the criterion measure for reading proficiency may be problematic. It is much harder to show improvement in a standardized score of decoding and comprehension. Informal reading inventories or teacher-made tests are far more sensitive in detecting improvement. In any case, given the vast individual differences in temperament, motivation, and learning style of the child on the one hand and the teaching style and personality characteristics of the remedial instructor on the other, it is truly amazing when a significant interaction effect is found. The joy of finding a shining needle in the haystack is overwhelming for the researcher!

TRAINING IN SIMULTANEOUS-SUCCESSIVE PROCESSING

We review here some past studies on remediation. The programs for remediation were earlier versions of PREP, except for the last two studies in which the current form was used.

LD Studies

The two initial LD studies within the PASS model utilized only successive strategy training tasks (Kaufman, 1978; Krywaniuk, 1974). A later study (Brailsford, 1981) incorporated both simultaneous and successive processing. All studies were conducted with elementary school age pupils who were either low achievers or reading disabled.

Krywaniuk Study

The initial study (Krywaniuk, 1974; see also Das, Cunnins, et al., 1979; Krywaniuk & Das, 1976), used 11 training tasks that emphasized successive more than simultaneous processing and which were context-free in that they did not reflect competence in any specific academic subject areas. The subjects were from grades three and four in a school located on a Canadian Indian reserve. All were considered underachievers. There were 18 low-achieving children who received 15 hours of remedial training and 20 low-achieving children who were in the control group. The control group received minimal training of 3 hours of interaction with the experimenter. During training the teacher encouraged the pupils to verbalize their thinking. The teacher encouraged the use of appropriate strategies and attempted to point out the ways in which the strategies were of use in the solution of the problem. Tasks included Sequence Story Boards, Parquetry Boards, Serial Recall, Matrix Serialization (Number Matrix), and five filmstrips designed to focus on visual training skills (Krywaniuk & Das, 1976).

The Sequence Story Boards required the pupil to arrange 12 pictures in a sequence to tell a story. Verbalization was encouraged as the pupil examined the pictures and arranged them. Following the completion of the task, the pupil was required to tell the story in the order of the scenes he had determined. Parquetry Designs involved the use of geometric shapes to build patterns, initially on the template and later using the template as a reference only. Serial Recall was a memory task to recall 12 shapes that had been shown and then hidden. The task required no specific order of recall and encouraged the grouping of objects to increase the chance of recall. The five filmstrips covered visual discrimination and spatial orientation, visual-motor coordination, visual memory, figure ground discrimination, and visualization. The filmstrips were used with the minimum training group as their total (3 hour) training, but only as part of the program for the experimental group.

The posttest results indicated that the experimental group had significantly higher scores than the control group in Serial Learning and Visual Short-Term Memory, the two successive tests in the battery. Improvement was also found in the Schonell Word Recognition Test. The results of the study indicated both near transfer to other nontaught examples of successive processing and far transfer to reading. In comparison to other studies claiming transfer, the results obtained by Krywaniuk represent strong examples of transfer. Additionally they illustrate that a training program focusing upon a weak skill can permit the pupil to use that skill more efficiently (Krywaniuk, 1974).

Kaufman Study

D. Kaufman (1978; see also Das, Cummins, et al., 1979; D. Kaufman & P. Kaufman, 1978), also conducted a predominantly successive strategy training program. A total of 17 above average and 17 below average pupils were assigned to experimental and control groups. The below average group can be considered to be a learning-disabled group (Das, Cummings, et al., 1979). The training group received 10 hours of individual training, using a total of 11 tasks. The tasks included the five filmstrips used previously by Krywaniuk and in addition People Puzzle, Matrix Letters, Numbers and Pictures (based on Krywaniuk's Matrix Serialization), Serial and Free Recall of Pictures, and Follow the Arrow.

The People Puzzle required the child to sort out the jumbled horizontal pieces of the puzzle and construct faces from it. In Serial Recall of pictures, the children were trained to recall an increasingly long series of picture cards, while in Free Recall the cards could be remembered in any order. In Follow the Arrow, the children learned to join pictures with arrows to show the correct sequence of events. The sequence had been shown to the child before on the master card that was to be studied by the child.

The results of the training showed that the experimental group had significantly higher scores on all successive marker tests and one simultaneous test, which was Memory for Designs. Near transfer could be considered to have been obtained in the case of the successive marker tests, and far transfer in the case of the Schonell Word Identification Test. The experimental group's posttest score was significantly higher in the Mathematical composite of the Metropolitan Achievement Test, reflecting far transfer to mathematics as well.

Brailsford Study

Brailsford (1981; Brailsford, Snart & Das, 1984), incorporated both simultaneous and successive processing strategies in her training program with reading-disabled children from upper elementary classes. Twelve pupils were assigned to each of the experimental and control groups. The experimental group took part in 15 hours of training, conducted individually. Twelve simultaneous processing tasks were utilized, including four that were subtests in the trial edition of the K-ABC. In addition, six successive processing strategy tasks were used including, Matrix Letters and Number, Picture Story Sequencing, Serial Recall and Associative Pairing based on previous studies. Also included were Tracking I and II and Joining Shapes; these tasks were devised by Venger and Kholmovskaya (1978) of

Moscow, who include them in a preschool psycho-diagnostic battery; they are described in the last section of this chapter.

The training program focused not only on simultaneous and successive processing but also on verbalization. Children were encouraged to verbalize during the tasks and also to explain their strategies following the completion of a task. As with the Krywaniuk and Kaufman studies, all tasks were free of reading skill content and were primarily designed to reflect either simultaneous or successive processing. Following training, in the posttest phase, all pretest measures were readministered. These comprised the reading tests, which were the Gates-MacGinitie and the Standard Reading Inventory (McCracken, 1966), and the simultaneous and successive processing tests. Analysis of variance was performed using the two groups and the pre/posttests as the main effects.

The posttest results showed improvement for Memory for Designs; a significant interaction between groups and prepost effects was obtained. In all successive marker tests, the experimental group was significantly higher as evidenced by the interaction term. Far transfer was also obtained for instructional reading levels as measured by the Standard Reading Inventory (McCracken, 1966). Far transfer to the Gates-MacGinitie Prose Comprehension subtest was not obtained probably due to the multiple-choice format of the test, which constricts access to the text and does not rely on the active organizational strategies that were emphasized in the training tasks (Brailsford, Snart, & Das, 1984). In contrast, the Standard Reading Inventory required reading, reconstruction, and answering questions. All of these involve the use of the coding and retrieval strategies that were taught in the training program.

The Success of LD Studies

The three LD studies conducted within our model of training have clearly demonstrated both near transfer to tests of simultaneous and successive processing and very far transfer to reading and mathematics. Unlike many studies of transfer, the near transfer tasks are clearly different from the training tasks. Far transfer tasks require the application of strategies, learned in context-free tasks, to context-specific tasks of reading and mathematics, a far more substantial degree of transfer than has been demonstrated in other cognitive training programs. In addition, the studies have demonstrated the viability of teaching context-free processing strategies to low achievers and the reading disabled.

Studies with the Mentally Handicapped

Parmenter Study

Parmenter (see Conway, 1985) trained educable mentally retarded (EMR) adolescents on four successive processing tasks. The sessions lasted for 50 hours. These training sessions were held over a period of 4 months. The tasks selected had previously been successfully utilized in either the Kaufman or Krywaniuk study.

Following the completion of training, the group was unable to demonstrate transfer to either successive or simultaneous processing tasks or to academic tests of reading. Parmenter explained the failure as the inability of the EMR subjects to utilize strategies appropriate for attempting marker tests even after remedial training. Instead, they continued to use their own inefficient strategies. A further reason advanced was that the EMR adolescents may have failed to learn the strategy to a level of proficiency that would allow them to apply it to an alternate task.

Conway Study

Conway (1985) incorporated an equal number of simultaneous and successive processing tasks in a training study for EMR children attending special classes in two elementary schools. The training took part in small groups of four children over a total of 18 hours. The training model differed from the previous LD studies in that after the introduction of two simultaneous and two successive processing strategy tasks, the children were reintroduced to one simultaneous and one successive task in order to teach discrimination between the two processing strategies and to demonstrate that one strategy was more appropriate than the other for a given task. This concept of discrimination was considered an important skill in attempting alternate novel tasks.

As in the Brailsford study, the emphasis was on the *child's solution to the task,* not on rehearsing an adult instructed verbal sequence. The role of the group was to provide both a more natural learning environment and feedback and models for the training program. Like Brailsford, Conway found that the verbalization of some children revealed that the less appropriate processing strategy was employed to solve a particular task. The group situation provided the opportunity for another group member to demonstrate the more appropriate strategy using a language and conceptual framework understood by the group members.

Facilitating Transfer for the Mentally Handicapped

The results of Conway's study failed to demonstrate transfer either to other simultaneous or successive tasks or to academic tasks of reading and mathematics. The failure to demonstrate transfer was considered by Conway to be due to the inability of the children to perceive the need to apply the learned strategies to novel tasks.

These studies with mentally retarded students suggest that PASS strategy training is of little value for promoting transfer to academic tasks. However, research in this area is limited, and further exploration may reveal that such training is more useful if directly applied to concrete activities such as vocational skills (see Ashman, 1985). When intelligence is limited, access to strategies learned in different tasks and situations is not flexible (Campione & Brown, 1984; Das, 1985). Transfer of principle or rule learning to any significant extent is not expected of the mentally handicapped. Salomon and Perkins (1989) have discussed the conditions of narrow and broad or far transfer. *Narrow transfer* is easier, nearly automatic, and demands minimal effort on the part of the learner. This is the kind that we can expect to achieve for the mentally retarded individual of moderate to severe retardation. In a subsequent section we discuss the problem of transfer and the limited language capacity of mentally retarded individuals. How can the remedial program assist in training them in spite of their language handicap?

Considering the PASS remedial program specifically, the global training tasks will be useful to guide vocational training. To proceed step by step, the vocational training tasks have to be analyzed in terms of the PASS processes; each task grouped as predominantly requiring one, two, three, or all PASS processes. Then the next step would be to add specific vocational task content to the global tasks, thus developing semi-automatic processing skills through practice. However, the skill should not be so "welded" to the specific task that it cannot be used in another task. We are suggesting a delicate balance between overlearning of a skill and maintaining some flexibility for transfer of the skill to a new, albeit similar, task. Learning the global tasks alone in the first stage of the training is supposed to "prime" the learning of content-related cognitive processes—attending, coding the information, and planning a course of action. The other components of the PASS model, as given in Chapter 2, play an important part in structuring the training experience as well: Input must be appropriate; knowledge base should exist before training; one or the other PASS processes is to be made preeminent in each task; and, finally, the method of output should be appropriately structured, taking the processing strengths and knowledge base of the individual into consideration.

Bridging the Gap between Global and Specific Process Training: Examples from a Spelling Study

Learning to spell requires attention to the letter sequences in the word that is to be spelled, which especially involves successive processing. A deficiency in successive processing is therefore observed in poor spellers. Given such a deficiency, a training program to improve spelling should promote successive processing. Planning also needs to be the object of training so that the process can be appropriately organized and applied in learning the spelling for new words. A study by Spencer (1987) attempted to test improvement in spelling by including both global and specific training. The global processes, successive coding and planning, were chosen for remediation by selecting five training tasks. The bridging tasks were five spelling tasks, which were modeled after the training tasks in keeping with the spirit of successive processing and planning. *Bridging*, as the name suggests, provides a connection between processing and context; examples are given to make the concept clear.

Twenty children between 8 and 12 years (mean 10.8 years) who were very poor in spelling served as subjects. Their spelling level was at grade 2.5, some two and a half grades below the level expected of their age. Ten of these children were placed in the group that received remedial training; the other 10 continued with standard instructions in reading and spelling in the resource room.

As examples of the global and specific tasks, consider the following: Bead Threading requires the child to thread a bead pattern by recalling the order in which different beads were dropped by the teacher. The beads were large or small (size) and yellow, red, blue, or green (color). The teacher drops the beads in predetermined serial orders. The child copies the order using his or her frame, then checks if the order was correct by lifting the cover off the teacher's frame. Interactions between the child and the teacher occur frequently. These focus on the processing demands of the task, identification of blocks in processing, and providing an opportunity for verbalizing the processing strategies (but not forcing the child to verbalize).

Spencer observed significant gains for every student involved in the remediation program. Significant improvement in their ability to spell words accurately is shown in the illustration provided in Figure 10-1. The *t*-test calculated between the first and second eight blocks indicated that the students' performance improved significantly over time. This finding was further substantiated by the results of the analysis of variance in which a significant main effect for pre–post improvement was found. The gain in spelling words during intervention *was retained by the students even after a 2-week break* from remediation (Spencer, Snart, & Das, 1989). Therefore, it can be assumed that the intervention program was effective. In summary, the students in the experimental group made significant progress in mastering spelling.

Improving Decoding Skills in Gifted LD Children: A Study of Three Cases

Successive processing deficits frequently appear in reading-disabled children who have high IQs (Snart, Das, & Mensink, 1988). A training program developed by Crawford (1990) involved global instruction in suc-

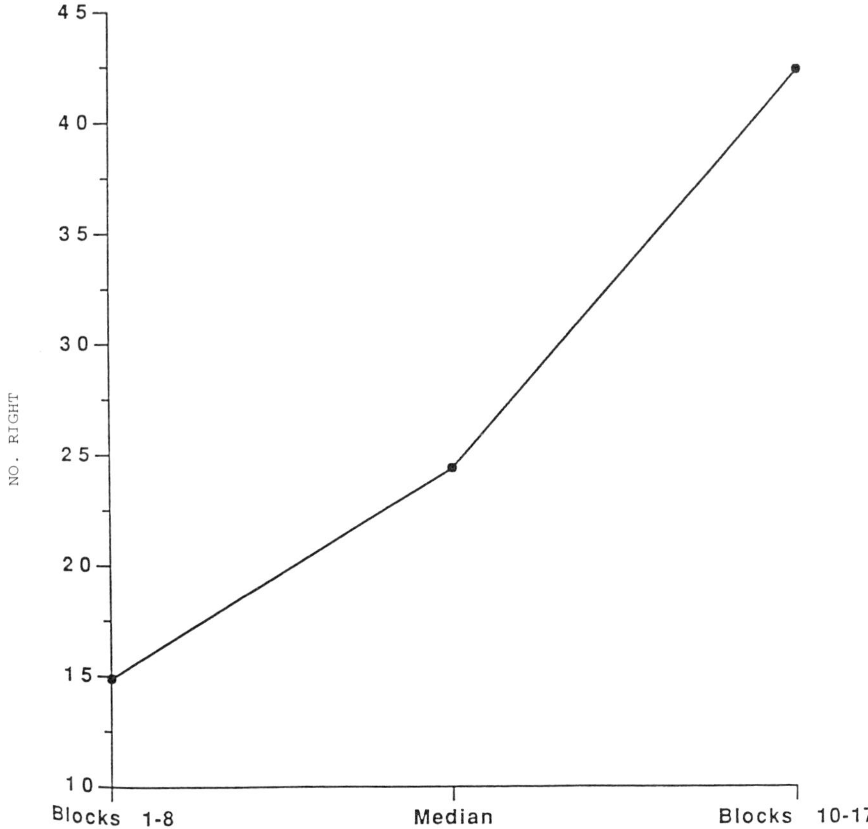

FIGURE 10-1 Mean Scores for Spelling Blocks 1 to 8 and 10 to 17 for the Total Group

cessive processing, coupled with bridging tasks designed to highlight the application of successive strategies to reading/decoding skills. A long description of Crawford's study (supervised by Snart and Das) is given here to illustrate individual differences in response to remedial training. Three boys (Brian, Mathew, and Colin) were involved in this study. These boys, who ranged in age from 10-0 to 12-3 years, possessed Full Scale IQ scores on the WISC-R of equal to or greater than 120 and displayed significant delays (at least 2 years) in basic reading skills. Remediation involved approximately 15 hours of individual instruction using six global and corresponding bridging tasks. Verbal mediation played a major role in the instruction. Before beginning the task, students were given directions as to the requirements, which they were required to repeat back to the instructor in their own words. During the performance of the task, increasingly explicit prompts were provided to assist the students in successfully completing the problems. The students were also allowed and assisted to verbalize what they were doing during the performance of tasks. After the task was completed the instructor and student discussed the strategies required to perform the tasks and their application to reading.

A case study design was used to examine individual changes in successive processing, reading/decoding skills, and confidence in school abilities. Performance in successive processing was measured using three selected marker tasks from the PASS tests: Naming Time, Speech Rate, and Successive Word Recall. In reading, students were assessed with the Woodcock Reading Mastery Test—Revised (WRMT-R) (Woodcock, 1987) and the Burns and Roe Informal Reading Assessment (IRA) (Burns & Roe, 1980). The students' self-concept with respect to their academic abilities was assessed using the Student's Perception of Ability Scale (SPAS) (Boersma & Chapman, 1989).

On PASS successive processing marker tasks, two of the students demonstrated considerable improvement. Brian displayed significant improvement on one CAS task (Speech Rate) and a trend toward improvement on the other two tasks. Colin also displayed significant improvement on Speech Rate as well as improvement approaching significance on another successive task, Successive Word Recall. Mathew did not demonstrate significant improvement on successive processing tasks.

In reading, Colin demonstrated improvement that approached significance on the WRMT-R Word Attack subtest. On the IRA he showed an improvement in the number of words read correctly on the Graded Word Lists, as well as substantial improvement in Oral Comprehension instructional level (grade 4 to grade 5). Brian did not display significant improvement on any of the reading measures but did improve substantially in listening comprehension (grade 6 to grade 9). This task involved sequential organization of ideas, concepts, and relationships, as well as short-term sequential memory for themes, details, and events. It was inferred that training in successive processing may have improved Brian's ability to organize concepts and events and therefore resulted in an improvement in listening comprehension. However, these skills did not transfer to reading. Mathew did not demonstrate appreciable improvement on any of the reading measures.

Both Colin and Mathew demonstrated substantial improvement in the perception of academic achievement as measured by the SPAS. In Colin's case this improvement was inferred to stem from improvements in successive strategy use in reading, which in turn improved his confidence in his reading skills. For Mathew this result was initially a mystery, since he did not improve in his successive processing or reading. However, some anecdotal evidence suggested why this improvement may have occurred.

At one point in the intervention Mathew said that he felt that the training was "useful." When asked to explain what he meant, he said that it was helpful in remembering series of details and sequences of information presented in class lessons. He recalled a specific science lesson in which he was required to remember a sequence of events, stating that the training tasks assisted him in remembering the information. Therefore, Mathew's increased perception of abilities may have been due to the application of successive strategies to academic areas other than reading. Brain's perception of his academic abilities did not improve.

The variability in performance among the three students indicated that, while the intervention had an impact in each case, the nature of that impact was different for each child. Crawford inferred that the specific strategies and processing abilities that children bring into remediation interact with instruction in order to produce change in performance. He suggested that, although the PASS instructional model can improve processing and reading performance, other factors must be taken into account in order to maximize the benefit of cognitive remediation.

One important consideration involved the impact that noncognitive factors, such as motivation, appeared to have on performance. A substantial degree of inconsistency was noted in processing and reading results within each of the children, indicating that fluctuations in attentiveness and motivation may have adversely contributed to their performance. This notion was supported by behavioral observations of distraction during intervention as well as teacher and parent reports of attentional problems in all students. It was suggested that motivational factors must be taken into consideration in any successful remedial program. This sentiment is also reflected in the work of researchers such as Carr and Borkowski (1989), who found that the incorporation of attributional training into a reading comprehension strategy training program resulted in greater improvement and generalization of strategy use than did a strategy-only group.

Reading Improvement for Underachievers

The factors highlighted in the studies discussed here have been incorporated into a follow-up remediation project, which was recently conducted with children in California. Underachieving ("Chapter 1") children who were neither mentally handicapped nor classified as learning disabled participated in a program similar to the one previously described. Instruction involved primarily successive strategies and bridging to decoding, since this appears to be the area of greatest deficit in these children. However, some instruction in simultaneous processing and bridging to comprehension was also included. Quantitative and qualitative reading measures are given in order to examine the nature of the relationship between simultaneous/successive processing and reading, as well as the relationship between the children's reading strategies and their improvement in the program.

An experimental (treated) group of 22 children was compared to a control (not receiving PASS Remedial Program or PREP) group of 15 children on measures of decoding. The treated group had received 15 hours of remedial training involving global and bridging tasks, while the untreated group was getting the regular resource room instruction. Following an analysis of variance design, 2 (groups) × 2 (pre/post performance) on decoding tasks, the results showed an improvement in decoding measures for both groups, but a significantly greater improvement for the treated group. This interaction effect is critical in intervention studies and is hard to achieve. The treated children gained the equivalent of 1.5 grades in word attack, the decoding of pseudowords, following 15 weeks of training.

Concluding Notes on PREP and Reading Achievement

Now that cognitive process training has distanced itself sufficiently from the discredited methods of Frostig and Kirk (Wong, 1992), it is possible to examine empirically the effectiveness of programs such as PREP. The program is based on theories found in both cognitive psychology and neuropsychology. It aims at enhancing the processing strategies that underlie word-reading, while at the same time avoiding direct teaching of word reading skills, for we believe that the teachers have tried direct teaching with Chapter 1 children and found that it did not improve their reading. In fact, direct teaching involving more-of-the-same kind of work has turned off the interest and motivation of the Chapter 1 children to learn. In contrast, the PREP has attractive materials that engage the children. PREP leads them to applying appropriately successive and to a lesser extent simultaneous processing skills in word reading while their planning and attention improve.

When confronting a word a child cannot read, his or her key activities are (1) to code it phonologically as a series of spelling-to-speech activities, (2) to assemble a pronunciation, and (3) to utter the word. Each of these predominantly requires successive processing. As suggested before, planning and simultaneous processing are involved as well. A prerequisite of course, is arousal-attention.

Dealing with arousal-attention first, the PREP materials, as we said before, were immensely interesting; our remediation therapists had unequivocally enthusiastic responses from the children. Attention was also demanded and obtained in performing every task; not so much by exhortations of the teacher-therapist, but by structuring the task in such a way that selective attention would be elicited. Next, planning was built into the structure of the tasks and was augmented by allowing the children to engage in discussion with the teacher-therapist throughout their performance. Then, as mentioned earlier, the tasks were structured in such a way that *appropriate* use of successive and simultaneous strategies will likely occur. The distinctive feature here was the tacit acquisition and use of the appropriate processing strategies in contrast to instructed learning; this is the inductive rather than the deductive rule-learning approach central to PREP.

An important point to note is the extent of transfer or generalization. This was shown, of course, for the learning-disabled samples, not for the mentally retarded. The value of a minimal IQ, a threshold for facilitating transfer, has been observed by many other researchers including Brown and Campione (1981). Lovett, Benson, and Olds (1990) also reported that within the normal IQ range of learning-disabled individuals, improvement was seen only for those with a higher IQ. All our studies showed far transfer. Improvement in decoding and comprehension test performance occurred even though these skills were not included in remedial training. Improvement in spelling test performance also occurred in the study where bridging to curriculum content was used, but the content did not overlap with the material of the spelling test. We suggest again the importance of including global process training for ensuring far transfer, but we do not know yet exactly how far transfer may occur.

Remediation and Instructional Design

The PASS theory and the perspectives on cognitive development and learning we have presented in this chapter provide guidelines for the design of remedial instruction. It is important to recognize that school achievement is complexly determined, being a function both of general processes and specific content learning. For example, we have argued that decoding in reading is heavily dependent on successive processing; it is also, of course, dependent on the child's knowledge of phonic rules and sight words. We emphasize general process instruction here, but we do not deny the importance of content knowledge.

Several general principles can be given. The first, which we have discussed extensively in the preceding section, is that *strategies must be acquired*—they cannot be given. Strategy acquisition is an inductive and gradual process; we do not see that it is possible to provide the learner with an abstract general principle or strategy and expect that the naive learner will be able to apply this in all appropriate instances (Kirby, 1989). A learner who understands the nature of a strategy and when it is likely to be useful is more likely to retain and use it (Paris, Newman, & McVey, 1985).

Second, it is important that the experience upon which strategy induction is to be based be coherent and that transfer be provided for. Learning based in a very narrow context is unlikely to be generalized, and far transfer becomes more likely when the learner is shown the way (Kirby, 1989; Salomon & Perkins, 1989).

Third, instruction should begin by understanding the child's initial approach to the task (Case, 1980); until misconceptions are eliminated, new learning will be fragile. It is necessary that the child sees the insufficiency in the old approach or strategy and the need for developing a new strategy.

Fourth, strategy or skill acquisition should proceed in small steps, beginning with familiar and nonthreatening content (Case, 1980). Complexity should be added gradually, and always after a return to easier content. If children have had little success with academic content (e.g., reading), then process instruction should begin with nonacademic content.

Fifth, while process instruction should often begin with nonacademic content, there is no reason why academic content should be avoided, and many reasons why it should be included. This is the way in which bridging occurs, by beginning with general processes in nonacademic contexts and then by gradually including academic content, at each stage showing how the general process may be applied.

INTERACTION BETWEEN CHILDREN AND TEACHERS/THERAPISTS

The idea of having a teacher or a therapist who intervenes between the learner and the material to be learned is not a new one. The role of the teacher is well recognized by ancients such as Socrates and moderns like Tolstoy and John Dewey. But how exactly should the intervention be carried out? What should be the common and essential properties of the procedure of intervention, mediation, or teaching? First, the children must be helped to develop appropriate orientation and attitude to accept the benefits of teaching. What must the teacher do to bring out a proper orientation to learning? Here are four suggestions for the teacher/therapist.

- *Be interactive.* Elicit from the student what he or she thinks the purpose of a lesson (e.g., reading a narrative or expository text) is and what his or her own intentions are. What does the teacher want? What is the best way to approach the task; what is the worst way? Give praise when it is due, but the praise must be informative, not platitudinal.

- *Remember, principles are transferable, skills are not.* Teaching specific skills on how to decode a given group of words, for example, or teaching a particular list of concepts will of course improve a student's competence in decoding those particular words or learning those particular concepts, but the skill will not necessarily generalize or be transferred. Too much practice with the list may promote welding of the skill to the task, which works against transfer. Let the student develop through inductive inference the underlying principles in decoding or comprehension; this inference occurs insidiously. Inductive inference is an offshoot of the old "discovery learning."
- *Relate formal instructional knowledge to spontaneous knowledge.* To facilitate maintenance and transfer, book knowledge must interface with the spontaneously acquired knowledge of the student. Initially, the student needs help in constantly relating the two as he or she learns. This is easier to do in some subject matters, as in comprehension of text, and harder to do in science and math, but it still is possible.
- *Aim at global process training and combine it with content-specific curriculum teaching.* To facilitate the development of induction in regard to simultaneous or successive processing of information to be learned (e.g., spelling), first expose the student to a number of successive tasks (if there is deficiency in spelling and in successive processing); then design spelling instructions that map on to the global training task.

These recommendations are not meant to be followed rigidly. The main object of these directives is to facilitate improvement in children's cognitive functions, and the ultimate goal is to restructure their habits of thought.

AN EXERCISE IN DETECTING TECHNIQUES OF MEDIATED INSTRUCTION

The following is a sample of interactions we have collected; they were recorded while a teacher-therapist was giving the Tracking task to three children. What we could retrieve from the tape was mostly the teacher's but not the children's speech. But the verbatim transcripts will serve our purpose, which is for the reader to identify the objectives of the teacher. Given the six things the teacher was trying to do, the reader is asked to check which statements of the teacher serve one of these particular objectives.

The teacher's intentions were to:

1. Encourage active guessing
2. Ask for children's reasons behind the choice of response
3. Elicit alternate responses
4. Make children verify if the response was right
5. Provide affective support
6. Anticipate the difficulty level of the next problem and thus prepare the children to expend their efforts accordingly

Tracking (see Figure 10.2) is being used here as a training task given to three reading-disabled children. The reader is asked to label each of the following statements by choosing one or more of the six intentions. The teacher is talking to the three children:

- Now, what we are going to do here on this game is, I am going to give you each a card and you have to try and get to the house. So let's just work on this together and then see if you all have it. OK.?
- You know which one it is? What about you, Robert? Which one do you think?
- Oh, right here, is the one you thought? Is that the one you thought?
- Good. OK. Now how did you guess that that was the one?
- OK. Very good. And when you did this one, did you use your fingers or did you use your eyes, Ricky?

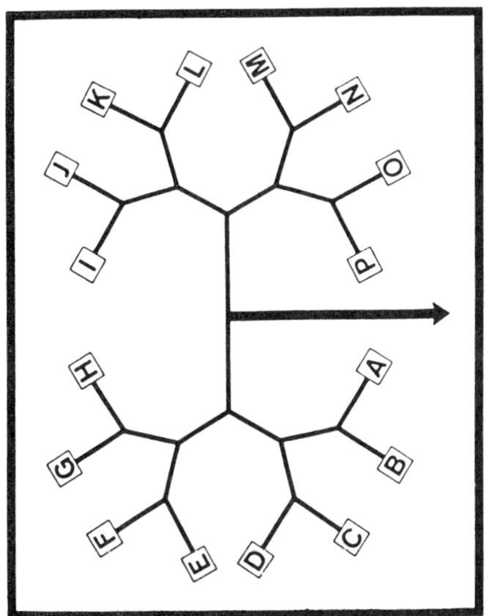

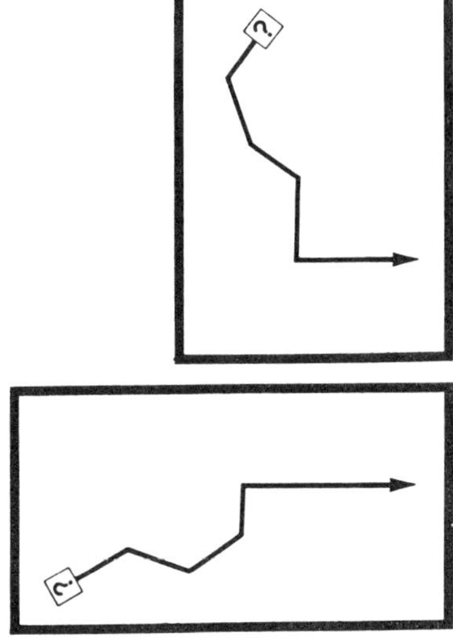

FIGURE 10-2 Tracking

- (I used my finger.) And did you use your finger or your eyes, Robert?
- You used your eye, right?
- And Tammy, what did you use?
- OK. Why did you use your eyes?
- OK, that's one of the reasons. Why did you use your finger?
- So you traced it? Good.

The final sections of this chapter present detailed instructions for facilitating two remediation tasks that exemplify the PREP approach.

EXAMPLES OF PREP: A GLOBAL AND BRIDGING TASK

Joining Shapes

Purpose

The student's task is to join a series of geometric shapes with a pencil line in response to a series of verbal instructions and following a set of rules. The shapes are triangles, squares, and hexagons. They are presented in rows, with a row of circles between each row of other shapes (see Figure 10-3, for example). There are three forms, corresponding to the number of rows of shapes. Form A consists of one row of triangles and one row of squares, with a row of circles between. Form B consists of one row of triangles, one row of squares, and one row of hexagons, with rows of circles between. Form C consists of a row of hexagons, a row of triangles, a row of squares, and another row of hexagons, with rows of circles between. There are also three levels of difficulty corresponding to the number of instructions given at any one time, which are one, two, or three instructions for difficulty levels 1, 2, and 3, respectively.

Focus

Successive strategies include visual scanning, rehearsal of rules, and talking aloud.

Materials

Response sheets, instructions and answer key, record form

Steps

1. Instructor shows the student the example and gives directions:
   a. In this task the purpose is to learn to draw a pattern by joining triangles, squares, and hexagons. The student will be given instructions as to how to construct the pattern. There are four rules to remember when drawing the pattern:

JOINING SHAPES – GLOBAL

Legend: T = Triangle S = Square H = Hexagon

Difficulty Level 2

Item 1a

Join:

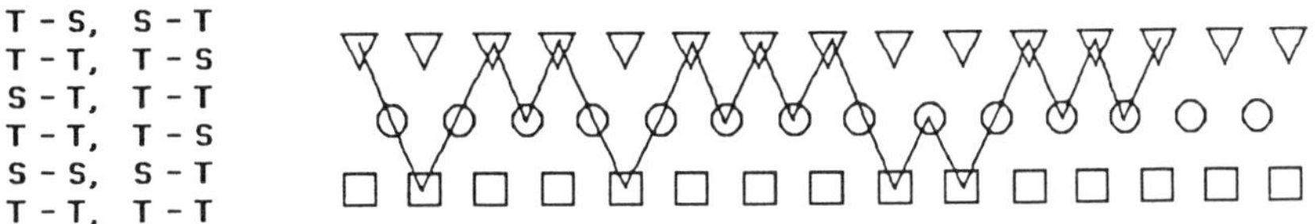

Item 2a

Join:

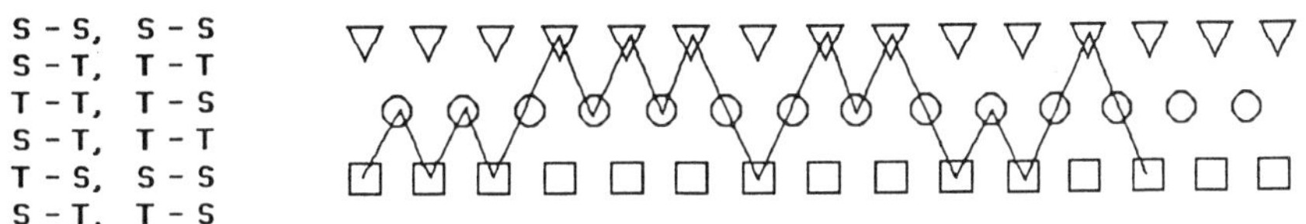

FIGURE 10-3 Joining Shapes—Global

I. To join squares, triangles, and hexagons together, the student must always pass through a circle.
II. The line drawn must always go forward on the page (left to right) and never backward.
III. The line drawn must be continuous from the beginning to the end of the page, so the student should not lift the pencil during the task.
IV. The student must join the closest shapes that correspond to the instructions.

As the rules are provided, the instructor demonstrates their application on the sample item. The instructor then provides some instructions for the student to follow to ensure that he or she understands the task and the rules. Any ambiguities in the task requirements are clarified. The student is asked to repeat the instructions to ensure that the task is understood.

2. The instructor gives the student the response sheet and provides the directions for constructing the pattern. For example, "Join a

triangle to a square, join a square to a triangle, join two triangles, join a triangle to a square."

3. The student follows the instructions and connects the shapes to produce the pattern. Each correct response to instructions is scored 2 points.
4. Instructor provides feedback.
   a. If all responses are correct, instructor acknowledges and praises correct responding. The instructor then asks the student how he or she performed the task and if any special strategies were used.
   b. If mistakes are made, the instructor asks the student to stop and look carefully at his or her response, then repeats the instruction and allows the student to correct the response. A correct response here is awarded 1 point.
   c. If the student still does not correctly respond, the instructor demonstrates the correct response, and the student is given 0 points. The instructor reminds the student of strategies such as scanning ahead before proceeding and rehearsing the rule. The task is then continued from the corrected response.
6. The procedure is followed for six items (two of each form) using the same difficulty level.
7. The instructor and student summarize the task and discuss strategies used. The parts of the task that the student found most difficult or simple are discussed, as well as ways in which the task could have been performed easily by the student. The instructor then tells the student that he or she is now going to perform the same type of task, but this time joining letters to make words.

Bridge to Joining Shapes

Purpose

The student's task is to join letters to make words. Letters are presented to the student in several rows, and the task is to join the letters from the top row to the bottom row, moving from left to right diagonally, to form a word. When the student reaches the bottom he or she is to start with the last letter of the word that was made and proceed back up to the top to make another word (see Figure 10-4). This series is continued until the student reaches the end of the sheet. The student is required to say the words aloud.

Focus

Successive strategies include visual scanning, rehearsal, sound blending, and prediction.

b p m g d b d t k y h

d a a n r e i e i c r

a t u a o f e a j n a

w i h d l g w u e n g

FIGURE 10-4 Joining Shapes—Bridging
Difficulty Level 2
Card 4a

Materials

Stimulus sheets, scoring guide

Steps

1. Instructor shows the student an example and gives directions:
   a. In this task the purpose is to learn to make words by joining letters. The student will be given instructions as to how to make the words. There are five rules to remember when drawing the pattern:
      I. The student must always start in the upper lefthand corner of the page and proceed from the top to the bottom, or vice versa, of the letter sheet to make a word.
      II. All words on a sheet will be the same length, which corresponds to the number of lines on the page, and the student must make a connection to only one letter on each line to form each word.
      III. The line drawn must always go forward across the page (left to right) and never backward (right to left).
      IV. The line drawn must be continuous from the beginning to the end of the page, so the last letter of each word is always the first letter of the next word.
      V. The student must look for the closest letter that will make a word. The instructor demonstrates the application of the rules on the sample item. The student then attempts to find other words on the sample page. The instructor provides feedback and clarifies any ambiguities in the task requirements. The student is asked to repeat the instructions to ensure that the task is understood.

2. The instructor provides the student with the first stimulus sheet and the student joins the letters according to the rules provided. The student then states the words spelled. Spontaneous corrections of wrong connections are permitted. Two points are awarded for a correct response.
3. Instructor provides feedback.
   a. If all connections for a word are correct, instructor acknowledges and praises the correct response. The instructor then asks the student how he or she performed the task and if any special strategies were used.
   b. If incorrect connections are made, the instructor first asks the student to look carefully at the word that he or she has produced and say it. If the student states a word that is not spelled, the instructor points out that the spelling is not correct. If the student gives a nonsense word, the instructor asks the student what the word means and points out that it is not a real word. In each case the instructor then asks the student to try again from the last correct connection and reminds the student to sound out the letters and scan ahead before making a connection. If the student makes the correct connections but cannot state the word, the instructor informs the student that the connections are correct and asks the student to start at the beginning of the word and try again to sound out the word. If the student makes the proper connections and says the word on the second trial, 1 point is awarded.
   c. If the student still cannot make the connections, the instructor demonstrates the correct connections and/or helps the student to sound out the word. Zero points are awarded here. The instructor then reminds the student of strategies such as scanning ahead before proceeding, sounding out letters, and sound blending.
6. The procedure is followed for each task in the session. For difficulty level 1, the session consists of three- and four-letter words. For level 2, four- and five-letter words are used. For level 3, five- and six-letter words are used.

CONCLUSION

The credibility of empirical results showing the effectiveness of PREP was established in this chapter. The program is based on theories found in both cognitive psychology and neuropsychology. It aims at enhancing the processing strategies that underlie word-reading while at the same time avoiding direct teaching of word-reading skills. Direct teaching, involving more-of-the-same kind of work, has turned off the interest and motivation of many children to learn. In contrast, the PREP has attractive materials that engage the children. PREP leads them to applying appropriately, successive processing skills and, to a lesser extent, simultaneous processing skills in word-reading. At the same time, improvement in planning and attention also occurs. Adopting PREP for the classroom and extending it to rehabilitation of brain-damaged individuals are the two topics for PREP research in the future. Taking children out of the class in two's and devoting one teacher to teach them for 15 45-minute sessions may not be deemed cost-effective. Therefore, research on extending PREP to instruct 8 to 10 pupils at a time should be worthwhile.

Can PREP be used generally for the early elementary school grades of 1 and 2 for all children so that those who may not be significantly reading-disabled but are weak in reading can also benefit from the training exercises? Some enthusiastic practitioners may even extend it below to kindergarten children. Now that early childhood education has received special support of the government, as well as the community, a program such as PREP ought to be tried for even kindergarten children. The program has a distinction which very few other programs have, that is, its base is in well-accepted theories of child development and cognitive functions associated with reading.

A possibility for PREP to be adapted for training individuals with brain damage should be explored. The global part of the PREP training is suitable, after adaptation, for brain-damaged individuals who may show a deficit in one or more of the PASS processes. New bridging tasks would have to be devised from the life skills that are required for rehabilitating these individuals. Thus, instead of bridging tasks that relate to reading or spelling curriculum, life skills requiring attention, planning or one of the two coding processes could be identified and used to construct the bridging tasks.

The alleviation of the cognitive deficits such as successive processing present in the common problems of reading disability (or brain damage) is the aim of PREP training. The success of training will be measured by the extent to which word decoding, word naming and other core problems are removed. Effectiveness of remediation, of course, would be modified by the individual's experience, maturation, compensation, and motivation, as Frith (1992) observed. As a first step, the cognitive deficits require to be identified in terms of a theoretical model. Then appropriate tasks are chosen to develop structured experiences for amelioration of the deficit. The emphasis here in PREP is on inductive learning of strategies.

11

THE RAFT

We think the following Buddhist story about a raft reflects an appropriate symbolic and cultural message for this final chapter.

Once upon a time a man was returning to his village. He had to cross a stream to reach the village. However, it had rained the night before and the stream was suddenly full and the current was swift. He needed a raft. Collecting wood from the nearby forest and twines from creepers, he started to make a raft. It wasn't easy. When the raft was finally constructed, he put himself on it and crossed the stream.

What does he do now with the raft? The raft was so useful! He could pull it up, place it on the bank, and leave it for someone else. He could hide it in a bush and save it for himself for another day when he might need it. He may carry it with him on his shoulder to his house and keep it as a memento. He could leave it in the stream and not bother with it anymore because it had served his purpose.

What to do with our raft? The three authors answer the question.

J.P.D.

IQ as a Raft

The concept of IQ was useful in classifying children into those who need to be taken out of regular classes. It was useful as a classificatory criterion, and not as an explanatory construct. In recent years, however, IQ has fallen into disuse for classifying special populations of children in school. For example, children with mental retardation of any level of severity are being put in schools for regular children, and their placement is guided by their special needs. Appropriate services are provided for them, irrespective of their IQ. In regard to children with learning disabilities, the usefulness of IQ is seriously questioned both in diagnosis and treatment. Special tests try to locate specific learning deficits, and the instructional programes are never determined by the children's IQ, which is in the normal range anyway. The banning of IQ tests in many school districts in the United States is evidence that IQ has become a burden, a raft that should be cast away.

The concept of IQ has diminished usefulness because it does not have a fixed connotation that we can agree with. A connotation is the common and essential properties of a word. IQ is untenable as a word because it has a variety of connotations; Sternberg (1991), in *Metaphors of Mind,* shows how very different these connotations of IQ or intelligence are.

We have left the IQ raft behind and have dealt, instead, with some major cognitive processes. Yet we often refer to IQ in the book, and in some of our experiments we "control" for IQ. Are we trying to keep it as a souvenir or, worse, hiding it behind the bush? I hope we will not be perceived to be doing that. The reference to the term *IQ* reflects a cultural practice, that helps us communicate our results to other psychologists who have grown up dealing with IQ. In a few years the culture should fade away; neuropsychology and cognitive psychology will have spread their general influence, and reference to IQ will not be necessary. This IQ raft would fade from our memory.

Factor Analysis as a Raft

> *The almost ubiquitous occurrence of positive correlations among scores on various tests and scales led early to various conceptions of general ability, ranging from Spearman's* g *to various systems of multiple factors . . . on the whole there seems to be increasing disillusion with the original idea that intercorrelations and factor analyses would lead to uncovering the basic structures of the mind as determined by the underlying neural organization. (Estes, 1976, pp. 295–297).*

In spite of this realistic observation made many years ago, factor analysis has dominated the field of test construction. To take a recent example, the "theory" in Binet:Four is still a post hoc product of their factor structure only because the sole basis for these contemporary scales was factor analysis. The scales did not aim for uncovering the basic structure of mind. Whatever they were measuring was measured by a set of specific tests and its factorial composition. It is no wonder that the revisions and re-revisions of old IQ tests have not aimed at discovering mental structures and their possible neural basis. The statistical procedure of factor analysis and its variations are grossly inadequate for advancing the understanding of intelligence or mental functions. A satisfactory prerequisite for using factor analysis is to work within a theoretical framework of cognitive processes as we have done, and then to construct tasks according to the theoretical model. We have followed such a procedure wherever factor analysis is used in this book.

A recent paper by Guttman and Levy (1991) reiterates the statistical limitations of factor analysis as a tool to discover mental structures. Consider why tests may load on the same factor. They may do so due to several reasons, as pointed out by Guttman (a veteran psychometrician) and Levy. Spearman's *g* is discussed as an example. The authors point to the failure of Spearman to prove the existence of a *general* factor alone because specific factors also appeared in his factor analysis. Some of the variance of each test remained unexplained. As Das, Kirby, and Jarman (1979) have observed: "Disagreements about the nature of that specific variance were to characterize the psychological study of intelligence for a long time . . . rival techniques of factor analysis were developed that tended to produce a larger number of factors" (p. 5).

But, we may ask, what about the positive manifold, the positive intercorrelations of mental tests, the ubiquitous fact that provided a strong evidence for "g"? Is that an artifact, a confusion promoting our attachment to factor analysis? Guttman and Levy would think so. The positive to zero intercorrelations arise simply because the test items share a common range of being scored objectively; as long as the test scores indicate various degrees of accuracy according to a certain rule, positive intercorrelations will appear. Given an objective rule for scoring performance in a common range of very right to very wrong answers, items in the tests *should* show positive correlations!

The objective rules in WISC items, for example, are mainly three inferences (Guttman & Levy, 1991) such as in analogical reasoning, general knowledge (Who is the president of the USA?), and semantic (tell me the numbers exactly as I said them). What is crucial here is the *construct of intelligence on which the rules are based.* Should intelligence consist of simple analogical reasoning, general knowledge, and instant learning? What justifications are given by the makers of WISC or its many innocuous revisions for choosing only these rules for making the items in the scale?

Like positive manifold, another twine that gives strength to the *g* raft is the size of the correlations among tests; the size of loading on the *g* factor is its reflection. But this itself can be determined by different conditions that are equally atheoretical. Consider the three reasons determining the size of correlations among Wechsler test items:

1. *The format of communication.* It is either verbal, numerical, or pictorial. Correlations are larger among verbal tasks than between verbal and nonverbal tasks.

2. *The rule applied to the task.* Similarities, general knowledge, and instant learning items will have a higher correlation among themselves because they represent tests within each rule category.
3. *Mode of output required by the tasks.* Similar modes enhance intercorrelations; the modes in WISC are oral, manual manipulation, and paper-pencil output.

Which of these three conditions has contributed how much to the size of intercorrelations is difficult to determine. Since intercorrelation size, in its turn, is the basis of factor loadings, the size of factor loadings cannot be attributed to expression, rules, or mode of output with any certainty. In any case, it seems to me that two of the three facets, expression and mode of output, that contribute to the size of loadings, have little to do with general mental ability.

To reiterate, an atheoretical use of exploratory factor analysis is not a raft for crossing the distance between the conceptualization of cognitive functions on one bank of the river and the tests on the other bank.

Confirmatory factor analysis, on the other hand, seems to hold more promise. It is used to support theoretical constructs regarding cognitive functions. Path analysis is an offshoot of the procedure. These are the refinements of factor analytic procedure that we have used. The time has come to abandon factor analysis, after it has provided us with some clues to carry out empirical investigations. Some examples of empirical studies are provided throughout this book. The investigation of the PASS constructs does not need more factor analyses.

Luria's Theory as a Raft

The functional organization of brain into three blocks provided us with the major cognitive processes of the PASS model. Throughout this book, however, we have gone beyond Luria's initial observations as new knowledge from neuropsychology and cognitive psychology has come to our notice. We view PASS as a framework for research, inviting further elaboration. As we incorporate new discoveries in each of the PASS processes, especially in Attention and Planning (see, for example, Posner [1991]), Luria's notions will be left behind. For Luria (1969) this would be what he predicted. He envied the future generation of researchers who would discover the workings of the frontal lobe and conceptualize planning and consciousness in scientific experiments.

The PASS model does not include motivation, affect, and personality as these influence "cognitive" functions. It has to, as it is applied to everyday learning, memory, and thinking. More importantly, its application to rehabilitation of cognitively impaired individuals and prescription for the amelioration of certain deficits such as reading disability will compel the model to connect to affect, motivation, and personality. Assessment of these components will be difficult and most certainly will require a drastic-change in the procedure we have adopted for PASS. Instead of the current practice of assessing a cognitive function within a short span of a few minutes, we may have to adopt long-term observation and monitoring of an individual's activities in everyday situations. Autobiographical records and data provided by co-workers and family members may need to be collected and assessed. We have both the tools and the rules for this purpose; the difficulty is to utilize them. A major obstacle is the traditional assessment procedures that psychologists currently follow. We may have to leave them behind as well.

Our attitude toward the PASS model is not to defend it. As theoretical views of cognitive functions and their applications evolve, we should be reminded of the inherent in the raft metaphor: The true picture of mental functions that will emerge could be neither PASS, nor its alternatives, nor the dimension defined by PASS and its alternatives.

J.R.K.

In what follows I review key issues raised in this book from a number of angles provided by the raft allegory. Mostly these angles relate to the dilemmas faced in raft construction before the river is crossed. The issues derive partly from what I am and what I do: I teach psychology to students becoming teachers and to teachers becoming (again) students. I have a particular interest in literacy and in some students' failure to acquire it.

So Who Needs to Cross Rivers?

As we have indicated, there is a great deal of controversy over intelligence and its measurement. On one side there are the concerned parents and practitioners, who fear the effects of mismeasurement and perhaps even the effects of accurate measurement. On the other side are the scientists, who see intelligence as a construct to be measured just like any other construct, and the professional testers and test developers, who see an established use for their measures. In terms of our parable, those opposed to intelligence testing question the need to cross this particular river (the "river of intelligence"), while those blindly in favor are inclined to cross any river.

We have taken a middle path, as the Buddha suggests, between these two extremes. Yes, it is true, measurement has its effects, and mismeasurement, or the measurement of the wrong things, can have very undesirable effects. But ignorance is no solution. Valid measurement of the appropriate constructs, followed by competent interpretation and application of the results, is critical if we are to advance in solving the problems of low achievement.

Lacking a theory, traditional IQ testing relied upon correlation for its justification; because the test scores correlated with, for instance, school success, they were good measures of the cognitive processes underlying school success. Yet race and home background are also good correlates of achievement in many societies, and no one seriously believes they are good *measures* of cognitive processes (if they are *correlates,* then we seek to discover *why* so that education can minimize negative effects of the correlations). We suggest that theory is essential; not only is it a raft, but it leads you to understand which rivers need to be crossed (which constructs need to be measured).

The wise person carefully chooses which river to cross.

Before the Flood, Who Needed Rafts?

The concept of intelligence as a general cognitive process seems to have emerged only in the middle to late nineteenth century. Perhaps some enterprising classical scholar will locate a reference to something like intelligence in the works of ancient Greece, or India, or Mesoamerica; even so, there is no doubt that the notion of intelligence only became prominent in the last 150 years or so.

I doubt that you could go into a traditional oral society (one that we condescendingly term "primitive") and ask for the "most intelligent" individual to be identified. While I haven't tried to do this, I suspect that there would be great difficulties in translating the word *intelligent,* and that once it had been translated, there would be great confusion. I can imagine an informant asking whether we wanted the best hunter, or best weaver, or the most powerful person in the village, but denying that there was any purpose in looking for the person who was generally the best. Our local consultant might even indicate that hunters don't weave and weavers don't hunt, so who could tell? If theories are rafts and phenomena are rivers, why was the river of intelligence not discovered, or seen to need to be crossed, for so many years of human history?

Intelligence refers to generalized cognitive processes, ones that are fundamentally decontextualized. This is not to deny that they are measured in a context—everything has to be—or that school represents a very particular context. They are decontextualized in the sense that they are transsituational; we want students to be able to read, write, do arithmetic, solve problems, and more generally think across a broad range of contexts, not just the ones encountered in school, and probably including ones we cannot even imagine yet. The purpose of schooling is to develop those generalized, decontextualized processes (Kirby & Biggs, in preparation).

Deconceptualized processes and schooling are intimately linked to literacy, especially to literacy that is widespread and well established (cf. Ong, 1982), and alphabetic (cf. Logan, 1986). Societies require that more basic needs be satisfied before literacy and schooling can become goals; similarly, persons within a society need options regarding careers and options within careers before generalized cognitive processes become critical. This does not mean that preliterate societies or illiterate individuals are "unintelligent" either in their context or on our tests; the point is simply that intelligence is in those cases neither a societal nor personal goal.

The wise person waits for the river before building her raft; she also considers the shape of the land, and does not wait in the path of the coming river.

The Right Twine, the Right Logs

Critical in raft or theory building are that components to use. Should one go for large logs or small ones? Broad theoretical constructs or narrow ones? And how should we tie them together?

We have opted for a middle path here, too. The psychologists behind traditional approaches to intelligence can be faulted for relying upon constructs that are too broad: The obvious case is that of intelligence as a one-dimensional scale of merit (Das, 1991), but "verbal ability" is another good candidate. As raft builders these psychologists seem to favor very large logs. One wonders how they would maneuver the raft into the water, get atop it, and stop it from rolling over on them.

Others have tended to very narrow, task-specific theories (e.g., of particular reading skills) or to theories of intelligence that fragmented it into many narrowly defined factors (e.g., Guilford's 1967, cube of 120 forms of intelligence). As raft builders these psychologists have favored twigs; they may be easy to maneuver, but you need too many to make a raft, and too much theoretical twine to bind them together. Alternatively, they may only be good for crossing very small rivers.

The four major components of PASS represent constructs of moderate generality and specificity. As we have indicated, there may often be value in analyzing each of these components into distinctive parts (see also Kirby, 1989; Kirby & Williams, 1991). For example, planning may be quite different for some subjects in different domains, and it may be possible to identify distinct clusters of planning skills (Kirby & Ashman, 1984). The twine that holds our raft together is theory. Optimally our theory is like good twine, flexible enough to take some empirical bumps, but not so elastic that the logs escape.

The wise man designs his raft to fit the river, and worries as much about the twine as the logs.

. . . To Get to the Other Side

Like the proverbial chicken, we should keep in mind that the purpose of our raft building is to get to the other side. Educational psychology and school psychology are fundamentally *applied* psychologies, aiming to make an impact in the real world. It is essential that our theories be valid, that they float. But we must not forget about applicability. An intricate theory may be too complex to be applied, or even to be understood by practitioners. Alternatively, the role of applied psychologists may be to translate complex theory into forms that can be understood and applied. We have little time for attractive rafts if they won't float or carry us to our goal.

We have tried to show how the PASS theory leads to the assessment of strengths and weaknesses (one form of application), the understanding of these results (diagnosis, another form of application), and, finally, how diagnosis may lead to remediation (a third aspect of application). We hope the days are over when the world of psychological assessment and the world of remediation are separated by an uncrossable river.

Good theory is definitely the raft to make the crossing. Is PASS the right raft? So far it seems to work better than any other we know, but the real test will come in application. Even if it is the right raft, only application will tell us which logs are loose or need replacing and whether we are steering in the right direction. We should keep our mind on the goal, however, and not be too obsessed with the raft.

The best raft is one that works.

J.A.N.

The Buddhist parable of the raft is an appropriate frame within which to set the problems facing those who study and use intelligence tests. This story can help guide our thinking today as it has since the third century before the birth of Christ. The components of the story—the journey already completed, the river, the raft, and the dilemma—all can be interpreted as elements of problems that have been faced by people in all professions, countries, and cultures of the world. Perhaps discussion of this parable can help us see its meaning in relation to the theme of our text—changing from traditional to more modern views of intelligence.

What are the important components of this Buddhist story? As you may recall, a person is returning home after a long journey and comes upon an unexpected obstacle, a swollen river. In order to complete the journey, the traveler builds a sturdy raft out of branches, logs, and vines from the forest and proudly uses it to cross the river. Upon reaching the other side, the traveler is faced with a dilemma—what to do with the raft? It was so well made and it was so valuable to overcome the obstacle posed by the swollen river, and so much was learned about how to use it during the trip. How can it now be left on the other side of the river bank to fall into disrepair? But if it is kept, completing the journey home would be made more difficult because there is still some distance to travel, and the raft is too big and heavy to move over land. Of course this story can be interpreted to tell us much about transitions in our personal life, but in this case, what does it tell us about professional transitions?

The Past

The journey already taken can be interpreted as the knowledge the individual has acquired from past experience. This includes all the beliefs that have been accumulated, the habits developed, and the things one does on a daily basis to function effectively. Clearly, the person's knowledge influences what the traveler thinks and does because it provides the basis for decision making. Simply put, the person's experiences and know-how guide current opinions and future actions.

The knowledge gained during the journey can provide the traveler with important and useful information—how to build a raft that will float and not sink, how to tie the logs together so that they do not loosen in the middle of the river, how to steer the raft to the desired goal, and so on. The person's past may also help guide the decisions of what to do once the river has been crossed.

Now, if the person has learned the lesson that the Buddha stressed regarding the value of all objects, then the decision of what to do with the raft after it has served its purpose would be simpler to make. Buddha encouraged people to recognize that the value of everything is not constant; it is "impermanent [and] subject to change" (Kalupahana & Kalupahana, 1987, p. 19). This same concept appears in the Sanskrit writings of the ancient Hindu sages (about 600 B.C.), in *The Upanishads*. Here all things are described as having three types of values: first, as an object of love that brings joy; second, as an object that can give us knowledge and power; and third, as an object seen as a possession that provides the "chains that bind us to matter . . . [and] drag us down" (Mascaro, 1965, p. 18). If the traveler clings to the raft as an object of attachment, the journey ends on the other side of the river. Further travel is not possible. If the traveler is too attached to the object and is unwilling to leave it behind, the object that at one time liberated the traveler from the bounds of the swollen river becomes repressive and a burden for the future even though the river has been crossed.

Thus, although the transition has been begun (the river crossed), fulfillment (completion of the voyage home) will be blocked. The raft could become a limit on future achievements because of past advantages.

The Present

How should the traveler view the raft? Clearly, the raft was very valuable, but the value was finite. Forging the river, which represents confusion, stress, and ignorance, would not have been possible without the cherished raft. It was needed to avoid the endless confusion that certainly would have emerged in an attempt to cross the turbulent river unassisted by the raft. If the traveler places value on the raft based on its past utility, then its present and future values are overestimated. It is not as valuable once the river has been crossed as it was before the river was crossed. That is, all current objects will, in time, become outdated and their usefulness reduced because everything changes and, as a result, nothing has permanent value. The current value of the raft, therefore, is different from its past value.

The traveler is faced with a decision: Retain the raft and carry it as a relic of the past or leave it as a once useful object that no longer has the same value? Like the poem by Robert Frost "The Road Not Taken" (Frost, 1979), two divergent paths lie before the traveler, and the one taken makes all the difference. If the traveler's mind is confused by the need to be overly attached to the raft because of familiarity, sentimentality, or comfort, then the conflict begins. If the traveler is unwilling to consider alternatives to carrying the raft, insists on its permanent value and stubbornly clinging to the well-trodden path, then the decision to retain the raft will become the burden of the future.

The Future

The raft story is a simple one and at the same time a complex one that illustrates the need for acceptance of change. In our profession, and in the field of intelligence testing particularly, we have seen little change since the beginning of this century. Do we cling to the past and let this become the burden of the future, or do we recognize the value of our past accomplishments as positive steps taken some 75 years ago and look for further advances to better understand those we work with? Of course I feel that the lesson of the story of the raft is that we must change and adapt to the ever evolving demands of professional life, as in our personal life, to achieve more effective practice. We need to use our intellect, described by Aquinis as "the best activity of man, and that [which] is of his highest potency" (Bourke, 1960, p. 43) to solve the problems we face so that we can move forward unencumbered by emotional ties and biases about past methods of practice. To me, the future looks good because we are on the edge of a major transition from old theories that limited us to new approaches that offer alternatives. Perhaps the information contained in this book and others like it (e.g., Kirby & Williams, 1991) will encourage the reader to consider our alternative.

REFERENCES

Achenbach, T. M., & Edelbrock, C. (1983). *Manual for the Child Behavior Checklist and Revised Child Behavior Profile.* Burlington, VT: Achenbach.

American Psychiatric Association: *Diagnostic and Statistical Manual of Mental Disorders,* Third Edition, Washington, DC: APA, 1980.

American Psychiatric Association: *Diagnostic and Statistical Manual of Mental Disorders,* Revised Edition, Washington, DC: APA, 1987.

Anastasi, A. (1988). *Psychological testing* (6th ed.). New York: Macmillan.

Arlin, P. K. (1977). Piagetian operations in problem finding. *Developmental Psychology, 13,* 297–298.

Ashcraft, M. H. (1982). The development of mental arithmetic: A chronometric approach. *Developmental Review, 2,* 213–236.

Ashman, A. (1978). *The relationship between planning and simultaneous and successive synthesis.* Unpublished doctoral dissertation. Department of Educational Psychology, University of Alberta, Edmonton.

Ashman, A. F. (1982). Cognitive processes and perceived language performance of retarded persons. *Journal of Mental Deficiency Research, 26,* 131–141.

Ashman, A. (1985). Problem solving and planning: Two sides of the same coin. In A. Ashman & R. Laura (Eds.), *The Education and Training of the Mentally Retarded* (pp. 169–214). New York: Nichols.

Ashman, A. F., & Das, J. P. (1980). Relation between planning and simultaneous-successive processing. *Perceptual and Motor Skills, 51,* 371–382.

Atkinson, R., & Shiffrin, R. (1968). Human memory: A proposed system and its control processes. In K. W. Spence & J. T. Spence (Eds.), *The psychology of learning and motivation: Advances in theory and research* (vol. 2). New York: Academic Press.

Baddeley, A. D. (1986). *Working memory.* Oxford, UK: Oxford University Press.

Baddeley, A. D. (1990). *Human memory: Theory and practice.* Boston: Allyn and Bacon.

Baddeley, A. D., & Hitch, G. (1974). Working memory. In G. Bower (Ed.), *The psychology of learning and motivation: Advances in research and theory* (vol. 8) (pp. 47–89). New York: Academic Press.

Bardos, A. N. (1988). *Differentiation of normal, reading disabled, and developmentally handicapped students using the Das-Naglieri cognitive processing tasks.* Unpublished doctoral dissertation. Ohio State University, Columbus, Ohio.

Barkley, R. A. (1990). *Attention-deficit hyperactivity disorder:* A handbook for diagnosis and treatment. New York: Guilford Press.

Belmont, J., & Butterfield, E. (1971). What the development of short-term memory is. *Human Development, 14,* 236–248.

Belmont, J., & Butterfield, E. (1977). The instructional approach to developmental cognitive research. In R. Kail & J. Hagen (Eds.), *Perspectives on the development of memory and cognition.* Hillsdale, NJ: Erlbaum.

Biggs, J. B. (1987). *Student approaches to learning and studying.* Melbourne, Australia: Australian Council for Educational Research.

Biggs, J. B., & Kirby, J. R. (1984). Differentiation of learning processes within ability groups. *Educational Psychology, 4,* 21–39.

Boder, E. (1973). Developmental dyslexia: A diagnostic approach based on three atypical reading-spelling patterns. *Developmental Medicine and Child Neurology, 15,* 663–682.

Boersma, F., & Chapman, B. (1989). *Students' perception of abilities scale.* Unpublished manuscript. Department of Educational Psychology, University of Alberta, Edmonton.

Bogen, J. E. (1969). The other side of the brain: Parts, I, II, and III. *Bulletin of the Los Angeles Neurological Society, 34,* 73–105, 135–162, 191–203.

Borkowski, J., & Cavanaugh, J. (1979). Maintenance and generalization of skills and strategies by the retarded. In N. R. Ellis (Ed.), *Handbook of mental deficiency: Psychological theory and research.* Hillsdale, NJ: Erlbaum.

Bourke, U. J. (1960). *The pocket Aquinas.* New York: Simon & Schuster.

Bradley, L., & Bryant, P. (1983). Categorizing sounds and learning to read: A causal connexion. *Nature, 301,* 419–421.

Brailsford, A. (1981). *The relationship between cognitive strategy training and performance on tasks of reading comprehension within a learning disabled group of children.* Unpublished master's thesis. University of Alberta, Edmonton.

Brailsford, A., Snart, F., & Das, J. P. (1984). Strategy training and reading comprehension. *Journal of Learning Disabilities, 17,* 287–290.

Broadbent, D. E. (1958). Perception and communication. Elmsford, NY: Pergamon Press, London.

Broadbent, D. E. (1977). The hidden preattentive processes. *American Psychologist, 32,* 109–118.

Broadbent, D. E. (1984). The Maltese cross: A new simplistic model for memory. *Behavioral and Brain Sciences, 7,* 55–94.

Broadbent, D., Fitzgerald, P., & Broadbent, M. (1986). Implicit and explicit knowledge in the control of complex systems. *British Journal of Psychology, 77,* 33–50.

Brown, A. (1977). Development, schooling and the acquisition of knowing about knowledge. In R. Anderson, R. Spiro, & W. Montague (Eds.), *Schooling and the acquisition of knowledge.* Hillsdale, NJ: Erlbaum.

Brown, A., Bransford, J., Ferrara, R., & Campione, J. (1983). Learning, remembering, and understanding. In J. H. Flavell & E. M. Markman (Eds.), *Carmichael's manual of child psychology* (vol. 3) (pp. 142). New York: Wiley.

Brown, A., & Campione, J. (1981). Inducing flexible thinking: The problem of access. In M. Friedman, J. P. Das, & N. O'Connor (Eds.), *Intelligence and learning.* New York: Plenum.

Brown, A., & Campione, J. (1986). Psychological theory and the study of learning disabilities. *American Psychologist, 14,* 1059–1068.

Bruck, M. (1990). Word-recognition skills of adults with childhood diagnoses of dyslexia. *Developmental Psychology, 26*(3), 434–454.

Bryden, M. P. (1990). Choosing sides: The left and right of the normal brain. *Canadian Psychology, 31*, 297–309.

Budoff, M., & Friedman, M. (1964). "Learning potential" as an assessment approach to the adolescent mentally retarded. *Journal of Consulting Psychology, 28*, 434–439.

Burns, P. C., & Roe, B. D. (1980). *Informal reading assessment: Preprimer to twelfth grade*. Boston: Houghton Mifflin.

Campbell, S. B., Douglas, V. I., & Morgenstern, G. (1971). Cognitive styles in hyperactive children and the effect of methylphenidate. *Journal of Child Psychology and Psychiatry, 12*, 55–67.

Campbell, S. B., & Werry, J. S. (1986). Attention deficit disorder (hyperactivity). In H. C. Quay & J. S. Werry (Eds.), *Psychopathological disorders of childhood* (3rd ed). New York: Wiley.

Campione, J., & Brown, A. (1984). Learning ability and transfer propensity as sources of individual differences in intelligence. In P. Brooks, R. Sperber, & C. McCauley (Eds.), *Learning and cognition in the mentally handicapped* (pp. 137–150). Baltimore, MD: University Park Press.

Campione, J., & Brown, A. (1987). Linking dynamic assessment with school achievement. In C. Lidz (Ed.), *Dynamic assessment* (pp. 82–115). New York: Guilford Press.

Carr, M., & Borkowski, J. G. (1989). Attributional training and the generalization of reading strategies in underachieving children. *Learning and Individual Differences, 1*, 327–341.

Carroll, J. B. (1976). Psychometric tests as cognitive tasks: New "structure of intellect." In L. B. Resnick (Ed.), The nature of intelligence. Hillsdale, NJ: Erlbaum.

Carroll, J. B. (1983). Studying individual differences in cognitive abilities: Through and beyond factor analysis. In R. F. Dillon (Ed.), *Individual differences in cognition* (pp. 1–33). New York: Academic Press.

Case, R. (1980). The underlying mechanism of intellectual development. In J. R. Kirby & J. B. Biggs (Eds.), *Cognition, development and instruction* (pp. 5–38). New York: Academic Press.

Cohen, J., Dunbar, K., & McClelland, J. (1990). On the control of automatic processes: A parallel distributed processing account of the Stroop effect. *Psychological Review, 97*(3), 332–361.

Cohen, N. J., Weiss, G., & Minde, K. (1972). Cognitive styles in adolescents previously diagnosed as hyperactives. *Journal of Child Psychology and Psychiatry, 13*, 203–209.

Conners, C. (1969). A teacher ratings scale for use in drug studies with children. *American Journal of Psychiatry, 126*, 884–888.

Conway, R. F. (1985). *The information processing model and the mildly developmentally delayed child: Assessment and training*. Unpublished doctoral dissertation. Macquarie University, Newcastle, Australia.

Copeland, A., & Reiner, E. (1984). The selective attention of learning-disabled children: Three studies. *Journal of Abnormal Child Psychology, 12*, 455–470.

Corballis, M. C. (1980). Laterality and myth. *American Psychologist, 35,* 284–295.

Corballis, M. C. (1989). Laterality and human evolution. *Psychological Review, 96,* 492–505.

Cormier, P., Carlson, J. S., & Das, J. P. (1990). Planning ability and cognitive performance: The compensatory effects of a dynamic assessment approach. *Learning and Individual Differences,* 2(4), 437–449.

Cowan, N. (1988). Evolving conceptions of memory storage, selective attention, and their mutual constraints within the human information-processing system. *Psychological Bulletin, 104*(2), 163–191.

Crawford, S. A. S. (1990). *Decoding in gifted/LD children: A process-based remedial approach.* Unpublished master's thesis. University of Alberta, Edmonton.

Cronbach, L. J. (1957). The two disciplines of scientific psychology. *American Psychologist, 12,* 671–684.

Cronbach, L. J., & Snow, R. E. (1977). *Aptitudes and instructional methods: A handbook for research on interactions.* New York: Irvington.

Cummins, J., & Das, J. P. (1977). Cognitive processing and reading difficulties: A framework for research. *Alberta Journal of Educational Research, 23,* 245–256.

Cummins, J., & Das, J. P. (1978). Simultaneous and successive syntheses and linguistic processes. *International Journal of Psychology, 13,* 129–138.

Cummins, J. P., & Das, J. P. (1980). Cognitive processing, academic achievement, and WISC-R performance in EMR children. *Journal of Consulting and Clinical Psychology, 48,* 777–779.

Daneman, M., & Carpenter, P. A. (1980). Individual differences in working memory and reading. *Journal of Verbal Learning and Verbal Behavior, 19,* 450–466.

Das, J. P. (1969). Development of verbal abilities in retarded and normal children as measured by Stroop test. *British Journal of Social Clinical Psychology, 8,* 59–66.Das, J. P. (1970). Vigilance and verbal conditioning in the mildly and severely retarded. *American Journal of Mental Deficiency, 75,* 253–259.

Das, J. P. (1972). Patterns of cognitive ability in nonretarded and retarded children. *American Journal of Mental Deficiency, 77,* 6–12.

Das, J. P. (1973a). Cultural deprivation and cognitive competence. In N. R. Ellis (Ed.), *International review of research in mental retardation* (vol. 6) (pp. 2–53). New York: Academic Press.

Das, J. P. (1973b). Structure of cognitive abilities: Evidence for simultaneous and successive processing. *Journal of Educational Psychology, 65,* 103–108.

Das, J. P. (1980). Planning: Theoretical considerations and empirical evidence. *Psychological Research* (W. Germany), *41,* 141–151.

Das, J. P. (1983). Process training and remediation of reading disability: Examples of some Soviet tasks. *Mental Retardation and Learning Disability Bulletin, 11,* 32–41.

Das, J. P. (1984a). Aspects of planning. In J. R. Kirby (Ed.), *Cognitive strategies and educational performance* (pp. 13–31, 35–50). New York: Academic Press.

Das, J. P. (1984b). Cognitive deficits in mental retardation: A process approach. In P. H. Brooks, R. Sperber, & C. McCauley (Eds.), *Learning and cognition in the mentally retarded* (pp. 115–128). Hillsdale, NJ: Erlbaum.

Das, J. P. (1984c). Simultaneous and successive processing in children with learning disability. *Topics in Language Disorders, 4,* 34–47.

Das, J. P. (1984d). Simultaneous-successive processes and K-ABC. *Journal of Special Education, 18,* 229–238.Das, J. P. (1985a). Aspects of digit span. *American Journal of Mental Deficiency, 89,* 627–634.

Das, J. P. (1985b). Remedial training for the amelioration of cognitive deficits in children. In A. Ashman & R. Laura (Eds.), *The education and training of the mentally retarded* (pp. 214–244). London: Croom Helm.

Das, J. P. (1988a). Coding, attention, and planning: A cap for every head. In J. W. Berry, S. H. Irvine, & E. B. Hunt (Eds.), *Indigenous cognition: Functioning in cultural context* (pp. 39–56). NATO ASI Series. Dordrecht, The Netherlands: Nijhoff.

Das, J. P. (1988b). Simultaneous-successive processing and planning. In R. Schmeck (Ed.), *Learning Styles and learning strategies* (pp. 101–129). New York: Plenum.

Das, J. P. (1992). Beyond a unidimensional scale of merit. *Intelligence, 16,* 137–149.

Das, J. P. (1993). Differences in cognitive processes of children with reading disabilities and normal readers. *Developmental Disabilities Bulletin, 21,* (1) pp. 42–59.

Das, J. P., Bisanz, G. L., & Mancini, G. (1984). Performance of good and poor readers on cognitive tasks: Changes with development and reading competence. *Journal of Learning Disabilities, 17,* 549–555.

Das, J. P., & Conway, R. N. F. (1992). Reflections on remediation and transfer: A Vygotskian perspective. In H. C. Haywood & D. Tzuriel (Eds.), *Interactive assessment.* New York: Springer.

Das, J. P., & Cummins, J. (1979). Academic performance and cognitive processes in EMR children. *American Journal of Mental Deficiency, 83,* 197–199.

Das, J. P., & Cummins, J. (1982). Language processing and reading disability. In K. D. Gaddow & I.+Bailer (Eds.), *Advances in learning disabilities* (vol. 1). Greenwich, CN.: JAI Press.

Das, J. P., Cummins, J., Kirby, J. R., & Jarman, R. F. (1979). Simultaneous and successive processes, language and mental abilities. *Canadian Psychological Review, 20,* 1–11.

Das, J. P., & Dash, U. N. (1983). Hierarchical factor solution of coding and planning processes: Any new insights? *Intelligence, 7,* 27–37.

Das, J. P., & Heemsbergen, D. B. (1983). Planning as a factor in the assessment of cognitive processes. *Journal of Psychoeducational Assessment, 1,* 1–16.

Das, J. P., Kirby, J. R., & Jarman, R. F. (1975). Simultaneous and successive synthesis: An alternative model. *Psychological Bulletin, 82,* 87–103.

Das, J. P., Kirby, J. R., & Jarman, R. F. (1979). *Simultaneous and successive cognitive processes.* New York: Academic Press.

Das, J. P., Leong, C. K., & Williams, N. H. (1978). The relationship between learning disability and simultaneous-successive processing. *Journal of Learning Disabilities, 11,* 16–23.

Das, J. P., Mensink, D., & Janzen, H. (1990) The K-ABC, coding, and planning: An investigation of cognitive processes. *Journal of School Psychology, 28,* 1–11.

Das, J. P., Mensink, D., & Mishra, R. K. (1990). Cognitive processes separating good and poor readers when IQ is covaried. *Learning and Individual Differences, 2*(4), 423–436.

Das, J. P., & Molloy, G. N. (1975). Varieties of simultaneous and successive processing in children. *Journal of Educational Psychology, 67,* 213–220.

Das, J. P., & Naglieri, J. A. (1989). *Das-Naglieri: cognitive assessment system.* (Experimental ed.). Unpublished test.

Das, J. P., & Naglieri, J. A. (1993). Das-Naglieri: *Cognitive Assessment System Standardization Edition.* Chicago: Riverside Publishing Co.

Das, J. P., & Siu, I. (1989). Good and poor readers' word naming time, memory span, and story recall. *Journal of Experimental Education, 57*(2), 101–114.

Das, J. P., Snart, F., & Mulcahy, R. F. (1982). Reading disability and its relation to information integration. In J. P. Das, R. F. Mulcahy, & A. E. Wall (Eds.), *Theory and research in learning disabilities.* New York: Plenum.

Das, J. P., & Varnhagen, C. (1986). Neuropsychological functioning and cognitive processing. *Child Neuropsychology, 1,* 117–140.

Dash, U. N., Puhan, B. N., & Mahapatra, S. (1985). Information integration modes in concrete operational skills of grade two children. *Psychological Studies, 30,* 22–25.

Davies, D. R., Jones, D. M., & Taylor, A. (1984). Selective-and sustained-attention tasks: Individual and group differences. In R. Parasuraman & D. R. Davies (Eds.), *Varieties of attention* (pp. 395–447). Orlando, FL: Academic Press.

Davies, D. R., & Parasuraman, R. (1982). The psychology of vigilance. London: Academic Press.

Davydov, V. C., & Radzikhovskii, L. A. (1985). Vygotsky's theory and the activity-oriented approach in psychology. In J. V. Wertsch (Ed.), *Culture, communication, and cognition.* Cambridge, MA: Cambridge University Press.

Denckla, M., & Rudel, R. G. (1976). Rapid automatized naming (RAN): Dyslexia from other learning disabilities. *Neuropsychologia, 14,* 471–479.

De Sonneville, L., & Njiokiktjien, C. (1988). *Pediatric behavioural neurology.* Amsterdam: Suyi.

Douglas, V. I. (1980). Assessing the attentional deficit of hyperactive children. In C. K. Whalen & B. Henker (Eds.), *Hyperactive children: The social ecology of identification and treatment.* New York: Academic Press.

Douglas, V. I., & Peters, K. G. (1979). Toward a clearer definition of the attentional deficit of hyperactive children. In G. A. Hale & M. Lewis (Eds.), *Attention and the development of cognitive skills.* New York: Plenum.

Doyle, R. B., Anderson, R. P., & Halcomb, C. G. (1976). Attention deficits and the effects of visual distraction. *Journal of Learning Disabilities, 9,* 48–54.

Dunbar, K., & MacLeod, C. (1984). A horse race of a different color: Stroop interference patterns with transformed words. *Journal of Experimental Psychology, 10,* 622–639.

Duncan-Johnson, C. C., & Kopell, B. S. (1981). The Stroop effect: Brain potentials localize the source of interference. *Science, 214,* 938–940.

Dunn, L., & Markwardt, F. (1970). Examiner's manual: Peabody Individual Achievement Test. Circle Pines, MN: American Guidance Service.

Dykman, R. A., Ackerman, P. T., Clements, S. D., & Peters, J. E. (1971). Specific learning disabilities: An attentional deficit syndrome. In H. R. Myklebust (Ed.), *Progress in learning disabilities* (vol. 2). New York: Grune & Stratton.

Easterbrook, J. A. (1959). Effects of emotion on cue utilization and organization of behavior. *Psychological Review, 66,* 183–201.

Ekwall, E., & Shanker, J. (1988). *Diagnosis and remediation of the disabled reader.* Boston: Allyn and Bacon.

Ellis, N. R. (1979). *Handbook of mental deficiency, psychological theory and research* (2nd ed.). Hillsdale, NJ: Erlbaum.

Estes, W. K. (1976). Intelligence and cognitive psychology. In L. B. Resnick (Ed), *The nature of intelligence* (pp. 295–305). Hillsdale, NJ: Erlbaum.

Estes, W. (1982). Learning, memory, and intelligence. In R. Sternberg (Ed.), *Handbook of human intelligence* (pp. 170–224). Cambridge, MA: Cambridge University Press.

Eysenck, H. J. (1957). *The dynamics of anxiety and hysteria.* New York: Praeger.

Feuerstein, R. (1979). *The dynamic assessment of retarded performers: The Learning Potential Assessment Device, theory, instruments, and techniques.* Baltimore, MD: University Park Press.

Feuerstein, R., & Hamburger, M. (1965). *A proposal to study the process of redevelopment in several groups of deprived early adolescents in both residential and non-residential settings.* Unpublished report. The Youth-Aliyah Department of the Jewish Agency, Jerusalem.

Feuerstein, R., Rand, Y., Hoffman, M. B., & Miller, R. (1980). *Instrumental enrichment.* Baltimore, MD: University Park Press.

Flavell, J. (1970). Developmental studies of mediated memory. In H. Reese & L. P. Lipsitt (Eds.), *Advances in child development and behavior* (vol. 5). New York: Academic Press.

Fleisher, L. S., Sodak, L. C., & Jelin, M. A. (1984). Selective attention deficits in learning disabled children: Analysis of the data base. *Exceptional Children, 51,* 136–141.

Ford, C. E., Pelham, W. E., & Ross, A. O. (1984). Selective attention and rehearsal in the auditory short-term memory task performance of poor and normal readers. *Journal of Abnormal Child Psychology, 12,* 127–142.

Frith, U. (1986). A developmental framework for developmental dyslexia. *Annals of Dyslexia, 36,* 69–81.

Frith, U. (1992). Cognitive development and cognitive deficit. *The Psychologist, 5* (1), 13–19.

Fuster, J. (1989). *The prefrontal cortex.* New York: Raven Press.

Galton, F. (1883). *Inquiries into human faculty and its development.* London: Macmillan.

Gardner, H. (1983). *Frames of mind: The theory of multiple intelligences.* New York: Basic Books.

Gardner, H. (1985). *The mind's new science: A history of the cognitive revolution.* New York: Basic Books.

Garofalo, J. F. (1982). Simultaneous synthesis, behavior regulation and arithmetic performance. *Journal of Psychoeducational Assessment, 4,* 229–238.

Gazzaniga, M. S. (1970). *The bisected brain.* New York: Appleton Century Crofts.

Geschwind, N. (1982). Disorders of attention: A frontier in neuropsychology. *Philosophical Transactions of The Royal Society of London, 298,* 173–185.

Glidden, L. M. (1979). Training of learning and memory in retarded persons: Strategies, techniques, and teaching tools. In N. R. Ellis (Ed.), *Handbook of mental deficiency, psychological theory and research* (2nd ed.), (pp. 619–657). Hillsdale, NJ: Erlbaum.

Gordon, H. W., & Bogen, J. E. (1974). Hemispheic lateralization of singing after

intacarotid sodium amylobarbitone. *Journal of Neurology, Neurosurgery, and Psychiatry, 37,* 727–738.
Gordon, M. (1983). *The Gordon Diagnostic System.* Boulder, CO: Clinical Diagnostic Systems.
Graf, P., & Schacter, D. L. (1985). Implicit and explicit memory for new associations in normal and amnesic subjects. *Journal of Experimental Psychology, 11,* 501–518.
Graham, F. K. & Kendall, B. S. (1960). Memory-for-designs test: Revised general manual. *Perceptual and Motor Skills, 11,* 147–188.
Guilford, J. P. (1967). *The nature of human intelligence.* New York: McGraw-Hill.
Guilford, J. P. (1973). Theories of intelligence. In B. B. Wolman (Ed.), *Handbook of general psychology.* Englewood Cliffs, NJ: Prentice-Hall.
Guttman, L., & Levy, S. (1991). The structural laws of intelligence tests. *Intelligence, 15,* 79–103.
Hallahan, D. P., & Reeve, R. E. (1980). Selective attention and distractibility. In B. K. Keogh (Ed.), *Advances in special education* (vol. 1). Greenwich, CT: JAI Press.
Harris, A. J., & Sipay, E. R. (1980). *How to increase reading ability.* New York: Longman.
Hayes-Roth, B., & Hayes-Roth, F. (1979). A cognitive model of planning. *Cognitive Science, 3,* 275–310.
Haywood, H. C., & Tapp, J. T. (1966). Experience and the development of adaptive behavior. In N. R. Ellis (Ed.), *International review of research in mental retardation* (vol. 1), (pp. 109–151). New York: Academic Press.
Haywood, H., & Tsuriel, D. (1992). *Interactive assessment.* New York: Springer Verlag.
Hebb, D. O. (1960). The American Revolution. *American Psychologist, 15,* 735–745.
Hecaen, H., & Albert, M. (1978). *Human neuropsychology.* New York: Wiley.
Heemsbergen, D. B. (1980). *Planning as a cognitive process: An empirical investigation.* Unpublished doctoral dissertation. University of Alberta, Edmonton.
Hilgard, E. R. (1956). *Theories of learning.* New York: Appleton-Century-Crofts.
Hull, C. L. (1943). *Principles of behavior.* New York: Appleton-Century.
Hunt, E. (1975). Quote the raven? Nevermore! In L. Gregg (Ed.), *Knowledge and cognition.* Potomac, MD: Erlbaum.
Hunt, E. B., Frost, N., & Lunneborg, C. (1973). Individual differences in cognition: A new approach to intelligence. In G. H. Bower (Ed.), *The psychology of learning and motivation* (vol. 7). New York: Academic Press.
Hunt, E., & Lansman, M. (1986). Unified model of attention and problem solving. *Psychological Review, 93,* 446–461.
Hurt, J., & Naglieri, J. A. (1992). Delinquent and normal males' performance on planning, attention simultaneous, successive cognitive processing tasks. *Journal of Clinical Psychology, 48,* 120–128.
Huttenlocher, J. (1968). Constructing spatial images: A strategy in reasoning. *Psychological Review, 75,* 550–560.
Jacobs, J. E, & Paris, S. G. (1987). Children's metacognition about reading: Issues in definition, measurement, and instruction. *Educational Psychologist, 3 & 4,* 255–278.
James, W. (1890). *The principles of psychology.* New York: Holt, Rinehart & Winston.

Jarman, R. F. (1978). Patterns of cognitive ability in retarded children: A reexamination. *American Journal of Mental Deficiency, 82,* 344–348.

Jarman, R. F. (1980). Cognitive processes and syntactic structure: Analyses of syntagmatic and paradigmatic associations. *Psychological Research, 41,* 153–169.

Jarman, R. F., & Das, J. P. (1977). Simultaneous and successive synthesis and intelligence. *Intelligence, 1,* 151–169.

Johnston, W. A., & Dark, V. J. (1986). Selective attention. *Annual Review of Psychology, 37,* 43–75.

Joreskog, K. G., & Sorbom, D. (1986). *LISREL user's guide* (4th ed.). Mooresville, IN: Scientific Software.

Journal of Educational Psychology. (1921). *Intelligence and its measurement: A symposium, 12,* 123–147.

Kagan, J. (1965). Reflection-impulsivity and reading ability in primary grade children. *Child Development, 36,* 609–628.

Kahneman, D. (1973). *Attention and effort.* Englewood Cliffs, NJ: Prentice Hall.

Kahneman, D., & Treisman, A. (1984). Changing views of attention and automaticity. In R. Parasuraman & D. R. Davies (Eds.), *Varieties of attention* (pp. 29–61). New York: Academic Press.

Kalupahana, D. J., & Kalupahana, I. (1987). *The way of Siddhartha: A life of the Buddha.* New York: University Press of America.

Kar, B. C., Dash, U. N., Das, J. P., & Carlson, J. (1993). Two experiments on the dynamic assessment of planning. *Learning and Individual Differences, 5,* 13–29.

Karnes, F. A., & McCallum, R. S. (1983). Evidence for the Luria-Das model of information processing for gifted students: A preliminary investigation. *Educational and Psychological Research, 3,* 133–137.

Kaufman, A. S. (1975). Factor analysis of the WISC-R at eleven age levels between 6 1/2 and 16 1/2 years. *Journal of Consulting and Clinical Psychology, 43,* 135–147.

Kaufman, A. S. (1979). *Intelligent testing with the WISC-R.* New York: Wiley.

Kaufman, A., & Kaufman, N. (1983). *The Kaufman Assessment Battery for Children: Interpretative manual.* Circle Pines, MN: American Guidance Service.

Kaufman, A., & McLean, J. E. (1987). Joint factor analysis of the K-ABC and WISC-R with normal children. *Journal of School Psychology, 25,* 105–118.

Kaufman, D. (1978). *The relationship of academic performance to strategy training and remedial techniques: An information processing approach.* Unpublished doctoral dissertation. University of Alberta, Edmonton.

Kaufman, D., & Kaufman, P. (1978). Strategy training and remedial techniques. *Journal of Learning Disabilities, 16,* 72–78.

Keith, T. M., & Novak C. G. (1987). Joint factor structure of the WISC-R and K-ABC for referred school children. *Journal of Psychoeducational Assessment, 4,* 370–386.

Keogh, B. K., & Margolis, J. S. (1976). Learn to labor and wait: Attentional problems of children with learning disorders. *Journal of Learning Disabilities, 9,* 276–286.

Kirby, J. R. (1980). Individual differences and cognitive processes: Instructional application and methodological difficulties. In J. R. Kirby & J. Biggs (Eds.), *Cognition, development and instruction* (pp. 119–143). New York: Academic Press.

Kirby, J. R. (1982). Cognitive processes, school achievement, and comprehension of ambiguous sentences. *Journal of Psycholinguistic Research, 11,* 485–499.

Kirby, J. (1984). Educational role of cognitive plans and strategies. In J. Kirby (Ed.),

Cognitive strategies and educational performance (pp. 51–88). Orlando, FL: Academic Press.

Kirby, J. R. (1988). Style, strategy, and skill in reading. In R. R. Schmeck (Ed.), *Learning strategies and learning styles.* New York: Plenum.

Kirby, J. R. (1989). Generality and specificity in strategy instruction. *Canadian Journal of Special Education, 5,* 179–186.

Kirby, J., & Ashman, A. (1984). Planning skills and mathematics achievement: Implications regarding learning disability. *Journal of Psychoeducational Assessment, 2,* 9–22.

Kirby, J. R. & Becker, L. D. (1988). Cognitive components of learning problems in arithmetic. *Remedial and Special Education, 9*(5), 7–15, 27.

Kirby, J. R. & Biggs, J. B. (1981). *Learning styles, information processing abilities, and academic achievement.* Final report to the Australian Research Grants Committee. University of Newcastle, NSW.

Kirby, J. R., & Biggs, J. B. (in preparation). *The psychology of reading and writing* (working title). Clevedon, UK: Multilingual Matters.

Kirby, J. R., & Das, J. P. (1977). Reading achievement, IQ, and simultaneous-successive processing. *Journal of Educational Psychology, 69,* 564–570.

Kirby, J. R., & Das, J. P. (1978a). Information processing and human abilities. *Journal of Educational Psychology, 70,* 58–66.

Kirby, J. R., & Das, J. P. (1978b). Skills underlying Coloured Progressive Matrices. *Alberta Journal of Educational Research, 24,* 94–99.

Kirby, J. R., & Das, J. P. (1990). A cognitive approach to intelligence: Attention, coding and planning. *Canadian Psychology, 31,* 320–331.

Kirby, J. R., & Gordon, C. J. (1988). Text segmenting and comprehension: Effects of reading and information processing abilities. *British Journal of Educational Psychology, 58,* 287–300.

Kirby, J. R., & Lawson, M. J. (1983). Effects of strategy training on progressive matrices performance. *Contemporary Educational Psychology, 8,* 127–139.

Kirby, J., & Moore, P. (1987). Metacognitive awareness about reading and its relation to reading ability. *Journal of Psychoeducational Assessment, 2,* 119–137.

Kirby, J. R., Moore, P. J., & Schofield, N. J. (1988). Verbal and visual learning styles. *Contemporary Educational Psychology, 13,* 169–184.

Kirby, J. R., & Robinson, G. L. (1987). Simultaneous and successive processing in reading disabled children. *Journal of Learning Disabilities, 20,* 243–252.

Kirby, J. R., & Williams, N. H. (1991). *Learning problems: A cognitive approach.* Toronto: Kagan and Woo.

Klich, L. Z. & Davidson, G. R. (1984). Toward a recognition of Australian Aboriginal competence in cognitive functions. In J. R. Kirby (Ed.), *Cognitive strategies and educational performance* (pp. 155–202). Orlando, FL: Academic Press.

Koppitz, E. M. (1964). The Bender Gestalt Test for young children. New York: Grune & Stratton.

Krupski, A. (1980). Attention processes: *Research, theory, and implications for special education.* In B. K. Keogh (Ed.), *Advances in special education* (vol. 1).

Krupski, A. (1986). Attention problems in youngsters with learning handicaps. In J. K. Torgesen & Y. L. Wong (Eds.), *Psychological and educational perspectives on learning disabilities* (pp.161–192). New York: Academic Press.

Krywaniuk, L. W. (1974). *Patterns of cognitive abilities of high and low achieving school children.* Unpublished doctoral dissertation. University of Alberta, Edmonton.

Krywaniuk, L. W., & Das, J. P. (1976). Cognitive strategies in native children: Analysis and intervention. *Alberta Journal of Educational Research, 22,* 271–280.

Kuehne, C., Kehle, T. J., & McMahon, W. (1987). Differences between children with attention-deficit disorder, children with specific learning disabilities, and normal children. *Journal of School Psychology, 25,* 161–166.

LaBerge, D., & Samuels, S. (1974). Toward a theory of automatic information processing in reading. *Cognitive Psychology, 6,* 293–323.

Lachman, R., Lachman, J., & Butterfield, E. (1979). *Cognitive psychology and information processing: An introduction.* Hillsdale, NJ: Erlbaum.

Lansman, M., Poltrock, S. E., & Hunt, E. (1983). Individual differences in the ability to focus and divide attention. *Intelligence, 7,* 299–312.

Larson, S., & Hammill, D. (1986). *Test of written spelling.* Austin, TX: Pro-Ed.

Lathem, E. C. (1975). The poetry of Robert Frost. New York: Hold.

Lawson, M. (1980). Metamemory: Making decisions about strategies. In J. Kirby & J. Biggs (Eds.), *Cognition, development and instruction* (pp. 145–160). New York: Academic Press.

Lawson, M. (1984). Being executive about metacognition. In J. Kirby (Ed.), *Cognitive strategies and educational performance* (pp. 89–110). Orlando, FL: Academic Press.

Lawson, M. J., & Kirby, J. R. (1981). Training in information processing algorithms. *British Journal of Educational Psychology, 51,* 321–335.

Lazarus, P. J., Ludwig, R. P., & Aberson, B. (1984). Stroop color-word test: A screening measure of selective attention to differentiate LD from nonLD children. *Psychology in the Schools, 21,* 53–60.

Leong, C. K., (1980). Cognitive patterns of "retarded" and below-average readers. *Contemporary Educational Psychology, 5,* 101–117.

Leong, C. K., Cheng, S. C., & Das , J. P. (1985). Simultaneous-successive syntheses and planning in Chinese readers. *International Journal of Psychology, 20,* 19–31.

Leontiev, A., & Luria, A. (1972). Some notes concerning Dr. Fodor's "Reflections on L. S. Vygotsky's thought and language." *Cognition, 1* (1), 311–316.

Levine, J. M., Romashko, T., & Fleishman, E. A. (1973). Evaluation of an abilities classification system for integrating and generalizing human performance research findings: An application to vigilance tasks. *Journal of Applied Psychology, 58*(2), 149–157.

Levy, J. (1972). Lateral specialization of the human brain: Behavioral manifestations and possible evolutionary basis. In J. A. Kiger (Ed.), *Biology of behavior.* Corvallis, OR: Oregon State University Press.

Lezak, M. D. (1976). *Neuropsychological assessment.* New York: Oxford University Press.

Lidz, C. S. (1987). *Foundations of dynamic assessment.* New York: Guilford Press.

Logan, R. K. (1986). *The alphabet effect.* New York: St. Martin's Press.

Lovett, M., Benson, N., & Olds, J. (1990). Individual difference predictors and treatment outcome in the remediation of specific reading disability. *Learning and Individual Differences, 2,* 287–314.

Lovett, M., Ransby, M., Hardwick, N., Johns, M., & Donaldson, S. (1989). Can dyslexia be treated? Treatment specific and generalized treatment effects in dyslexic children's response to remediation. *Brain and Language, 37,* 90–121.

Lovett, M., Warren-Chaplin, P., Ransby, M., & Borden, S. (1990). Training the word recognition skills of reading disabled children: Treatment and transfer effects. *Journal of Educational Psychology, 82*(4), 769–780.

Luria, A. R. (1963). *The mentally retarded child.* New York: Macmillan.

Luria, A. (1966). *Human brain and psychological processes.* New York: Harper & Row.

Luria, A. R. (1969). *The origin and cerebral organization of man's conscious action.* Paper presented at the 19th International Congress of Psychology, London, England.

Luria, A. R. (1973). *The working brain: An introduction to neuropsychology.* New York: Basic Books.

Luria, A. R. (1980). *Higher cortical functions in man* (2nd ed.). New York: Basic Books.

Luria, A. R. (1982). *Language and cognition.* New York: Wiley.

Luria, A. R., & Vinogradova, O. S. (1959). An objective investigation of the dynamics of semantic systems. *British Journal of Psychology, 50*(2), 89–105.

Mascaro, J. (1965). *The Upanishads.* New York: Penguin Books.

Masson, M. E. J., & Miller, J. (1983). Working memory and individual differences in comprehension and memory of text. *Journal of Educational Psychology, 75,* 314–318.

McCallum. R. S., & Merritt, F. M. (1983). Simultaneous-successive processing among college students. *Journal of Psychoeducational Assessment, 1,* 85–93.

McCracken, R. A. (1966). *Standard reading inventory manual.* Klamath Falls, OR: Klamath Printing Co.

Melnyk, J. (1988). *The measurement of attention deficits in mildly mentally handicapped adolescents.* Unpublished master's thesis. University of Alberta, Edmonton.

Melnyk, L., & Das, J. P. (1992). Measurement of attention deficit: Correspondence between rating scales and tests of sustained and selective attention. *American Journal on Mental Retardation, 96,* 599–606.

Merritt, F. M., & McCallum, R. S. (1983). Sex-related differences in simultaneous-successive information processing? *Clinical Neuropsychology, 5,* 117–119.

Miller, G. A. (1956). The magical number seven, plus or minus two: Some limits on our capacity for processing information. *Psychological Review, 63,* 81–97.

Miller, G., Galanter, E., & Pribram, K. (1960). *Plans and the structure of behavior.* New York: Holt.

Miller, W. (1988). *Reading teacher's complete diagnosis and correction manual.* West Nyack, NY: The Center for Applied Research in Education.

Minick, N. (1987). The zone of proximal development. In C. S. Lidz (Ed.), *Foundations of dynamic assessment.* New York: Guilford Press.

Mwamwenda, T., Dash, U. N., & Das, J. P. (1984). A relationship between simultaneous-successive synthesis and concrete operational thought. *International Journal of Psychology, 19,* 547-563.

Naatanen, R. (1982). Processing negativity: An evoked-potential reflection of selective attention. *Psychological Bulletin, 92*(3), 605–640.

Naglieri, J. A. (1985a). *Matrix Analogies Test- Expanded form.* New York: The Psychological Corporation.

Naglieri, J. A. (1985b). Use of the WISC-R and K-ABC with learning disabled, borderline mentally retarded, and normal children. *Psychology in the Schools, 22,* 133–141.

Naglieri, J. A. (1989). A cognitive processing theory for the measurement of intelligence. *Educational Psychologist, 24,* 185–206.

Naglieri, J. A. (1993). Pairwise and ipsative comparisons of the WISC-III IQ and Index scores. *JCCP: Psychological Assessment, 5,* 113–116.

Naglieri, J. A., Braden, J. P., & Gottling, S. (1993). Confirmatory factor analysis of the Planning, Attention, Simultaneous, Successive (PASS) cognitive processing model for a kindergarten sample. *Journal of Psychoeducational Assessment,* in press.

Naglieri, J. A., Braden, J., & Warrick, P. D. (1991). *Confirmatory factor analysis of the Planning, Attention, Simultaneous, Successive (PASS) Cognitive Processing Model.* Manuscript submitted for publication.

Naglieri, J. A., & Das, J. P. (1987). Construct and criterion related validity of planning, simultaneous and successive cognitive processing tasks. *Journal of Psychoeducational Assessment, 4,* 353–363.

Naglieri, J. A., & Das, J. P. (1988). Planning-arousal-simultaneous-successive (PASS): A model for assessment. *Journal of School Psychology, 26,* 35–48.

Naglieri, J. A., & Das, J. P. (1990). Planning, attention, simultaneous, and successive cognitive processes as a model for intelligence. *Journal of Psychoeducational Assessment, 8,* 303–337.

Naglieri, J. A., Das, J. P., & Jarman, R. F. (1990). Planning, attention, simultaneous and successive cognitive processes as a model for assessment. *School Psychology Review, 19*(4), 423–442.

Naglieri, J. A., Das, J. P., Stevens, J. J., & Ledbetter, M. F. (1991). Confirmatory factor analysis of planning, attention, simultaneous, and successive cognitive processing tasks. *Journal of School Psychology, 29,* 1–18.

Naglieri, J. A., & Haddad, F. A. (1984). Learning disabled children's performance on the Kaufman Assessment Battery for Children: A concurrent validity study. *Journal of Psychoeducational Assessment, 2,* 49–56.

Naglieri, J. A., & Jensen, A. R. (1987). Comparison of Black-White differences on the WISC-R and the K-ABC: Spearman's hypothesis. *Intelligence, 11,* 21–43.

Naglieri, J. A., Prewett, P., & Bardos, A. N. (1989). An exploratory study for planning, attention, simultaneous and successive cognitive processes. *Journal of School Psychology, 27,* 347–364.

Neill, W. T., & Westberry, R. L. (1987). Selective attention and the suppression of cognitive noise. *Journal of Experimental Psychology: Learning, Memory and Cognition, 13*(2), 327–334.

Neisser, U. (1967). *Cognitive psychology.* New York: Appleton.

Nelson, T. F. (1969). The effects of training in attention deployment on observing behavior in reflective and impulsive children. (Doctoral dissertation, University of Minnesota). *Dissertation Abstracts, 29,* 2659.

Newell, A., & Simon, H. (1961). The simulation of human thought. *Current Trends in Psychological Theory.* Pittsburgh, PA: University of Pittsburgh Press.

O'Grady, K. (1989). Factor structure of the WISC-R. *Multivariate Behavioral Research, 24,* 177–193.

Ong, W. J. (1982). *Orality and literacy: The technologizing of the word.* London: Routledge.

Ownby, R. L., & Mathews, C. G. (1985). On the meaning of the WISC-R Third Factor: Relations to selected neuropsychological measures. *Journal of Consulting and Clinical Psychology, 53,* 531–534.

Paivio, A. (1975). Imagery and synchronic thinking. *Canadian Psychological Review, 16,* 147–163.

Palincsar, A. S., & Brown, A. L. (1984). Reciprocal teaching of comprehension-fostering and monitoring activities. *Cognition and Instruction, 1,* 117–175.

Parasuraman, R. (1984). Sustained attention in detection and discrimination. In R. Parasuraman & D. R. Davies (Eds.), *Varieties of attention* (pp. 243–271). Orlando, FL: Academic Press.

Parasuraman, R., & Davies, D. R. (Eds.). (1984). *Varieties of attention.* Orlando, FL: Academic Press.

Paris, S. G., Cross, D. R., & Lipson, M. Y. (1984). Informed strategies for learning: A program to improve children's reading awareness and comprehension. *Journal of Educational Psychology, 76,* 1239–1252.

Paris, S. G., Lipson, M. Y. & Wixson, K. K. (1983). Becoming a strategic reader. *Contemporary Educational Psychology, 8,* 293–316.

Paris, S., Newman, R., and McVey, K. (1982). Learning the functional significance and mnemonic actions: A microgenetic study of strategy acquisition. *Journal of Experimental Child Psychology, 34,* 490–509.

Pavlov, I. P. (1942). *Lectures on conditioned reflex* (vol. 2) (W. H. Gantt, Trans.). New York: International Publishers.

Pellegrino, J., & Glaser, R. (1979). Cognitive correlates and components in the analysis of individual differences. *Intelligence, 3,* 187–214.

Perecman, E. (1987). Consciousness and the meta-functions of the frontal lobes: Setting the stage. In E. Perecman (Ed.), *The frontal lobes revisited* (pp. 1–10). New York: IRBN Press.

Posner, M. I. (1973). Coordination of codes. In W. G. Chase (Ed.), *Visual information processing.* Orlando, FL: Academic Press.

Posner, M. I. (1978). *Chronometric explorations of mind.* Hillsdale, NJ: Erlbaum.

Posner, M. I. (1991). Editor's note: Attention as a cognitive neurosystem. *Journal of Cognitive Neuroscience, 3,* 303.

Posner, M. I., & Boies, S. J. (1971). Components of attention. *Psychological Review, 78,* 391–408.

Posner, M. I., & Petersen, S. E. (1990). The attention system of the human brain. *Annual Review of Neuroscience, 13,* 25–42.

Posner, M., & Snyder, C. (1975). Attention and cognitive control. In R. Solso (Ed.), *Theories of information processing* (pp. 55–85). Hillsdale, NJ: Erlbaum.

Pribram, K. H., & McGuinness, D. (1975). Arousal, activation, and effort in the control of attention. *Psychological Review, 82* (2), 106–149.

Proctor, R. W. (1981). A unified theory for matching-task phenomena. *Psychological Review, 88,* 291–326.

Ramey, G. W. (1985). *The role of planning in reading comprehension.* Unpublished Ph.D. thesis. University of Alberta, Edmonton.

Raven, J. C. (1956). *Coloured progressive matrices: Sets A, Ab, B.* London: Lewis.

Reardon, S. M., & Naglieri, J. A. (1991). PASS cognitive processing characteristics of normal and ADHD males. *Journal of School Psychology,* in press.

Resnick, L. (1981). Instructional psychology. *Annual Review of Psychology, 32,* 659–704.

Rogoff, B., & Wertsch, J. (Eds.) (1984). *Children's learning in the "zone of proximal development."* San Francisco: Jossey-Bass.

Rosenthal, R. H., & Allen, T. W. (1978). An examination of attention, arousal, and learning dysfunctions of hyperkinetic children. *Psychological Bulletin, 85,* 689–715.

Ross, A. O. (1976). *Psychological aspects of learning disabilities and reading disorders.* New York: McGraw-Hill.

Ross, D. J., & Ross, S. A. (1982). *Hyperactivity: Research, theory, and action* (2nd ed.). New York: Wiley.

Rosvold, H. E., Mirsky, A. F., Sarason, I., Bransome, E. D., & Beck, L. N. (1956). A continuous performance test of brain damage. *Journal of Consulting Psychology, 20,* 343–350.

Salomon, G., & Perkins, D. (1989). Rocky roads to transfer: Rethinking mechanisms of a neglected phenomenon. *Educational Psychologist, 24*(2), 113–142.

Samuels, S., & Miller, N. (1985). Failure to find attention differences between learning disabled and normal children on classroom and laboratory tasks. *Exceptional Children, 51*(5), 358–375.

Santostefano, S., Rutledge, L., & Randall, D. (1964). Cognitive styles and reading disability. *Child Development, 35,* 939–949.

Sapir, S., & Nitzburg, A. (1973). *Children with learning problems.* New York: Brunner/Mazel.

Sarason, S. B. (1949). Psychological problems in mental deficiency. New York: Harper.

Sattler, J. M. (1982). *Assessment of children's intelligence and special abilities* (2nd ed.). Boston: Allyn and Bacon.

Sattler, J. M. (1988). *Assessment of children* (3rd ed.). San Diego, CA: Sattler.

Schneider, W., & Shiffrin, R. M. (1977). Controlled and automatic human information processing: I. Detection, search, and attention. *Psychological Review, 84,* 1–66.

Schofield, N. J., & Ashman, A. F. (1986). The relationship between Digit Span and Cognitive Processing across ability groups. *Intelligence, 10,* 1–8, 59–73.

Seigelman, E. (1969). Reflective and impulsive observing behavior. *Child Development, 40,* 1213–1222.

Shallice, T. (1982). Specific impairments of planning. *Philosophical Transactions of The Royal Society of London, 298,* 199–209.

Shallice, T. (1988). *From neuropsychology to mental structure.* Cambridge, MA: Cambridge University Press.

Shankweiler, D., Liberman, I. Y., Mark, L. S., Fowler, C. A., & Fischer, F. W. (1979). The speech code and learning to read. *Journal of Experimental Psychology: Human Learning and Memory, 5,* 531–545.

Shannon, C. (1948). A mathematical theory of communication. *Bell System Technical Journal, 27,* 379–423.

Shiffrin, R. M., & Schneider, W. (1977). Controlled and automatic human information processing: II. Perceptual learning, automatic attending, and a general theory. *Psychological Review, 84,* 127–190.

Siegel, L. S. (1988). Evidence that IQ scores are irrelevant to the definition and analysis of reading disability. *Canadian Journal of Psychology, 42,* 201–215.

Siegel, L. S. (1989). IQ is irrelevant to the definition of learning disabilities. *Journal of Learning Disabilities, 22,* 469–479.

Siegel, L. S., & Ryan, E. B. (1989). Subtypes of developmental dyslexia: The influence of definitional variables. *Reading and Writing: An Interdisciplinary Journal, 2,* 257–287.

Simon, H. (1981). Studying human intelligence by creating artificial intelligence. *American Scientist, 69,* 300–309.

Simon, H. (1990). Invariants and human behavior. *Annual Review of Psychology, 41,* 1–19.

Snart, F., Das, J. P., & Mensink, D. (1988). Reading disabled children with above-average IQ: A comparative examination of cognitive processing. *Journal of Special Education, 22*(3), 344–357.

Snart, F., O'Grady, M., & Das, J. P. (1982). Cognitive processing in subgroups of moderately retarded children. *American Journal of Mental Deficiency, 86,* 465–472.

Sokolov, E. N. (1960). Neuronal models and the orienting reflex. In M. Brazier (Ed.), *The central nervous system and behavior.* New York: Josiah Macy, Jr. Foundation.

Sokolov, E. N. (1963). *Perception and the conditioned reflex.* New York: Macmillan.

Spearman, C. (1927). *The abilities of man.* New York: Macmillan.

Spencer, F. (1987). *The application of a process based approach to the remediation of spelling.* Unpublished doctoral dissertation. University of Alberta, Edmonton.

Spencer, F., Snart, F., & Das, J. P. (1989). A process-based approach to the remediation of spelling in students with reading disabilities. *Alberta Journal of Educational Research, 35*(4), 269–282.

Spong, P., Haider, M., & Lindsley, D. B. (1965). Selective attentiveness and cortical evoked responses to visual and auditory stimuli. *Science, 148,* 395–397.

Sprague, R. L., & Sleator, E. K. (1976). Drugs and dosages: Implications for learning disabilities. In R. M. Knights & D. J. Bakker (Eds.), *Neuropsychology of learning disorders: Theoretical Approaches.* Baltimore, MD: University Park Press.

Stankov, L. (1983). Attention and intelligence. *Journal of Educational Psychology, 75*(4), 471–490.

Stanovich, K. E. (1982a). Individual differences in the cognitive processes of reading I: Word decoding. *Journal of Learning Disabilities, 15,* 485–493.

Stanovich, K. E. (1982b). Individual differences in the cognitive processes of reading II: Text-level processes. *Journal of Learning Disabilities, 15,* 549–554.

Stanovich, K. (1988). Explaining the differences between the dyslexic and the garden-variety poor reader: The phonological-core variable-difference model. *Journal of Learning Disabilities, 21*(10), 591–604.

Sternberg, R. J. (1977). *Intelligence, information processing, and analogical reasoning: The componential analysis of human abilities.* Hillsdale, NJ: Erbaum.

Sternberg, R. J. (1991). *Metaphors of Mind.* Cambridge, MA: Cambridge University Press.

Stewart, K. J., & Moely, B. E. (1983). The WISC-R Third Factor: What does it mean? *Journal of Consulting and Clinical Psychology, 51,* 940–941.

Still, G. F. (1902). Some abnormal physical conditions in children. *Lancet, 1,* 1008–1012.

Strauss, A. A., & Lehtinen, L. E. (1947). *Psychopathology and education of the brain-injured child* (vol. 1). Orlando, FL: Grune & Stratton.

Stroop, J. R. (1935). Studies of interference in serial verbal reactions. *Journal of Experimental Psychology, 18,* 643–661.

Stuss, D. T., & Benson, D. F. (1986). *The frontal lobes.* New York: Raven Press.

Stutzman, R. L. (1986). A cross validation study of Das' simultaneous-successive-planning model. Unpublished doctoral dissertation. Ohio State University, Columbus, Ohio.

Swanson, H. L. (1983). A developmental study of vigilance in learning-disabled and nondisabled children. *Journal of Abnormal Child Psychology, 11*(3), 415–429.

Sykes, D. H., Douglas, V. I., Weiss, G., & Minde, K. K. (1971) Attention in hyperactive children and the effect of methylphenidate (Ritalin). *Journal of Child Psychology and Psychiatry, 12,* 129–139.

Sykes, D. H., Douglas, V. I., & Morgenstern, G. (1972). The effect of methylphenidate (Ritalin) on sustained attention in hyperactive children. *Psychopharmacologia, 25,* 262–274.

Sykes, D. H., Douglas, V. I., & Morgenstern, G. (1973) Sustained attention in hyperactive children. *Journal of Child Psychology and Psychiatry, 14,* 213–220.

Thorndike, R. L., Hagen, E. P., & Sattler, J. M. (1986). *The Stanford-Binet intellience scale: fourth edition.* Chicago: Riverside.

Titchener, E. B. (1908). *Lectures on the elementary psychology of feeling and attention.* New York: Macmillan.

Tolman, E. (1948). Cognitive maps in rats and men. *Psychological Review, 55,* 189–208.

Torgesen, J. (1989). Why IQ is relevant to the definition of learning disabilities. *Journal of Learning Disabilities, 22*(8), 484–486.

Tulving, E. (1986). What kind of a hypothesis is the distinction between episodic and semantic memory? *Journal of Experimental Psychology: Learning, Memory and Cognition, 12,* 307–311.

Tulving, E., & Donaldson, W. (1972). *Organization of memory.* New York: Academic Press.

Varnhagen, C. K., Das, J. P., & Varnhagen, S. (1987). Auditory and visual memory span: Cognitive processing by TMR individuals with Down syndrome or other etiologies. *American Journal of Mental Deficiency, 91*(4), 398–405.

Venger, L. A., & Kholmovska, V. V. (1978). *Diagnostika umstennago azvitiya doshkolnivok.* Moscow: Pedgogika.

Vernon, P. E. (1979). *Intelligence: Heredity and environment.* San Francisco: Freeman.

Vygotsky, L. (1934). *Thought and speech.* Moscow: Sotsekgiz.

Vygotsky, L. S. (1962). *Thought and language.* Cambridge, MA: M.I.T. Press.

Vygotsky, L. (1965). Psychology and localization of functions. *Neuropsychologia, 3,* 387–392.

Vygotsky, L. S. (1978). *Mind in society: The development of higher psychological processes.* Cambridge, MA: Harvard University Press.

Wachs, M. C., & Harris, M. (1986). Simultaneous and successive processing in university students: Contribution to academic performance. *Journal of Psychoeducational Assessment, 4,* 103–112.

Warm, J. S., & Birch, D. B. (1985). Sustained attention in the mentally retarded: The vigilance paradigm. In N. R. Ellis & N. W. Bray (Eds.), *International review of research in mental retardation* (vol. 13) (pp. 1–42). New York: Academic Press.

Warrick, P. D. (1989). *Investigation of the PASS model of cognitive processing and mathematics achievement.* Unpublished doctoral dissertation. Ohio State University.

Wechsler, D. (1974). *Wechsler intelligence scale for children—Revised.* New York: The Psychological Corporation.

Wechsler, D. (1991). *Wechsler intelligence scale for children—III.* New York: The Psychological Corporation.

Wender, P. H. (1987). *The hyperactive child, adolescent, and adult: Attention deficit disorder through the lifespan.* New York: Oxford University Press.

Wertsch, J. V. (Ed.) (1985). Culture, Communication and Cognition. Cambridge, MA: Cambridge University Press.

Wertsch, J. V., & Stone, C. A. (1985). The concept of internalization in Vygotsky's account of the genesis of higher mental functions. In J. V. Wertsch (Ed.), *Culture, communication, and cognition.* Cambridge, MA: Cambridge University Press.

Whalen, C. K. (1983). Hyperactivity, learning problems, and the attention deficit disorders. In T. H. Ollendick & M. Hersen (Eds.), *Handbook of child psychopathology.* New York: Plenum Press.

Whitman, T. (1990). Self-regulation and mental retardation. *American Journal of Mental Retardation, 94*(4), 347–362.

Wielkiewicz, R. M. (1990). Interpreting low scores on the WISC-R Third Factor: It's more than distractibility. *JCCP: Psychological Assessment, 2,* 91–97.

Witkin, H. A., Moore, C. A., Goodenough, D. R. & Cox, P. W. (1977). Field-dependent and field-independent cognitive styles and their educational implications. *Review of Educational Research, 47,* 1–64.

Wong, B. Y. L. (1992). On cognitive process-based instruction. *Journal of Learning Disabilities, 25,* 150–152.

Woodcock, R. W. (1987). *Woodcock reading mastery tests—Revised.* Circle Pines, MN: American Guidance Service.

Woodcock, R. W. (1990). Theoretical foundations of the WJ-R measures of cognitive ability. *Journal of Psychoeducational Assessment, 8,* 231–258.

Wundt, W. (1904). *Principles of physiological psychology.* New York: Macmillan.

NAME INDEX

SUBJECT INDEX